The Faith of Australians

Studies in Society

A series edited by Ronald Wild which sets out to cover the major topics in Australasian sociology. The books are 'readers', but original works—some cover new ground and present original research, some provide an overview and synthesis of source materials and existing research. All are important reading for students of sociology.

Titles include:

Studies in Society: 25
Series editor: Ronald Wild

The Faith of Australians

HANS MOL
*Professor, Sociology of Religion, McMaster University,
Hamilton, Ontario, Canada*

George Allen & Unwin
Sydney London Boston

First published in 1985
George Allen & Unwin Australia Pty Ltd
8 Napier Street, North Sydney, NSW 2060, Australia

George Allen & Unwin (Publishers) Ltd
18 Park Lane, Hemel Hempstead, Herts HP2 4TE, England

Allen & Unwin Inc.
Fifty Cross Street, Winchester, Mass 01890, USA

National Library of Australia
Cataloguing-in-Publication entry:

Mol, Hans, 1922-
    The faith of Australians.

    Bibliography.
    Includes index.
    ISBN 0 86861 628 1.
    ISBN 0 86861 636 2 (pbk.).

    1. Religion and sociology – Australia.   2. Australia – Religions.
    I. Title.   (Series: Studies in society (Sydney, N.S.W.); no. 25).

306'.6'0994

Set in 10/11 pt Times by Setrite Typesetters, Hong Kong
Printed in Hong Kong

Contents

Tables

Introduction

When a leave fellowship of the Social Sciences and Humanities Research Council in Canada came my way in 1983, I welcomed the opportunity to return to Australia and write a new book on religion in Australia. I had previously written a book with this title (Melbourne, Nelson, 1971). It had been widely received as the authoritative book on the subject but had been out of print for a decade.

The Department of Demography in the Research School of Social Sciences of the Australian National University in Canberra offered me a much appreciated visiting fellowship which gave me access to its excellent facilities. Allen & Unwin in Sydney proved to be interested in publishing the new book, and Nelson in Melbourne gave permission to use materials from the old one. It took several months to read whatever had been written on the subject since 1971 (and even so I am not sure that I covered everything), to analyse the 1981 census materials and to reanalyse the various surveys of the 1980s containing religious data. The latter were made available by Roger Jones and his staff of the Social Science Data Archives at the Australian National University.

The Faith of Australians is the result of these investigations. It uses some of the relevant materials of the old book. Often the 1966 Religion in Australia Survey proved to be still pertinent. Sections were added, for instance on sects and Sunday schools and the more recent data were compared with the old. In the intervening years at McMaster University, I had become particularly interested in the theories and assumptions underlying the social scientific study of religion. The books I had written on the subject guided me in fresh interpretations of the Australian findings.

I wish that it had been possible to also consider the data now being gathered for the National Social Science Survey and the Australian Values Study; only some of the preliminary material from the latter could be included. However a detailed reanalysis of both surveys can only be made in 1985 at the earliest. I hope that by then a revised edition of this book will be necessary, so that a better comparison can be made between the 1966 and the 1984 data.

At the request of the publisher I have reduced the number of tables in this book. There are still plenty left! But wherever possible I have described the main features of surveys and censuses instead of presenting the material in table form. I have also avoided detailed descriptions and histories of denominations and sects. Two excellent bibliographies (Mason, 1982; Hynd, 1982) are available to those readers interested in specific religious organisations.

The structure of the book is straight forward, moving from organisation and membership to religious practices, dealing with the relationships between education and religion and between beliefs and morality. Finally there is an analysis of the relation of religion to class, residence and politics. Distributed throughout the book are data on ethnicity and the family, but a full treatment of these topics will have to wait until I write the relevant articles for a forthcoming encyclopaedia on ethnic groups and a monograph commissioned by the Institute of Family Studies.

Finally, I would like to thank the typists and word processing personnel of the Australian National University, and particularly my daughter Margery and her boyfriend George Harpur who took over when, at a crucial stage, an epidemic of tenosynovitis befell the office staff. My wife, Ruth, proved to be her usual co-operative self when she took the indexation upon herself.

Canberra, June 1984

1 Denominations and sects

The faith motivating Australians in the 1980s is not necessarily Christian. Yet for most of Australian history 'faith' has been closely linked with churches, denominations and sects and it is therefore appropriate to begin with the distribution of religious organisations in the population. Later we will pay attention to the more 'secular' faith which propels some people.

Denominational distribution

When governor Phillip landed at Sydney Cove on 26 January 1788, there was no Christian ceremony to mark the occasion. The British flag was raised solemnly and the appropriate military rites were carried out, but chaplain Richard Johnson took no part in the proceedings. Bonwick wrote 'The baptism of the place was performed in libations of liquor and success to the settlement was duly honoured in the flowing bowl' (Bonwick, 1898:71).

By contrast, when the Pilgrim Fathers had landed at New Plymouth in 1620, Christian prayer, bible reading and the proclamation of the church covenant (the Mayflower Compact) were the only forms of celebration. Neither flag raising nor any military ceremony marked what many Americans regard as the beginning of their history.

The place of the Christian religion in those events symbolises the diverging ways Christianity functioned in subsequent days. In Australia it remained much more on the periphery, although eight days after the landing the first religious service was conducted and has been part of society ever since.

In Australia ethnic origin and fertility explain a good deal of denominational composition. That is to say the English, the Irish and the Scots transplanted their own Anglican, Catholic and Presbyterian religious organisations. The Cornish and the Welsh amongst others introduced Methodism. The relative strength of these denominations in the total population shows even now the original patterns of migration, provided one takes differences in fertility into account as

1

well. This is also true for other countries, such as Canada and New Zealand. The Historical Records of Australia (Series 1, Volume XIII:305) show that on 1 April 1827 the majority of the 4164 prisoners at the penal settlement were of English origin (53 per cent) and Anglican/Episcopalian (55 per cent). Most of the rest were of Irish origin (42 per cent) and Catholic (39 per cent). Way behind came the Scottish (4 per cent) and the Presbyterians (4 per cent). A century and a half later Anglicans and Catholics still form the two main denominations.

In the United States factors apart from ethnic origin and fertility operate strongly. The large numbers of Baptists and Methodists, for instance, are the result of vigorous evangelism and exuberant revivals. The American scene also spawned a variety of new denominations and sects such as Mormons, Seventh Day Adventists, Jehovah's Witnesses, Pentecostals, Churches of Christ, Christian Scientists, Scientologists, etc. I do not know of any new religion which has been initiated in Australia. In contrast with Australians, Americans are also more ready to change religious affiliations, but this factor seems to have less affect on the religious composition of the population as the outflow of members often cancels out the inflow.

The important difference is that since the nineteenth century, Australians were born into a religion, rather than changed by it as happened in particular episodes of American history. This is why demographical factors are a more reliable guide for the explanation of the denominational composition in Australia than in the USA.

Until recently Australians considered their religious affiliation in terms of national origin. The churches never actively discouraged this association and this contributed to an image of old world nostalgia rather than an independent stance.

Of the Church of England, Leicester Webb made the following observations:

> In the country districts of New South Wales and Victoria, it was, until fairly late in the nineteenth century, the Church of a dominant social class of landowners who consciously attempted to reproduce in Australia the conditions of an English rural parish. These men built the parish churches on English models and are commemorated on their walls by memorial inscriptions carrying the coat-of-arms of ancient families and recording connections with British regiments and with Oxford and Cambridge colleges. At the beginning of this century, all the Anglican bishops in Australia and a substantial proportion of the clergy were English born and trained. Even today, all the Archbishops and many of the diocesan bishops are Englishmen.
> The same dependence on England is apparent in the organization of Australian Anglicanism. (Webb, 1960: 104–5)

Today Webb's remarks are dated as the Church of England in Australia is now autonomous. Also at the time of writing (1984) 26 of 32 Anglican bishops in Australia received their basic training in Australia, five in England and one in New Zealand.

The Irish character of the Catholic Church has been documented by historians such as O'Farrell. He says that the doom of Irishism lay in its failure to separate nationality and religion (1968:45). From 1865 onwards there was an Irish episcopal invasion (ibid.: 90) and until the 1930s Irish priests dominated the Australian ministry, after which their number began to drop to below half the Australian total (ibid.: 243). However, even in the nineteenth century there were many moves afoot to make the Catholic Church Australian rather than Irish. Some of the Irish clerical imports failed to gain social acceptance by the Australian Catholic community and as a result influential prelates like Carr and Moran favoured an Australian-born priesthood (ibid.: 161). Even as late as 1924, Archbishop Mannix said that the more deeply Catholics breathed the Irish atmosphere the stronger and more vigorous would be the Australian faith (ibid.: 249). Certainly at present the Catholic Church is not behind any other major denominations in becoming a native church both in atmosphere and training.

The Presbyterian churches also relied rather heavily on personnel and ideas from overseas until World War II, particularly in theological seminaries. Last century the Presbyterians were as Scottish as the Catholics were Irish. This has changed now even to the extent that favourite anecdotes denigrate old world ties. One of these runs as follows:

> A Presbyterian congregation decided that the front of its sanctuary looked rather bare. A trusted elder, who was also a signwriter, said that he would adorn that area with an appropriate text. The congregation left the matter with him and the following Sunday when they entered the church they saw in big glaring letters: 'Scotland forever'. They made some gentle hints about the suitability of the text, and the elder promised that he would change it. The next week the congregation saw: 'Scotland for ever and ever, Amen'.

Since Presbyterians without exception laugh heartily at this anecdote feelings about the link between Presbyterianism and Scottishness are not sacred anymore. Yet, not without pride, some continuing Presbyterians (1984) speak about the fact that the three major Australian churches (Scots Church in Melbourne and Sydney, St Andrew's in Canberra) all have Scottish-born ministers.

In the case of Methodism only a small proportion (8 out of 93) of clergymen memorialised in J. Colwell's Illustrated History of Methodism at the beginning of this century were colonial born

(Bollen, 1973: 56). At present, however, the situation is almost reversed: there are few Methodist (or, since 1977, Uniting) ministers left who are overseas born.

This is not true for the Orthodox clergy. They, as well as the immigrants from Greece and Eastern Europe whom they serve, have arrived primarily since World War II and 'with very few exceptions, the majority of them at present are not indigenous and find it difficult to relate to the youth' (Chryssavgis, 1982, 104).

Like the other Protestant denominations, Congregationalism (now almost entirely absorbed in the Uniting Church) began as a replica of its English parent. Dale wrote that its churches were hardly to be distinguished from English Congregational Churches both in thought and interests (Dale, 1889: 218). This has not been true anymore for the past quarter of this century.

One of the Australian clergymen who tried to understand the reasons for the tenacious ties between religion and nationality was Kenneth T. Henderson:

> It was inevitable that English, Scotch, Irish and Welsh, given freedom, should reflect their racial traits in religious worship and belief. The complete intermingling of these originally distinct types in Australia has destroyed increasingly the distinctness of inherited national characteristics, and blurred national traditions. It has done away with the sense of tradition itself. National memories, as personal sympathies and prejudices, and attitudes 'in the blood' have nearly gone. But religious institutions are conservative, not only of ideas but of sentiments and the hearts of the Anglican or Presbyterian have turned for help in religion to England, Scotland or Ireland, as the case may be. This has hitherto been inevitable. Traditions of culture, as well as of religion, have been weakened. The native Australian has been very preoccupied with the making of a new country, and immigration does not come from the educated class. Leadership in religion and education has hitherto had to come from overseas (Henderson, 1923: 8–9).

Although Henderson's explanation has definite merits, one wonders about the assumption that religious leadership must be imposed rather than allowed to emerge from the ranks. The fact that this imposition was necessary in Australia may explain the peripheral nature of at least Australian Protestantism.

How has the denominational composition changed? Table 1.1 shows that between 1851 and 1981 important shifts in distribution have taken place. From being the denomination of the majority, Anglicanism now represents a little more than a quarter of the Australian population. Catholicism has maintained the 26 per cent share it had in 1851, but has had its own ups (27.0 per cent in 1971) and downs (19.6 per cent in 1933) in between.

Do these shifts parallel changes in migration patterns and consequent changes in the distribution of ethnic origins of the Australian population? The latter account for a great deal. There were large inflows of English migrants in the 1910s and 1920s (Price, 1970: 62) and this raised the percentage of Anglicans in the population to 43.7 in 1921. Catholic decline from 24.2 per cent in 1881 to 21.6 per cent in 1921 similarly followed the reduced influx of Irish immigrants during that same period (ibid.).

The situation was reversed after World War II. The relative decrease of approximately 5.5 per cent Anglicans from 1947–1966 and a similar increase of Catholics during the same period correlate with the large influx of immigrants from Catholic countries in southern and eastern Europe and a comparatively smaller inflow of English settlers (Price, 1963: 194; Price, 1957: 37; Pyne and Price, 1979: Table 2.1). The 1981 census provides further evidence in that the percentage of overseas born Catholics in that year (23.8) exceeded the corresponding figure for Anglicans (15.5) by 8.3 per cent. Fifteen years earlier (in 1966) the gap was even wider: 9.9 per cent.

Orthodoxy and Islam also came to Australia with post World War II migration waves. At the 1981 census 20.6 per cent of the Australian population was born overseas, but the corresponding figure for the Orthodox was as high as 59.8 per cent with 31.0 per cent being born in Greece and 11.8 per cent in Yugoslavia. Muslims are even more recent arrivals. As many as 72.1 per cent were born elsewhere, 23.1 per cent in Turkey, with Lebanon 20.3 per cent a close runner-up.

Fertility also affects denominational distribution. Denominations, such as the Catholic Church, objecting to artificial birth control, are (or certainly *were*) more likely to consist of larger families. Consequently their proportion of the population would rise faster than that of denominations which do not oppose artificial birth control. Yet prior to 1933 the ratio of 0–4-year-old Catholic children per 100 Catholic women over the age of fifteen was lower than the national average (Mol, 1971: 249). The reason was not that Catholic women practised birth control more, but that fewer Catholic women were married. Once they were married, they would generally have more children (Table 37.2, Mol, 1971: 250). To estimate the effect of fertility on denominational distribution it is therefore more useful to compare the denominational ratios of 0–4-year-old children per 100 women over the age of fifteen than to express the denominator of the ratio in terms of *married* women of the same age.

Doing that for Australia, we see that over the last 50 years (from 1933 onwards) the Catholic ratio has exceeded the national average. In 1961 there were as many as 38.0 children per 100 Catholic women over the age of fifteen compared with 26.8 for Anglican women of the same

Table 1.1   Religious denominations in Australia, 1851–1981 (%)

Denomination	1851a	1861b	1871c	1881	1901	1921	1933	1947	1961	1971	1981
1. Anglican[1]	175,643	428,759	624,738	819,645	1,497,576	2,372,995	2,565,118	2,957,032	3,668,931	3,953,204	3,810,469
%	52.7	42.8	38.4	38.4	39.7	43.7	38.7	39.0	34.9	31.0	26.1
2. Catholic[2]	87,357	236,152	400,828	516,503	855,799	1,172,661	1,300,908	1,586,738	2,620,011	3,442,634	3,786,505
%	26.1	23.6	24.6	24.2	22.7	21.6	19.6	20.9	24.9	27.0	26.0
3. Uniting	–	–	–	–	–	–	–	–	–	–	712,609
%											4.9
4. Presbyterian	34,249	134,549	201,345	246,666	426,105	636,974	713,229	743,540	976,518	1,028,581	637,818
%	10.3	13.4	12.4	11.5	11.3	11.7	10.8	9.8	9.3	8.1	4.4
5. Methodist[3]	18,768	78,498	191,582	241,963	504,101	632,629	684,022	871,425	1,076,395	1,099,019	490,767
%	5.6	7.8	11.8	11.3	13.4	11.6	10.3	11.5	10.2	8.6	3.4
6. Orthodox[5]									154,924	338,632	421,281
%									1.5	2.7	2.9
7. Lutheran[4]					75,021	57,519	60,803	66,891	160,181	196,847	199,760
%					2.0	1.1	0.9	0.9	1.5	1.5	1.4
8. Baptist[6]			33,021	47,242	89,338	105,703	105,874	113,527	149,819	175,969	190,259
%			2.0	2.2	2.4	1.9	1.6	1.5	1.4	1.4	1.3
9. Church of Christ[7]					24,192	54,574	62,754	71,771	95,641	97,423	89,424
%					0.6	1.0	0.9	0.9	0.9	0.8	0.6
10. Muslim[8]										22,311	76,792
%										0.2	0.5

11. Pentecostal[11]	72,148										
%	0.5										
12. Salvation Army[9]	71,570	65,831	51,084	37,572	31,210	31,589	31,100				
%	0.5	0.5	0.5	0.6	0.5	0.6	0.8				
13. Hebrew	62,126	62,208	59,343	32,019	23,553	21,615	15,239	8,815	6,924	5,054	1,778
%	0.4	0.5	0.6	0.4	0.3	0.4	0.4	0.4	0.4	0.5	0.5
14. Jehovah's Witness[10]	51,815	35,752									
%	0.4	0.3									
15. Other	731,074	600,304	354,859	247,691	218,003	236,673	192,360	256,073	169,199	118,925	15,402
%	5.0	4.7	3.3	3.2	3.3	4.4	5.1	11.9	10.4	11.9	4.7
16. No Religion[12]	1,576,718	855,676	37,550	26,328	15,417	20,544	6,779				
%	10.8	6.7	0.4	0.3	0.2	0.4	0.2				
17. No Reply[13]	1,595,195	781,247	1,102,930	824,824	848,948	92,258	56,191				
%	10.9	6.1	10.5	10.8	12.8	1.7	1.5				
TOTAL	14,576,330	12,755,638	10,508,186	7,579,358	6,629,839	5,435,734	3,773,801	2,136,912	1,627,637	1,001,937	333,197

Notes: a NSW Vic & Tas only
b NSW Vic, Qld & Tas only
c NSW Vic, Qld, SA and Tas only-Tas 1870

1 Includes 'undefined Protestants' for 1851
2 Includes Roman Catholics and Catholics unspecified
3 Includes Bible Christians, Primitive Methodists, Methodist New Connexion.
4 Included in 'Other' until 1891
5 Included in 'Other' until 1954
6 Included in 'Other' until 1871
7 Included in 'Other' until 1891
8 Included in 'Other' until 1971
9 Included in 'Other' until 1971
10 Included in 'Other' until 1981
11 Included in 'Other' until 1981
12 Included in 'Other' until 1891
13 Included in 'Other' until 1891

age group. Leicester Webb's prediction that 'Roman Catholicism will become the largest religious denomination in Australia within the next thirty years' therefore made good sense (Webb, 1960: 194). In the 1981 census there were indeed only 23 964 fewer Catholics than Anglicans in the Australian population. However in that same census the number of Catholic children aged 0–4 was 297 464 compared with 229 239 Anglicans of the same age group. The Catholic excess was 68 407 Catholic children, leading to the conclusion that at the time of writing (1984) the Catholic percentage of the population is likely to have surpassed the Anglican, provided that Catholic fertility since 1981 has continued to differ in the same proportion and that other variables (such as migration, death rate etc.) have remained the same.

Yet over the last fifteen years the Catholic fertility ratio (number of 0–4-year-old children per 100 women of child bearing age (15–45)) has diminished dramatically. In the 1966 census the ratio was 57.2. In 1981 it was 33.8. But the Anglican ratio has also diminished (from 44.4 to 27.2). And because the Catholic ratio is still higher, one can confidently assume that now the Catholic proportion of the Australian population is larger than the Anglican one.

Table 1.1 also shows patterns which have little, if anything, to do with either immigration or fertility. In 1977 the Uniting Church was formed out of three denominations which had hitherto been independent. The smallest was the Congregational Church, consisting of only 0.4 per cent of the population (1976 census). Much larger was the Methodist Church of Australia with 7.3 per cent of the population. Virtually all Methodists and Congregationalists joined the union, but approximately one third of Presbyterians (6.6 per cent of the population in 1976) continued a separate existence. This being the case one would expect the Uniting Church figures in 1981 to hover around 12.1 per cent (0.4 + 7.3 + 2/3 (6.6)). Yet in 1981 not even half (4.9 per cent) of this expected percentage of the Australian population put 'Uniting' on the census form.

What had happened from one census to another? One consideration is the significant erosion, even before 1976, of census membership in each of the participating denominations. All three combined still formed 22.2 per cent of the population in 1947, but their share dwindled to 21.3 per cent in 1954, 20.2 in 1961, 19.4 in 1966, 17.2 in 1971 and 14.3 in 1976. The reason for the decline of the census figures lies in comparatively less immigration, reduced fertility, but above all in an increasing number of nominal members who tended to fill in 'No Religion' on the census form. As there is no reason to think that this trend had been halted or reversed between 1976 and 1981 one could expect the combined 1976 figures to be below 14.3 per cent. The combined percentage of Uniting (4.9), Presbyterian (4.4), Methodist

(3.4) and Congregational (0.2) in the 1981 census (12.9) is probably a fairly accurate indicator of the sort of decline one could have expected in between censuses, given the trend since 1947.

Yet none of this explains the riddle of the unexpectedly low 4.9 per cent for the Uniting Church. The argument has been put forward that the participants continue to think about themselves as Congregationalists, Methodists and Presbyterians in the Uniting Church. After all, there are very few separate Congregational and Methodist organisations left. On the basis of voting one would expect the percentage of continuing Presbyterians to be more in the neighbourhood of 2.2 per cent (one third of 6.6) rather than the 4.4 per cent of the 1981 census. And so the argument goes that one would actually have to add almost all Congregational and Methodist percentages and half the Presbyterian (all in all 5.8 per cent) in order to arrive at the 'real' figures for the Uniting Church (10.7 per cent).

This argument is fallacious in that it assumes that nominal and active members act similarly and that, if anything, the active, aware members put 'Methodist' and 'Presbyterian' on the census form, although they are now part of the Uniting Church. The evidence goes contrary to these assumptions. It shows that nominal and active members have diverging loyalties and that the first tend to stick to the old designations, whereas the second have much more begun to think of themselves as 'Uniting'.

Ever since the 1977 union the percentage of regular church goers amongst those who regard themselves as 'Uniting' has shot way beyond the pre 1977 figures for Congregationalists, Methodists and Presbyterians (see the section on church attendance later in this book). By contrast the percentage of regular church goers amongst those who continue to regard themselves as Presbyterians has been at least halved. Similar evidence for the diverging loyalties of nominal and active members comes from the calculation of communicant/census membership ratios for specific census years. In 1981 there were in Australia 225 663 confirmed members of the Uniting Church. The number of individuals who regarded themselves as belonging to the Uniting Church at the time of the 1981 census is 712 609, making for a high ratio of 31.7. Of course the census figures include children, adherents and other non-confirmed members, but the point is that it includes far fewer of those than the corresponding ratio for Presbyterianism in 1981. Here there were 45 985 communicant members, only 7.2 per cent of the census figures (637 818) in that year.

Yet a similar ratio in pre-1977 census years at least doubled this figure. For 1976 it was 16.0 (144 061 out of 899 950 'census' Presbyterians) and for 1971 13.8 (141 730 out of 1 028 581). The inescapable conclusion from all this is that a much larger percentage of active rather than nominal members of the participating denominations put 'Uniting' on their census form in 1981 and vice versa, that a disproportionate larger percentage of nominal members stuck to the old designations. As the number of nominal members in all these denominations is much greater than the number of active members, the percentage of 'Uniting' proved therefore to be unexpectedly small while the percentage of individuals who filled in Congregational, Methodist and Presbyterian on the census form is unexpectedly large.

The finding that the Presbyterian communicant/census membership ratio increased from 13.8 in 1971 to 16.0 in 1976 deserves further comment. Bouma noticed a similar increase for Anglicans in the Diocese of Melbourne and, to a much lesser extent, for Lutherans in Australia:

> Although, according to census figures, the proportion of Melbournians who identify themselves as Anglican has declined from 37.2 per cent in 1951 to 19.5 per cent in 1981, the proportion of those calling themselves Anglicans who actually show up in church rolls has gone from a low of 9.2 per cent in 1956 to 14.8 per cent in 1976 and 16.9 per cent in 1981 (Bouma, 1983: 20).

As for the Lutherans, 'Confirmed members of the Lutheran Church made up the following proportions of persons identified as Lutherans in the Census: 1966 (38.9 per cent); 1971 (38.8 per cent); 1976 (39.6 per cent) and 1981 (39.7 per cent).

Michael Mason, who together with Georgina Fitzpatrick, produced a very valuable and exhaustive bibliography of research on religion in Australia in 1982, similarly noted (1983: 34) a fall in the proportion of Catholics from the 1971 to the 1976 census. Adding birth and migration figures for the period and deducting deaths of Catholics, he concluded that at least 266 000 individuals who described themselves as Catholic in 1971 did not do so in 1976. Yet in 1981 the process seemed to have reversed itself according to his calculations. 'At least 63 000 Catholics who did not describe themselves as Catholic in 1976 did so in 1981.' Mason has not, as far as I know, calculated similar ratios for Catholics as Bouma did for Anglicans and Lutherans and as I did for Presbyterians and members of the Uniting Church. My guess is that for all major denominations in Australia (including Catholics) in the last few decades the communicant/census membership ratios have gone up while the percentage increase (if any) has been below that of the population at large, keeping the migration and fertility variable constant.

My reason for saying so is that during that period the 'No Religion' category in the various censuses has risen from 0.4 per cent (1961) to 0.8 (1966), 6.7 (1971), 8.3 (1976) and 10.8 (1981). The increase in communicant/census membership ratios over at least some of this period (in so far as they have been calculated) appears to demonstrate that large numbers of inactive nominal individuals, vaguely and tenuously identifying themselves with particular denominations, now cut that tie and prefer to think of themselves as having 'No Religion'. Or, as Charles Price has it:

> The increase of No Religion amongst Australians does not necessarily mean a rapid increase in the number of atheists, but simply that more Australians are thinking about their religious position and are stating what it really is, instead of drifting along unthinkingly, content to put on the census schedule the long discarded religion of their childhood (Price, 1981: 4).

More can be said about the 'No Religion' category of the 1981 Australian census, using the cross tabulations from the 1 per cent personal sample file. Men (56.9 per cent) more than women (43.1 per cent), tend to prefer that designation. So do individuals in the 20–44 age bracket (37.3 per cent of the population is in this cohort, but 47.3 per cent of those who designate themselves as having 'No Religion'), while in the 45 and over age group the corresponding percentages are 27.4 and 17.2. More professionals and semi-professionals (nurses, teachers, etc.) are in that category (9.8 per cent) than in the population at large (6.0 per cent). Although the 'No Religion' segment forms only 10.8 per cent of the population, it has the largest share (23.6 per cent) of Australians with a university degree.

In the 1983 European Value Systems Study the 'No Religion' category was approximately the same as in Australia (13 per cent). It seems that European respondents who designate themselves as having 'No Religion' think primarily in terms of having no religious affiliation. Stoetzel (1983: 94) analysed the findings and found that as many as 18 per cent of those who claimed to be religious belonged in the 'No Religion' category. This seems very strange indeed, since the percentage of the West-Europeans involved in the survey who stated 'No Religion' was actually smaller. Only a detailed analysis of this category (when the data become available) can shed some light on the anomaly; this is certainly not clarified by another observation by Stoetzel (same page) that 'those who do belong to a religion do not all claim to be religious. This is true in the case of three quarters of all Catholics, but of only 57 per cent of Protestants'. As I did not have access, at the time of writing, either to the data or to the French manuscript of Stoetzel (the quote above was from a hasty translation), I do not know what this means. Stoetzel also states (ibid.: 94) that

36 per cent of those who never attend church consider themselves to be religious.

The 'No Religion' category in the Australian census is different from the 'No Reply' one. In 1933 the 'No Reply' option was introduced to the census form through the statement 'There is no legal obligation to answer this question' (on religion). As a consequence the percentage of the population using the opportunity rose from 1.7 per cent of the population to 12.8. Ever since, the percentage has hovered around the 10 per cent (1971 being the exception). At the time of introduction it was thought that the sensitive and private nature of the question would make optionality desirable. Yet there is evidence that nowadays it is used by many people 'who take little trouble over their census schedule and fill in as little as they can get away with' (Price, 1981: 5). Price's evidence (the respondents have a very high level of 'No Reply' in other questions as well) is corroborated by the fact that in sample surveys the category tends to disappear altogether when interviewers ask questions about denominational-belonging directly, without stressing its optionality.

Sects

Although I have argued that a great deal of denominational distribution in Australia hinges on ethnic origin and fertility, I have also qualified that argument by pointing to organisational factors (such as the formation of the Uniting Church) and the internal cohesion of some denominations (expressed in communicant/census ratios) making some of them prone to erosion and loss of members to the 'No Religion' category.

Usually one finds the internally cohesive religious bodies more on the sect side of the church–sect continuum. By the latter I mean the tendency of religious bodies to take a more inclusive view of the relation with society and its institutions (churches, denominations) or to adopt a more exclusive stance (sects). By 'continuum' I mean that there tends to be a fluid transition from one to the other, although at any given time it is possible to plot specific churches and sects on this line from exclusivity to inclusivity. When sociologists use the word 'sect' they use it in a neutral, non-pejorative sense. I use it to indicate that a particular religious body tends to stress its marginality and separateness in a particular society and tends to attract individuals who are marginal.

In Australia the churches long ago shed the image of being the moral police arm of the nation or the uncritical reinforcer of existing social values, practices and beliefs. In so far as they take a prophetic/critical stance they move more towards the sect end of the church–sect continuum. Yet implicitly these churches and denominations, through prayers, hymns and sermons, reinforce a great deal of what the culture regards as proper behaviour (for instance, being kind, altruistic, responsible, reliable, self denying, being a good citizen, being loyal to the elected, or even non-elected rulers). If they are critical it is because they have specific standards, passed on from the beginning of the Christian era, which they feel make for a better society, community, family.

The sects usually go a bit further than that. They glory in being the 'saving remnant', a biblical term meaning the small group of those who have remained faithful to God's covenant and therefore have become the core around which God will construct his new and better order. They usually defend many values which the culture regards as desirable: truthfulness, self denial, honouring parents and all the other prescriptions and proscriptions of the ten commandments. Yet the accent lies generally on the irredeemable perversion and degeneracy of the surrounding society which only God's drastic intervention can remedy.

These and similar religious organisations have, particularly in the United States, changed the denominational distribution map. In previous centuries they have increased their membership at a much faster rate than the population growth. Their appeal did not lie only in a note of urgency and the strong sense of belonging they emitted, but in their relevance for rapid social change. They managed to advance this change while minimising the traditional damage to moral integrity which usually accompanies upheavals of this kind.

Early in this chapter I stated that the effect of these kinds of religious organisations on denominational distribution had been much smaller than in the USA and that in Australia the demographic variables of ethnic origin and fertility could account a great deal for the shape of the religious map. Yet 'a great deal' does not mean 'all'. There are in Australia, too, instances of sects growing much faster this change while minimising the traditional damage to moral integrity which usually accompanies upheavals of this kind.

Early in this chapter I stated that the effect of these kinds of the period never fail to mention the abysmally poor relations between clergy and convict. Even those evangelical ministers, whose message of salvation elsewhere tended to appeal to outcasts, the deprived, the oppressed, the ne'er do well, in short, those on the margin of society, community and family, hardly made an impact. Very occasionally there were Methodist ministers who became popular with some of the convicts because they were felt to be on their side in the way family members or sympathetic mates were (Grocott, 1980: 252). Yet only very few managed to lose all sense of judgement and to convey a deep sense of common suffering, of being broken by sin, inhumanity, injustice, inner insecurity.

Methodism, 'perhaps the most successful cause in nineteenth-century Australian Christianity' (Bollen, 1973: 11), produced the few little revivals there were in Australia: in Sydney in 1835; Goulburn, 1871; Taree, 1879–80; Cobar, 1880, all in New South Wales. There was also one in the mining towns of Moonta and Wallaroo in South Australia in 1875 (ibid.: 29), but their effect was strictly limited, even though they contributed a little to the Methodist growth ('from 6.7 per cent of New South Wales population in 1861 to 10.2 per cent in 1901'), as Bollen (ibid.) suggests.

Certainly in the second half of the nineteenth century Methodists in both Victoria and New South Wales attended church much more often than Anglicans, Catholics and Presbyterians (Mol, 1971: 11) and the vigour of their organisations had its own, independent effect on their appeal to many outsiders who somehow felt a heartwarming affinity with those who were equally convinced of their unworthiness, moral weakness and physical frailty, but had somehow balanced their sense of sin with faith in Christ's whole-making.

In the twentieth century Methodism succumbed to the same institutionalisation of charisma (and therefore more limited appeal to the marginal fringes of society) as its offspring, the Salvation Army. The heydays of the latter were in the last two decades of the nineteenth century, when it grew from nothing to 0.8 per cent of the population, but Table 1.1 shows that in all censuses since 1901 the percentage of the population thinking of itself as belonging to the Salvation Army diminished, in spite of it continuing effectively to extend a helping hand to the down-and-outers of Australian society.

In the twentieth century other sect-type organisations seem to have taken over the socially important task of gathering to their bosoms those who feel deprived, powerless and unwanted. What is more, in the preceding quarter of this century the number of those who feel alienated from an increasingly looser woven, rudderless society appears to have expanded rapidly. Radical causes, feminism, ecology, marxist militancy were the antidote and shelter for many who were usually not economically deprived, yet felt that salvation of any kind was in grave jeopardy. Non-Christian or semi-Christian sects, the Hare Krishnas, Ananda Marga, the Scientologists, the Moonies, have all made an impact on those who expected existence to be more than titillating the senses, amassing consumer goods, power, fame or academic recognition.

It may be worthwhile to document this last observation from those who have observed these groups more closely. O'Brien (1983: 141) describes a sample of young members of the Hare Krishnas in Melbourne as ex-drifters, ex-experimenters with drugs, who subsequently gave up all material possessions in order to transcend and discipline their physical impulses and now realise their 'true essence' through union with Krishna. The sect (the official name is The International Society for Krishna Consciousness) was founded by an Indian guru Bhaktivedanti Swami Prabhupada in New York in 1966. It teaches that Krishna is the supreme God, that whatever one does should be done as an offering to this godhead and that chanting his name is the best way to acquire and spread His love. Hunter (1981: 35) notes that the core of the sect consists of 400 fully initiated members in Australia, but that it claims at least 30 000 sympathisers and other individuals who attend their temples in Perth, Adelaide, Melbourne, Sydney, Brisbane and in farm communities near Mildura, Windsor and Murwillumbah.

At first sight the Holy Spirit Association for the Unification of World Christianity (the Moonies) seems altogether different. The Hare Krishnas are Hindu (Krishna is a Hindu god figuring prominently in the Bhagavad Gita), the followers of Sun Myung Moon combine Christian scripture with the more esoteric doctrines contained in Moon's *Divine Principle* (Moon claims to be chosen by Jesus to complete the mission He began). Yet the disciples of both movements separate themselves from the world, usually reject parents and the values of their upbringing, and form highly disciplined communities with strong emphases on sacrifice and self denial (Hare Krishnas rise at 4.30 a.m., Moonies surrender their possessions to the organisation, both have strict taboos against premarital sex, both allow sex after marriage only sparingly and for procreation alone). The point is that these and other new sects are little cohesive islands—there are only approximately 300 full fledged members of the Unification Church in Australia, (Hunter, 1981: 31)—of mutual support in a non-caring, heterogeneous society. Through unifying commitment, clear goals and simple prescriptions, they compensate for lack of structure and meaning in the culture at large.

This is also true for the Church of Scientology which similarly appeals to the younger, well educated generation. If anything it sets itself off even more militantly from Australian society. It promises a sense of wholeness and integrity in a society which rewards competence and efficiency, but is disappointingly vague about other expectations. It uses 'auditors' (lay psychotherapists) to assist individuals in getting rid of aberrant imprints on the mind ('engrams'). But once these individuals have become 'clear' (capable of controlling their mind) they are encouraged to enrol in more advanced courses.

In Australia the Church of Scientology has a staff of 193, according to Hubbard (1978: 193) and claims membership of 100 000 (ibid.: 224). The organisation has been involved in a number of court cases, and in Victoria was subject to a public inquiry which left no doubt about the position of the investigator. Anderson (1965: 160) called the belief system delusional, the organisation enslaving, harmful medically, morally, socially and a menace to the health of the community. Its devotees, he said, possessed 'an invincible impediment to reason where Scientology is concerned'. The report seemed to be as high on condemnation as it was low on understanding the kind of society which gives rise to movements of this sort.

The sects just mentioned have emerged since World War II and are too small to have a separate category in the census tables. Some of the larger ones have been tabulated, but were still too small to be incorporated in our summary Table 1.1 which for reasons of space had to confine itself to denominations and sects with more than 50 000 adherents. One of these is the Seventh Day Adventist Church, deriving its name from the practice of having the sabbath on a Saturday. It has kept a constant 0.3 per cent of the population since 1961.

Also from the USA and also strongly abstemious are the Mormons (Church of the Latter Day Saints). Their Church was founded in 1830 in New York state by Joseph Smith Jr who was inspired to re-establish the defunct Church of Jesus Christ. Mormonism (the name derived from the Book of Mormon, found by Joseph Smith and providing particulars about the lost northern tribes of Israel which migrated to America) claims to be the only authentic Christian Church. It had only 3499 adherents in the 1947 census, but climbed to 32 444 (0.2 per cent of the population) in 1981. The LDS (Latter Day Saints) statistics (Hunter, 1981: 28) show an even more spectacular growth: from 2716 members in 1950 to 9192 (1960) to 32 581 (1970) to 52 166 (1980). This means that they increased by 238.4 per cent in the 1950s, 254.4 per cent in the 1960s and 60.1 per cent in the 1970s. Their strength lies both in the viability of the local organisation (all members are intricately linked in a network of activities) and in the dedication of their elders who customarily give two years of their life to the mission. It is through their visitation that the Mormons, like Jehovah's Witnesses, have become highly visible in communities throughout the nation.

Consistent and steady proselytising is also the main reason for the growth of the Jehovah's Witnesses. Although the prophecies about the pending end of the world may again and again have proved to be premature and the internal autocratic rule of the organisation from Brooklyn (New York) may lead to much internal dissension and even partition, nevertheless from 1971–1976 the census membership grew from 35 752 to 41 359 (15.7 per cent—the population increased by 6.2 per cent in that period) and from 1976–1981 the census membership rose from 41 359 to 51 815 (25.3 per cent—the population expanded with 7.6 per cent). During the 1970s nearly all denominations decreased in number or increased less than the population. If they sometimes increased more than the population (for instance Muslims), it was due to substantial immigration from Islamic countries. Yet the Jehovah's Witnesses, the already mentioned Mormons and also the Pentecostals about whom more will be said later, attracted thousands to their fold because the commitment of its membership, the clear delineation of a future and their disciplined behaviour in the present, impressed those on the margin of society.

How much on the margin of society the Jehovah's Witnesses are is shown not only by an extensive history of opposition to the state (for instance their refusal to salute the flag), but also by some of the cross tabulations of the 1981 census. For instance, the 500 Jehovah's Witnesses in the 1 per cent population sample did not have a single individual with a university degree, although in the population at large there were 3.0 per cent with such education. They had more than their share (7.2 per cent) of the unemployed (the population figure at the time was 5.4 per cent). Although 46.3 per cent of the population fell in the lower earning brackets of the population (annual family income less than $15 000), the Jehovah's Witnesses had 57.8 per cent in this category. Although 6.6 per cent of the population were professionals, semiprofessionals or graziers, only 1.8 per cent of the Jehovah's Witnesses entered any of these as their occupation. It is true that spectacular sectarian growth seems less impressive if one takes the small numbers into account. After all it is much easier to add 15 000 to one's membership in 5 years as the Jehovah's Witnesses did, than to add almost a million which the Anglicans would need in order to show comparable growth from 1976–1981. There is comparatively little membership erosion; the majority of those who indicate on the census form that they think of themselves as Jehovah's Witnesses are usually also active in their various Kingdom Halls. The ratio of publishers (Jehovah's Witnesses regard only those who regularly 'publish' God's word through witnessing, as bona fide members) to census members (which include children and the aged as well) was 65.4 in 1971 (23 387: 35 752); 70.4 in 1976 (29 101: 41 359); 61.6 in 1981 (31 898: 51 815). In case the 1980 drop is regarded as a slide down the slippery path of membership erosion, it should be added that the most recent publisher figures for Australia (1983) were 37 636, a whopping 18.0 per cent increase over 1981!

Another group of sects has recently grown much faster than the population and has also done so without the benefit of migration or fertility. Pentecostalism is a group name for people who belong to a variety of religious organisations, the largest of which is the Assemblies of God. Other major Pentecostal denominations are the Christian Revival Crusade, the Apostolic Church and the International Church of the Foursquare Gospel. All these groups stress the experience of the Holy Spirit as it was poured out on the apostles and converts on the day of Pentecost in Acts 2. They insist that evidence of being baptised by the Holy Spirit is speaking in tongues, greater holiness, more love and the ministry of healing. Pentecostalism increased between the 1976 and the 1981 census from 38 393 census members to 72 148 (88 per cent). It has done so also in other countries, such as Canada, New Zealand and the United States of America. Unlike the Jehovah's Witnesses its appeal does not stem from door to door visitation but from the exuberance, caring and evangelism of local congregations. It too has a decided outline for the future (Christ's return), but it is less inclined to calculate a date for the Armageddon. Glossolalia (speaking in tongues), as in Acts 2, is practised and regarded as evidence of the possession of the Holy Spirit. A historian of the movement (Barry Chant, 1982: 111) says that in 1979 there was an increase of 116 per cent of Pentecostal ministers registered as marriage celebrants compared with 1970 and that at the end of 1980 the Assemblies of God showed 'an increase of over 100 per cent in both number of churches and membership in the previous 18 months'.

As in most sects women are overrepresented amongst Pentecostal (53.2 per cent of the 1981 census members were female). The percentage of members with a university degree (2.2) is below the figure for the population as a whole (3.1). The majority (56.2 per cent) of those with degrees were born overseas or had parents who were born there (compared with 42.3 per cent of the population at large). They are overrepresented by 6.6 per cent amongst those whose family income in Australia was below $15 000 in 1981 (52.9 per cent–46.3 per cent) and underrepresented amongst those whose family income was above $22 000 (14.1 per cent–20.0 per cent). Also in the 1981 census the percentage of unemployed amongst the Pentecostals (4.9 per cent) was slightly lower than in the population at large (5.4 per cent). They are also slightly underrepresented (5.3 per cent as against 6.6 per cent) in the percentage of individuals who were classified as professionals, graziers and semi-professionals in the Australian population at the time.

The emphasis on experiencing the Holy Spirit is not confined to those belonging to the Pentecostal fold. There are large groups of 'charismatics' intent on renewing the church in all major denominations in Australia. The Catholic Charismatic Renewal fellowship is particularly strong and has its own journal, *Ruah*. So has the Uniting Church where the journal of the National Fellowship for Renewal is called *Renewing*. There are also interdenominational charismatic organisations, the best known one being Vision Ministries, based in Sydney (Chant, 1982: 114). Its director, Harry Westcott, used to be the minister of O'Connor Uniting Church in Canberra which attracted throngs of young people to its charismatic services on Sunday nights.

The increasingly looser weave of Australian society has reduced the social pressure to shape convictions, implement norms, enforce conformity, structure beliefs and delineate proscriptions. Therefore movements and sects of the kind just described are less impeded by public condemnations of weirdness and social disapproval of what would once have been regarded as lunacy. The major denominations have lost their monopoly on cultural definitions of decency, correctness and value structures. And so the young have no qualms of conscience while dancing in the streets and chanting Hare (meaning all pervading energy) Krishna, Hare Krishna, Krishna, Krishna, Hare, Hare, Hare Rama (also meaning Lord), Hare Rama, Rama, Rama, Hare, Hare. If they have retained some interest in traditional Christianity, they feel sufficiently unconstrained to roll in the aisles while being possessed by the Holy Spirit. These individuals are certainly the exception rather than the rule, but the point is that the public condones rather than condemns what is different.

And yet the viability and growth of some major sects is not even primarily the consequence of greater freedom to do one's thing. It is mainly caused by the very tolerance and colourless uniformity of urban culture, which creates a need for firm structures, clear certainties and secure outlines of what to expect. The sects fulfil this need and provide reciprocal love and care within their separate enclaves.

2 Relations between the churches

Basic to our argument in Chapter I has been the idea that the remarkable growth of many Australian sects goes together with the internal cohesion of their organisations. Their appeal seems to depend on the capacity to remain cosy shelters in a harsh world, caring communities in a thirsty land, affectionate refuges for the increasing number of individuals on the margin of Australian society, sources of commitment for the alienated and the confused.

If that is the case one can expect these religious organisations to be wary of congenial, open-hearted relations, not only with other sects or churches, but also with the other 'systems' of a society (nation, community, family, militant political or worker's organisations, personal identities). After all, survival depends on maximum loyalty of the membership and the more legitimate competing allegiances are considered, the greater the danger for one's own bailiwick. Mutual affection grows with separation from the 'without'. Boundaries are a prerequisite for being a shelter in inhospitable surroundings. Illustrations for this argument abound.

The Jehovah's Witnesses set themselves off against the state. They want their membership not to be excessively dedicated to their jobs. They alone will be saved at the pending armageddon. The deprogramming, headline-producing efforts by families to rescue their children from the clutches of some of the 'new religions' are the direct result of the Moonies, the Hare Krishnas and the Scientologists insisting that their organisation is now 'the new family' of the convert. The theology of uniqueness implicitly or explicitly pervading Moon's doctrines, Scientology dogma and Mormon history is a refined way of strengthening organisational boundaries and keeping the shelter intact. The Pentecostals' claim of a special line to God via the Holy Spirit and their denunciation of evil and sin in the world and individuals are, amongst other things, a boundary defence against society at large and against an overly proud ego.

Of course there are 'exclusive' elements in the churches and larger denominations as well. Ministers and priests who preach against sport on Sunday morning, glory in the uniqueness of their history, spend countless hours and effort on increasing both quality and quantity of their core members, are also (whatever else they may be doing) bolstering the organisational machinery. They are often rewarded for their pains with higher salaries or appointments to larger parishes. Nevertheless the churches and major denominations are decidedly less exclusive than the sects. They are much more loath to flout expectations of tolerance in society at large and are therefore also much more amenable to fraternal relations with other churches. The culture respects them for this open mindedness and accords them higher status. Even so they do not always go the whole way. Ever since Vatican II from 1962–1965 the Catholic Church has relaxed its boundaries. Yet it has recently drawn the line with Freemasonry.

The drawback of inclusiveness (and the accompanying bolstering of social integrity) is that it tends to attract those who have arrived and can afford to be less bounded. By contrast, those who are marginal according to canons of attractiveness, success and status, will be more drawn to organisations which themselves are marginal. Both inclusiveness and exclusiveness have their own, quite separate, consequences for the differences in cohesion of churches and sects. Both inclusiveness and exclusiveness have their separate and diverging kinds of appeal for sections of the populations. Both inclusiveness and exclusiveness can equally find sources of legitimation in the Christian tradition. If this were not so, Christianity would not have survived as long as it has: a dialectic with openness and closed-ness, differentiation and integration, chaos and order, hell and heaven, is of the essence of any surviving religion.

With all this in mind, let us now look at the history of ecclesiastical unions in Australia and at anti-Catholic, anti-Protestant and anti-Semitic sentiments of the various sections of the population.

Church union in Australia

As expected there have never been unions of sects in Australia. Also the conservative/evangelical wings of the major denominations have been less inclined to contemplate mergers with other denominations than the more liberal sections. The reason is that both sects and conservatives are more exclusive as defined above, and that the liberals have always treasured a long standing tradition of open mindedness towards (and indeed implicit respect for) the surrounding culture, its beliefs and values. However, let us start from the beginning.

There is a neat historical division between the various attempts to unite the denominations in Australia. In the nineteenth century almost all efforts of this kind were directed to mergers within groups of similar denominations. After 1900 they were almost exclusively concerned with inter-denominational unions.

Methodists and Presbyterians were particularly prone to ecclesiastical divisions. Often these intra-denominational separations originated in Britain and were brought to Australia by the new settlers. The Methodist migrants, for instance, belonged to at least six separate organisations. There were Primitive Methodism, the United Methodist Free Church, the New Connexion, the Wesleyan Methodist Church (the largest of all) and another group called Bible Christians. It soon became apparent that however much historical reason there was for the division in Britain, they were out of place in a new country. The shortage of institutional and clerical provisions and the mingling of migrants soon made this clear. Still Methodist unity came relatively late. In Canada union was accomplished in the early 1880s, but in Australia efforts were confined to overtures of good intention. An important impetus for greater action was provided by the various Ecumenical Methodist World Conferences of 1881, 1891 and 1901. In 1898 Queensland became the first state to have a united Methodist Church, but there were considerable controversies within the Wesleyan Church in New South Wales. However when the first General Conference of the Methodist Church of Australia was held in Melbourne in 1904, all parties were represented.

The Presbyterian divisions were of a different order. They were a direct consequence of the 1843 Disruption in Scotland whereby a large minority of the Church of Scotland ministers formed the Free Church of Scotland because they felt that congregations should have the right to refuse a minister nominated by landowners or the Crown. In Australia the Church was not 'established' in the Scottish sense, so the issue was not as pertinent. However the Scottish churches did not relish Australian neutrality in the matter and so disruption was imported. It did not last long and in 1859 the Free Church, the Synod of Victoria and two Synods of the Presbyterian Church formed the General Assembly of the Presbyterian Church of Victoria. A similar union was accomplished in Queensland in 1865 and in Tasmania in 1896, whereas in Western Australia Presbyterianism was so late in coming that it avoided disruption altogether. The various state assemblies soon felt the need for 'more frequent intercourse'. This resulted in the First General Assembly of Australia in 1901.

The Congregationalists were earlier than either the Methodists or the Presbyterians. The first assembly of the Congregational Union of Australia and New Zealand was held in Wellington, New Zealand in 1892, but in this church with its distrust for non-congregational authority, union apparently meant little. When the Queensland

Congregationalists wanted to ask the Union to assemble in Brisbane in 1903 at the occasion of their Jubilee celebration, they found the Union practically non-existent. It was then revived and has been meeting ever since.

The period of inter-denominational attempts to merge begins about the same time as political federation in 1901. In that year the General Assembly of the Presbyterian Church expressed interest in a United Evangelical Church of Australia. But in 1918, at the culmination of years of discussions on union, only 60 per cent of the voting Presbyterians were in favour compared with 90 per cent of voting Methodists and 84 per cent of Congregationalists. In 1923 three of the Presbyterian state assemblies disapproved of the basis for union and although the General Assembly of 1924 declared that in principle there was no barrier separating the three negotiating churches, it felt it was inadvisable to press forward to organic union because of the 'divided state of feeling and opinion among the office-bearers and people of the Presbyterian Church of Australia'. Almost twenty years later, in 1942, attempts were renewed. This time the emphasis was on a united rather than an evangelical church. Again the Congregational Union of Australia and New Zealand and the Methodist General Conference favoured the proposal, but in 1951 the Presbyterian General Assembly considered it impossible to continue negotiations, partly because of the opposition of a sizeable minority. The Methodists and Congregationalists then considered going alone, but the Presbyterians showed some interest again, and in 1957 a 21 man Joint Commission on Church Union was appointed by all three denominations. This commission had no trouble agreeing on the theological issues of the first report, but its second report published in 1963 on *the Church; its Nature, Function and Ordering* was controversial from the start. A sizeable minority (seven) of the commission wrote a reservation to the report because they could not agree with some proposals, the main one being the introduction of bishops. None of the three negotiating churches had bishops in Australia. However, the Church of England which had sent observers to some meetings of the Joint Commission and which had shown a more than perfunctory interest in the proposed union, was organised on episcopal lines.

This was not the first time Anglicans were involved in unity discussions with other denominations. In 1906, for instance, conversations were held in Melbourne on the possibility of the Union of Anglicans and Presbyterians (Latourette, 1963: 247). In 1913 there was an unofficial Congress of Churches in Melbourne, formed of Anglicans, Brethren, Baptists, Church of Christ, Congregationalists, Methodists, Presbyterians and Society of Friends, to consider combined theological education, control of home missions and organic union (Spurr, 1918: 249). In 1943 Anglican, Methodist, Presbyterian and Congregational leaders formulated what were known as the Australian proposals for intercommunion.

However, none of these negotiations came to much. Even the only successful one (leading to the formation of the Uniting Church in 1977) did anything but unite Congregationalists, Methodists and Presbyterians. Of the first, about 15 per cent of congregations (mainly in New South Wales) stayed out of the union. The Fellowship of Congregational Churches had 768 members in 1979 (Berthelsen, 1982: 289). Of the second, almost all went in. The Wesleyan Methodist Church of Australia had only 348 members in 1979 (ibid: 293). But of the 1437 Presbyterian congregations 522 stayed out (Black, 1983b: 101). As few as one third of all voting members in each congregation could prevent entrance into the union and this rule favouring the die-hards undoubtedly increased the number of continuing Presbyterian parishes.

We will come back later to the census and other materials allowing us to speculate about the differences between those who went into and those who stayed out of the Uniting Church. Before doing so, however we must have a look at the pre-1977 polls and surveys regarding interdenominational mergers. They may help us to understand better the later data.

One suggestion fitting in rather well with the assumptions of our introduction is that the clergy, being mobile and less attached to local communities and to the niches of specific religious organisations in those communities, will be more ecumenical than the laity often linked since birth to the local church. This was articulated by the former Primate of the Anglican Church in Australia, Archbishop H. Gough when he said:

> The leaders of the churches want unity. The majority of the lay people do not. They are the grass roots and you can't force the grass roots ... (Trengrove, 1965: 16).

Still, Gallup polls on church union seemed to deny this. A 1963 poll established that a majority of the Australian population (55 per cent) doubted that the day would ever come when all Christians of the world, that is Catholics, Protestants and all other Christian groups, would be united into one church, but a 1965 poll showed that an even larger majority (70 per cent) felt that Catholic and Protestant Churches should at least try to unite. Seventy-four per cent of this majority considered their uniting very important. Similar responses were obtained in two 1966 polls. In the teenage poll in February of that year, 61 per cent of respondents felt that Catholics and Protestants should try to unite. In the adult poll in July 1966, 66 per cent gave that response. In all these polls there was not much variation between the major denominations. In all three polls Catholics were the most union minded.

It is interesting that the teenagers were less inclined to advocate union. This should make us suspicious of a widely held opinion that it is the older generations who hold out against 'progress' in ecumenical relations.

Table 2.1   Percentage of respondents in various Gallup polls who think that Catholics and Protestants should try to unite, by denomination

	1965	1966	1966
	Adult Gallup Poll	Teenage Gallup Poll	Adult Gallup Poll
Anglican	68	60	65
Catholic	82	72	76
Methodist	69	59	63
Presbyterian	72	59	65

Who are the people who favour or disfavour church union? Are they the staunch, church going Anglicans, Catholics, Methodists and Presbyterians? Where does the resistance to merger lie?

The Religion in Australian Survey based on a 1966 sample of 68 per cent of the population (New South Wales, Victoria and Tasmania) (Mol: 1971) attempted to shed light on this issue by asking the following question:

Would you like to see your own denomination (if you belong to one) merge, or join together with any other denomination?

Twenty-one per cent of the respondents (n = 1825) said that they did not want their denomination to merge with another. Another 15 per cent had no opinion or said that they did not belong to any denomination. The rest (64 per cent) said that they favoured merger of their denomination with others. The respondents who favoured mergers were then asked whether there were any denominations with which they would not like to see their church unite. Thirty-seven per cent of the sample did not want to make any exceptions, but 12 per cent wanted to exclude Catholics and 8 per cent wanted to exclude one or more of the fringe sects such as Mormons, Jehovah's Witnesses, etc. A further 6 per cent gave other or several replies.

As we began to expect after the analysis of the Gallup polls, age made hardly any difference. All age groups came within 1 per cent of the average who favoured unqualified mergers (37 per cent).

The denominational differences were more significant: Methodists (82 per cent, n = 172) were more union minded than Presbyterians (68 per cent, n = 280). The latter, however, did not differ much from the Catholics (64 per cent, n = 407) or Anglicans (62 per cent, n = 734). Methodists were least inclined to be against any merger at all (9 per cent). Methodists (21 per cent) and Presbyterians (23 per cent) were significantly more ready than Anglicans (14 per cent) to exclude Catholics from any merger attempts. This seems to confirm the traditional self-image of Anglicanism as a bridge between Catholics and Nonconformists (Webb, 1960: 105).

Those respondents who were familiar with other denominations and religious orientations could reasonably be expected to favour mergers more than those who were ignorant of what is going on in other churches. People are not likely to advocate closer ties with organisations that are strange to them. Radio and television seem to be appropriate candidates for familiarising people with other religious beliefs. The Australian Broadcasting Commission and most of the commercial stations follow a policy of scrupulous neutrality in religious matters, and it is inevitable that the audience has ample opportunity to hear and watch religious services and lectures of other denominations. Would those respondents who favoured mergers be more inclined to listen to or watch religious services on radio or television regularly? Yet of those who were for unqualified mergers, 16 per cent listened to or watched these programmes regularly, but so did 20 per cent of the respondents who did not want any mergers at all. Although the finding did not help the attempt to discover discriminating variables, it confirmed the generalisation of mass media research that programmes reinforce, rather than change existing orientations and attitudes of an audience (Schramm, 1949: 404–7).

As with age and radio listening, church going proved to have little effect. Of the regular church goers (n = 604) 23 per cent were against any merger, but so were 20 per cent of those who never went to church or went, at the most, a few times a year (n = 1218). In the same way as one could reasonably assume that older people were more entrenched in denominational divisions, so one could also expect the church goers to have a greater stake in the established ecclesiastical order than those who rarely, if ever, attended church. Yet this was not the case. Table 2.2 summarises the findings on mergers of the Religion in Australia Survey.

Firstly, items 1 to 4 are significantly related to attitudes towards merger, but not to church going. There are more educated people amongst those who favour mergers than amongst those who disapprove of them. This is not surprising. People who are highly educated tend to feel friendly and at ease with foreigners, and to have a diverse circle of friends rather than belong to a small clique of friends most of whom are from the local church. This presumably has helped the educated to be less afraid of people and organisations with a different religious orientation.

Secondly, there is a strong relationship between opposing mergers and condoning differential treatment according to a person's importance. Respondents who are against mergers seem to be people for whom 'getting ahead' is a personal adage and who adhere to the doctrine that whatever another person does is his business and therefore 'think it is all right', irrespective of whether this other person is very patriotic, anxious to be an intellectual, wants to gamble heavily, or treats people according to how important they are. They accept things as they are without illusion and enthusiasm. The issue of mergers and unions between denominations seems to fall into this realm of enthusiastic hopes of which they want no part. As one respondent said: 'Why should I want to put a lot of effort in changing things when the result makes no difference anyway?'

An alternative interpretation of the differences is suggested in the literature on the 'authoritarian personality'. There seems to be an overrepresentation of the 'closedminded personality' among those who are against mergers. He or she seems to derive security from being intolerant. To this person, belonging to the in-group is an antidote to anxiety and the outgroup is to be kept at a distance (Rokeach, 1960: 349). This interpretation fits in with the fact that those who have the majority of their closest friends in the local church are over-represented amongst those who are against mergers. This explanation has considerable merit. It becomes clear when we look at those respondents who agree that the most important thing for a child to learn is to obey rather than to think for himself, and approve of the person who treats people differently according to how important they are ($n = 201$). Only 22 per cent of these respondents favour any merger while 48 per cent reject all forms of merger. On the other hand for those who disagree with the obedience statement and disapprove of this particular kind of inegalitarian treatment ($n = 748$), the respective percentages are 41 per cent favouring mergers with 14 per cent against any of them. These differences are very significant indeed.

Thirdly, contrary to items 1–4, items 5–7 of Table 2.2 are classic examples of two variables, in our case 'church going' and 'favouring mergers', strengthening one another. Respondents who have the

Table 2.2   Percentage of respondents in the categories which correlate significantly with attitudes to mergers and/or church going (1966)

Percentage of respondents who	Respondents favour any and all mergers		Respondents are against any and all mergers	
	attend church regularly $n = 272$	attend church irregularly (if at all) $n = 409$	attend church regularly $n = 140$	attend church irregularly (if at all) $n = 239$
	(a)	(b)	(c)	(d)
1 have completed a secondary education	35	34	23	21
2 think it is all right if a person treats people differently according to how important they are	10	11	31	33
3 admire the person who is very patriotic	56	49	37	38
4 agree that the most important thing for a child to learn is to obey rather than to think for himself	38	43	60	56
5 have the majority of their 5 closest friends in the local church	40	23	67	33
6 disapprove of the person who is against any Asians migrating to Australia	74	60	64	52
7 feel friendly and at ease with a Jew	74	60	64	50
8 never attend non church meetings or activities	52	64	65	62
9 agree that it is more important to try to get ahead than to be satisfied with what one has	58	67	71	74
10 often attend other church meetings (not worship and at least once a week)	13	0	17	0
11 disapprove of the person who has a a small job on the side and does not declare it for income tax purposes	49	32	54	34
12 disapprove of the person who has zex relations before marriage	83	58	80	59
13 pray daily	61	23	56	21
14 report that they have ever had a sense of being saved in Christ	49	24	46	26

**Table 2.2 Percentage of respondents in the categories which correlate sig-
nificantly with attitudes to mergers and/or church going (1966)
(cont)**

15 are of the opinion that on the whole the Church stands for the best in human life, in spite of shortcomings found in all human institutions	27	40	20	37
16 are of the opinion that the Church is appointed by God	53	22	48	26
17 know that God really exists and have no doubts about it	78	37	79	51
18 while they have doubts, feel that they do believe in God	14	28	9	21

Source: Religion in Australia Survey, 1966

majority of their friends in the local church, tend to attend church regularly and to be against mergers. Respondents who disapprove of the person who is against any Asian migration to Australia or feel friendly and at ease with a Jew (and other minorities generally) tend to favour mergers and attend church regularly.

Fourthly, items 8 and 9 are related to the combination of our two variables but not with each separately. The person who never attends meetings or activities of a non-religious nature tends not to attend church regularly and to favour any and all mergers. In other words lack of sociability is likely to have a negative effect on both church going and favouring mergers, not just on the one or the other. The largest difference is between column (a) and all the others; there is no significant difference between (b) (c) and (d).

Fifthly, items 10–18 have the reverse effect of items 1–4. They correlate significantly with church going, but not with being for or against mergers. Column (a) differs significantly from (b). So does (c) from (d), but column (a) does not differ significantly from (c), or (b) from (d). Yet item 17 is an interesting exception. It follows the pattern of the others, but column (b) differs significantly from column (d). How can this be explained? Those who are against mergers and who are irregular church goers tend to affirm God's existence without doubt more than those who favour mergers and are irregular church goers. The most crucial characteristic of those who are against merger seems to be 'closed mindedness' rather than belief or participation in public or private acts of worship. Maybe this group finds it more difficult to entertain doubts (see item 18) and projects its own need for unchangeability in the authority figure.

It is interesting that again there is an important clustering of ethical and religious responses in items 10–18. Favouring or not favouring merger is outside this cluster. It in turn is part of a different set of responses all related to education, egalitarianism, need for authority and negative feelings towards minorities.

Whether respondents look upon the church as a sacred or as a human institution has nothing to do with whether or not they favour mergers. This is indeed surprising! One could have expected those who prefer the theological definition of the church as appointed by God, to look upon the merging of such sacred institution from a different point of view from the person who thinks of the church in terms of a human institution with shortcomings. Also surprising is the absence of any trace (see item 14) of disfavour of mergers by those who claim to have had an experience of being saved in Christ. This experience is associated usually in Protestantism with evangelicalism which has taken a conservative, ambivalent, if not absolutely negative, view of merger attempts.

Yet another hypothesis that prejudice is associated with the security of the in-group (Mol, 1966: 255) seemed to be borne out by the finding that opposition to any merger was strongly associated with having the majority of one's closest friends in the local church.

Some important hypotheses regarding ecumenicity are presented in a book by Bryan Wilson, who felt that ecumenism had become a new faith, something to believe in.

> There has been something like a mass conversion of the clergy. It is not a spirit which has suddenly overtaken the churches, it is a campaign which has been actively, almost aggressively, canvassed (1966: 125)

This campaign has been instigated by the weakness of the denominations (ibid: 124). Therefore the healing of division restores the morale of churchmen. 'The energy which churchmen have put into the ecumenical movement has been perhaps in rough proportion as they have lost hope of evangelisation of the world' (ibid: 176). Wilson speaks primarily about England, where the number of church supporters was in decline, and the USA where the decline was less in numbers than in Christian influence over behaviour and morality, politics and education. His remarks appear applicable to Australia as well, where the Anglican church seemed to suffer from a decline similar to its sister church in England. The real motives for ecumenicalism among the Australian Protestant clergy may well be the same as those of their overseas brethren. Of course the survey did not provide any insight into the how and why of Australian ecumenicalism, only about the grass roots reaction to proposals of union. Although these reactions were supposedly influenced by church leaders, there was no indication that the latter had been able to make any appreciable headway. There was hardly any difference between the regular church goers, whom the clergy could conceivably influence and the irregular church goer who did not know the name of the minister of his denomination. The reactions to proposals of union of religious denomination seemed to have as secular a source as alleged initial motivation of the leadership. Apart from the fact that the issue of mergers appeared to be less relevant in proportion to the lesser religious involvement, most respondents seemed to identify religion vaguely with what unified morality. To them unity of religious denomination was a good thing. But to others who are against it, irrespective of their religious involvement, these merger attempts undermined their need for a fixed localised authority providing security in a world by which they felt threatened. In both instances favouring or disfavouring mergers and unions of denominations seemed to have nothing to do with theology or even religion. This seemed to be the major surprise of the 1966 survey.

Since the Religion in Australia Survey more detailed research on ecumenism has been carried out, partly substantiating its major findings, but also going beyond it. Kaill (1971) similarly found that theology was not related to the attitudes of laymembers to possible union of the Anglican and United Church of Canada. However, his research showed that the perceived views of the local clergymen and civil liberalism (for instance belief in the freedom of expression) were. In the United States, Roof (1976) showed that support for church union correlated negatively with 'localism' (commitment to the community and its boundaries) and positively with 'cosmopolitanism' (respondent's involvement in, and concern for, the larger society).

Black (1983b; forthcoming) made an important contribution to the debate by using all these findings, by refining the measurements and by linking them to a larger context. The questionnaire he constructed in 1979 was sent to approximately one thousand Congregational, Presbyterian and Uniting Church members in New South Wales. He found strong correlations between authoritarianism/dogmatism, civil conservatism and localism on the one hand and ecumenism on the other. He also discovered that theological conservatism (measured not by the view that the Church was appointed by God as the Religion in Australia Survey did, but by such items as the inerrancy of the Bible, Christ's return, predestination to damnation, original sin, opposition to the Darwinian view of evolution and women's ordination, etc.) was the best predictor of opposition to church union, of church attendance and of moral conservatism (measured, for instance, by condemnation of alcohol, premarital sex, divorce, abortion, suicide). Black took the dogmatism of the Religion in Australian Survey, Kaill's civil conservatism and Roof's localism as aspects of what he called 'narrowness of perspective', that is to say (and here I interpret Black) the narrower attachments to local rather than national or cosmopolitan authority structures, or as it was put in *Identity and the Sacred* (Mol, 1976: 87ff), the need for commitment to concrete, discernible, closer-at-hand rather than abstract, wider, vaguer and more remote, structures. Black found that 'narrowness of perspective' was the better predictor for lack of concern for social activism.

Another important finding by Black was that the continuing Presbyterians were now much more conservative theologically than the Presbyterians generally had been before 1977, which suggests that the Uniting Church (similar to the United Church of Canada in 1925) now possessed a stronger share of the more liberal social activists. He also observed that in New South Wales (where 54 per cent of the Presbyterians continued as compared with the 24 per cent in Victoria (Black: 1983b)) there was a relatively larger contingent of continuing Presbyterians with more liberals views of theology than in other states. Blaikie (1979: 232) found that in Victoria the continuing Presbyterians were consistently more conservative theologically than were those former Presbyterian clergy who joined the Uniting Church.

Apart from theological conservatism, ethnic allegiance also seems to have played at least some part. Black (1983b: 102–3) quotes from sources which are against mergers of Presbyterians for fear of seeing the Scottish traditions swallowed up. He feels that this factor is not very strong among later generation Australians, even though it may apply to individuals born in Scotland. Yet (ibid: 106) he also mentions a Uniting Church leader who typified the new denomination as 'the first distinctively Australian Church'.

At first sight the 1981 census seems to bear out this spokesman. Although in 1976 the percentage of individuals born in the United Kingdom was 7.7 for Congregationalists, 4.4 for Methodists and 8.7 for Presbyterians, the corresponding percentage for those putting 'Uniting' on the 1981 census form was only 3.7. Or to put this in a slightly different form: The ratio of United Kingdom born to Australian born individuals was as small as 0.039 (26 221: 668 710) for the Uniting Church, but 0.088 (1805: 20 594) for the Congregational, 0.053 (24 083: 452 522) for the Methodist and as high as 0.101 (55 265: 547 613) for the Presbyterian Churches. Although this seems to prove the point about the 'Australianness' of the Uniting Church, the evidence becomes somewhat less convincing when one considers that the major component of the Uniting Church (Methodism) also in previous censuses was very much the church of the Australian born (94.2 per cent in 1961, 93.8 per cent in 1976 and 92.2 per cent in 1981). By contrast also in previous censuses the percentage of Australian born Presbyterians was lower (86.5 per cent in 1961, 87.7 per cent in 1976 and 85.9 per cent in 1981). The comparable figures for

Congregationalists are 90.3 per cent in 1961, 90.3 per cent in 1976 and 89.5 per cent in 1981. Actually the percentage of United Kingdom born Presbyterians in 1981 (8.7 per cent) did not increase over the 1976 percentage (8.8), although the percentages of Presbyterians born in the Netherlands and New Zealand did (from 2.0 per cent in 1976 to 3.6 per cent in 1981).

Summarising the Australian findings on ecumenism, there is good evidence that the more exclusive (attached to cohesive bodies of local religious communities) the sects or churches are, the less they are likely to merge, and the more they think of themselves as separate from, or marginal to, society at large. And, conversely, the more inclusive (attached to larger units of social organisation, their values and norms), the more likely they are to break the bonds of specific ecclesiastical organisations and engage in inter-denominational cooperation.

Pride and prejudice

Sectarian hatred and inter-denominational squabbles have been evident throughout most of the almost 200 years of Australian settlement. They were already apparent by the end of the eighteenth century when the first Irish convicts arrived in Sydney. The Protestant establishment 'began to take alarm not only at a people who threatened English rule in Ireland and who were in that sense disloyal, but also at a people whose religion and way of life threatened "higher civilization" ' (Clark, 1963: 35). For long periods of early Australian history Catholics did not have even the services of a priest.

Catholic convicts were sometimes forced to attend Protestant services under penalty of twenty-five lashes for the first refusal, fifty for the second, and for the third, transportation to Norfolk Island. Murtagh, (1959: 11) mentions that this period has been called the 'catacomb era' of the Catholic Church in Australia and that at that time the faith was kept alive by laymen alone.

One of the first Irish priests to arrive in Australia, J.J. Therry in 1820, was met with great suspicion. The Church of England was regarded as official and established and so Father Therry was confined by many regulations. He could not perform mixed marriages and could not attend Catholic children in state institutions where they were taught the Anglican religion. Catholics did not have the right of association, except attendance at mass (O'Brien, 1922: 28–32). However, this *de facto* Anglican establishment was disliked by the other denominations in the colony of New South Wales and when in 1825 the government conferred the sole right for primary education on the clergy of the Church of England, Catholics, Methodists and Presbyterians were 'driven into an alliance of expediency to destroy the Anglican monopoly' (Clark, 1963: 70). Usually, however, the alliance was all Protestants versus Catholics. Ullathorne was Vicar-General of Australia between 1833 and 1840 and he earned the title 'Agitator General' for his fierce fight against the anti-Papists. He spoke at length in his autobiography about the 'old English anti-Catholic prejudices' in the colony, and how Government officials spoke at assemblies of the Protestant Tract Society which distributed anti-Catholic tracts at the very doors of Catholic houses (Ullathorne, 1981: 163). In 1848 two Anglican clergymen were received into the Catholic Church and Protestant congregations throughout New South Wales declared the day 'a day of mourning'. Catholic priests in return called John Calvin a sodomite and all the leaders of the Protestant revolt in the sixteenth century were branded as slaves of sensual lust (Pike, 1957: 109).

It was in this period that the fiery Presbyterian minister John Dunmore Lang wrote his pamphlet *Popery in Australia and the Southern Hemisphere; and how to check it effectually*, and that the *Australian Banner* in its first issue published a poem about Pope Pius IX which began:

> This big-bellied Pope,
> Like a pig in a rope
> Plumped into the Vatican sty; (Molony, 1969: 59, 61)

In South Australia the anti-Catholic sentiment of the population was voiced by David McLaren who testified before the Lords' Select Committee on ways in which colonisation could ameliorate conditions in Ireland. He said plainly that the colonists in South Australia wanted no more emigrants from Southern Ireland (Pike, 1957: 378).

Reilly reports a similar sentiment in his reminiscenses of Western Australia:

Protestants of the day were so intolerant that they could not brook the idea that Catholics could be on an equality with themselves, and it was only after many years of combating deeply-rooted prejudices that the press and the non-Catholics abandoned the notion that Catholics were only living here on sufferance, and were not capable of asserting and exercising social and political rights as well as members of the other sections of the community (Reilly, 1903: 31).

There is evidence for further sectarian controversy in the second half of the nineteenth century. The anti-Catholic stance of the Melbourne *Age* in the 1860s is well documented by Pawsey, 1983.

In 1867 George Higinbotham expressed the belief that 'the clergy of all Protestant denominations were united in a sort of suspicious terror and cordial detestation of the clergy and doctrine of the Church of Rome and he had no doubt that these feelings were 'reciprocated by the clergy of the Church of Rome' (Fogarty, 1957: 143). In 1872 the Protestant Political Association was formed to stem the advance of 'that political conspiracy against the rights and liberties of man, commonly called the Church of Rome' (ibid.: 143).

In that period O'Farrell (1968: 114, 46, 79) describes anti-Catholicism as 'even more vigorous among non-Anglican Protestants'. Vice versa, when on Cardinal Moran's first voyage to Australia in 1884, a Protestant service held on the deck was doused by a fresh wave, he seriously felt this to be a judgement upon heretics (ibid.: 170). Again in 1916 the conscription referendum which was opposed by the Catholic Bishop Mannix aroused enormous anti-Catholic feeling.

Nevertheless, there were some instances of Catholic-Protestant co-operation. In 1817 Governor Macquarie forced Father O'Flynn who had arrived without formal credentials to leave, and Protestants as well as Catholics signed petitions on behalf of the Catholic priest (Murtagh, 1959: 13).

A few years later when the Catholic priests Therry and Conolly arrived in New South Wales, they were helped by a Protestant to find board and lodging (O'Brien, 1922: 23-4). Manning Clark describes the episode as follows:

> At a public meeting held on 30 June at the court house, Protestants agreed to unite with Catholics to raise funds to build a church, and three of the Protestants present were appointed to collect funds from the members of their own persuasion. For the memories, the anger, and the bitterness engendered by 1798 and 1803-4 had faded, while the sectarian sentiment stirred up by the tractarian movement and the Catholic revival were still in the womb of time. So the Catholic clergy began their pastoral work in what was to prove to be, in Australia, one of those rare calms between sectarian storms (Clark, 1962: 350).

In Adelaide in 1838 when a fund was opened for a Catholic Church 'Anglican, Presbyterian, Wesleyan, Independent, Baptist and Quaker donations outnumbered Catholic' (Pike, 1957: 276). A sense of justice and charity sometimes prompted Protestants to side with Catholics as in the case of the first group of Irish orphan girls who arrived in Adelaide in 1848. The newly arrived Anglican clergymen visited the boat to say that 'no Catholics were wanted in the colony and they should all become Protestants'. The outraged Scottish editor of the *South Australian* thereupon wrote indignantly:

> If this is the vaunted freedom of the Church of England, it is not to be wondered at that so rotten a church should require all the aids and props that state patronage can bestow to prevent its utter annihilation (ibid.: 276).

One wonders whether in this particular instance an ostensible tolerance of Catholicism was not a subterfuge for a strong anti-Anglican sentiment.

Cardinal Moran made a tour of the southern areas of his Sydney diocese in 1886 and was impressed by the welcome he received from Protestants. 'In a little town called Wallumba there were four triumphal arches ... all erected by the Protestants of that district' (O'Farrell, 1968: 172-3). When he preached in Brisbane in 1887, half the congregation was Protestant (ibid.: 173).

There are historical accounts of the Protestant clergy turning against bigotry, a case in point being Cardinal Moran's candidature to represent NSW at the second National Australasian Convention in Adelaide.

> The Anglican primate refused to have anything to do with organised opposition to the cardinal and many Protestant ministers publicly supported his nomination, while the *Christian World*, a leading Protestant journal, defended the Cardinal's candidature in its issue of 12th February (1897). But a junta of Orangemen and bigots formed a United Protestant Conference and held a meeting of protest at which a clergyman announced that 'they would have to use the devil's weapons to defeat Cardinal Moran'. A group of clergymen even held a day of prayer to avert the disaster of electing a Cardinal to write the Australian Constitution! (Murtagh, 1959: 129)

What is the situation in the second half of the twentieth century? Scores of writers have attested to a virulent strain of anti-Catholicism in Australia and some of their observations are worthy of extensive quotation for the interesting hypotheses they contain. The author of the *Current Affairs Bulletin* on church going (22 (4), 16 June 1958: 64) wrote:

> Many Australians who give no visible support to any Protestant church nevertheless carry the torch of 'anti-Popery'. In at least one State it is impossible for a Catholic lawyer, however talented and learned, to be appointed as a judge.

John Douglas Pringle regarded anti-Catholic feeling in Australia as extremely strong. He says:

> From time to time it bursts out like lava from a sleeping volcano, burning and destroying everything it touches. The fire is kept alive in the Protestant Churches and Masonic Lodges, many of which are dominated by men descended from Ulster, but once allowed to escape it is inclined to sweep with it a very large proportion of the population who have no religious view at all (Pringle, 1963: 86).

Although Pringle's observation is certainly dated, it is of interest to

see what he feels has caused this deplorable state of affairs. He feels
that the Protestants are more to blame. He says:

> The stupidity and ferocity of their hatred is often beyond belief. Even a
> responsible body like the Australian Council of World Churches (SIC)
> committed itself, as late as 1953, to the extraordinary statement that Rome
> and Moscow must be considered as equal menaces. The Anglican Church,
> which should take a lead in fighting these views, is itself dominated by low
> churchmen and evangelicals, some of Ulster origins, who often add fuel to
> the fires.
>
> This Protestant prejudice is only partly religious. Much of it is inspired by
> a fear and jealousy of the Catholic Church, which is strong, militant, highly
> organised and steadily increasing in strength. Some of it, regrettably, is
> racial—a hangover from the English prejudice against the Irish. (Even
> today Catholics in Sydney are often referred to as "Micks"). On the other
> hand, the Catholic Church often seems to go out of its way to provoke these
> fears. Though it is always most careful not to attack the Protestant
> Churches directly and restricts itself almost entirely to replying to attacks
> made upon it, it too often behaves in its ordinary business as it if were an
> invading army in a hostile country. Unfortunately it has inherited from
> Ireland, not only a great deal of the narrowness, Puritanism and bigotry of
> the Irish Catholics, but also a great deal of their minority consciousness
> (ibid.: 87–8).

Pringle feels that Catholic schools have something to do with this
attitude:

> Catholic children are also specially coached for the public service, which
> they enter in large numbers much to the alarm of the Protestants who see
> this as a subtle attempt to get more influence than their numbers deserve.
> (Catholics reply that other professions and businesses are barred to them).
> Too often the Church seems to prefer to act by intrigue and secret influence
> rather than by openly stating its views. In this way, of course, it unwittingly
> stirs the ancient Protestant fears of the Catholic Church as a "State within
> the State" whose loyalty cannot be relied upon (ibid.: 88).

Like Pringle, Horne (1964: 54) seems to interpret the situation of
the 1960s with history in mind and one suspects that this is the reason
why some of his remarks have an old-fashioned ring. To say that 'the
single most significant aspect of Protestantism now is its anti-
Catholicism' seems to misrepresent Protestantism. However, Horne is
aware that times have changed.

> Anti-Catholicism is not as overt as it was in the nineteenth century when
> fear and hatred of Rome led secularists and Protestants to combine to
> secularise the State and education; those who have not grown up in
> Australia do not now always detect the significance of anti-Catholicism and
> it may at last be declining; but bitter distrust of the Catholic Church is still
> part of the system of beliefs of most non-Catholic Australians. It is

nurtured by some of the Protestant clergy; it is an article of faith among many intellectuals (anti-Catholicism is the anti-Semitism of the intellectuals); it is a matter of considerable importance in the lower levels of many government departments; there is an anti-Catholic bias in a significant section of the Liberal Party; many business leaders are anti-Catholic; it is a most important factor in the struggle for the Labour movement (ibid.: 55).

Although Horne seems to find an intellectual quality in the Australian variety of anti-Catholicism, Knopfelmacher is unimpressed with it:

It should also be added that Australian anti-Catholicism, with the partial exception of the politically uninfluential Andersonian variety, is of a shamefully low intellectual calibre, using sources and arguments which no serious American or European intellectual would touch (Knopfelmacher, 1961: 148).

Knopfelmacher also locates at least one source of anti-Catholicism in some Protestant churches who have lost or watered down most of their positive beliefs but who still retain the traditional hatred of the 'Romanish' Church—and a distaste for the Irish—an interesting reflection on the psycho-social basis of Christian zeal among some Calvinists.

He feels that the other source consists of the 'Stalinoid liberals who hate the Catholics for their anti-communism' (ibid.).

The author of the 1958 *Current Affairs Bulletin*, 'Church-going in Australia' (p. 12) observed that times were beginning to change when he mentioned the reduction of tension among Catholic and Protestant university students. Since that time attendance of Catholics and Protestants at one another's meetings and conferences has increased. Of all the commentators in the early sixties Professor Spann (1961: 126–7) seems to be most aware of an impending change. He mentions that there are still clubs that will not admit Catholics and that the Australian 'Establishment' in many sectors, including business and non-Labor politics, is still Anglo–Scottish Protestant. However, although residual bigotry and suspicion persist, the era of militancy is now passed. Craig McGregor feels that these sectarian splits are mainly a matter of generation. He uses as an example a young Anglican acquaintance who became engaged to a Catholic girl:

... neither of them cared very much about which church they married in; it was their parents who were worked up about it. They ended by marrying first in a registry office and some weeks later in a Catholic Church (McGregor, 1966: 280).

Often squabbles are local rather than national.

When the Rev. J. Arthur Lewis of the Collins Street Baptist Church in Melbourne reputedly said that there was no greater menace to human society than the Rome Catholic Hierarchy (the *Age*, 21 March 1958) a lot of dust blew into the local press.

In November 1967 the Australian Capital Territory Teachers' Association raised the possibility of strike action if the Minister of the Interior persevered with his plans to provide temporary accommodation for Catholic school children and teachers in a Woden Valley state school. The Minister backed down and found a different solution for the accommodation problems of the Catholic schools in the area. However, the teachers were severely criticised in the local press for raising the issue, as was the Minister for backing down.

> Are the old sectarian fires a-burning up when elsewhere they are dying down? What principle are the teachers standing on? If it is simple opposition to any form of State aid for denominational schools, then it is a principle that has been overthrown, and the community has acquiesced in the change. For teachers then to deny a few unlucky children the tiny temporary help sought in the Woden Valley cannot even be dignified as a rearguard action (the *Canberra Times*, 16 Nov. 1967: 2).

The effect of the Second Vatican Council on the Australian community has become quite apparent. Catholics and Protestants now cooperate in a large number of local and national committees from the Australian Society for Theological Studies to a local inter-church committee exhibiting the entries for the Blake Art prize. Catholic clergymen are now invited to, and attend, installation and ordination services of Protestant ministers and vice versa. Protestant ministers address local Catholic meetings and Catholic priests address the youth clubs of the local Anglican parish. In 1970 the Universities Catholic Federation and the Student Christian Movement had a combined conference in Canberra.

Some Australian Catholics criticise their church for not running fast enough to the ecumenical encounter. They agree with the Dutch bishop who uncharitably suggested that travel agencies should promote tours to Australia to see 'the last example of a pre-conciliar Church' (the *Australian*, 23 Sept. 1967: 7). This criticism seems unfair. On 13 October 1967, the top representatives of all major Australian denominations, among whom were Hobart's Catholic Archbishop Young and Melbourne's Archbishop Woods, met for a three-day conference to hammer out concrete proposals for ecumenical action. During the conference, Protestants knelt with Catholics at three masses and the Catholic delegates attended an experimental Anglican liturgy, a Greek Orthodox and a Methodist service (the *Canberra Times*, 13 Oct. 1967). The leaders proposed the sharing of lectures and facilities of their respective theological colleges. The Catholic Archbishop Young justified this particular proposal by asking 'Who could better explain Calvin's doctrine of justification than a Presbyterian scholar?'

A little town in Western Australia, Jerramungup, population 120, 274 miles south-east of Perth, went one further. It built a church to be used on a roster basis by Anglican, Catholic, Methodist, Presbyterian and Lutheran organisations and financed it from a special property rate on the 280 ratepayers in the eastern ward of the Shire of Gnowangerup where the township was situated. In a referendum the ratepayers overwhelmingly approved this action, but the few who did not took legal action. They lost and had to meet the council's legal costs. However, there was much national support for their position, not only by the Humanists, but also by prominent clergymen for whom the separation of church and state was an important principle (*Canberra Times*, 26 June 1969).

There is little in the way of survey or opinion poll material to affirm or deny the many historical and contemporary interpretations. In February 1964 Father Smith published an article entitled Catholics and Protestants: A Survey. Father Smith does not make any claims regarding the representativeness of the sample, consisting of 330 Catholics and 100 Protestants, all church goers, and not including Anglicans. Beyond this, there is no mention as to how and where the sample was drawn (*Social Survey*, 1964: 5). However, some of the results showed some interesting differences which should not be left unmentioned. Father Smith asked both Catholics and Protestants to choose which of five words they thought best expressed the general attitude of the adherents of the one denomination to the other. The result is shown in Table 2.3. Regarding the other persons' ceremonies, Catholics were much more inclined to characterise Protestant services as 'scriptural' (78.6 per cent versus 6.0 per cent of Protestants who selected this word for Catholic services). On the other hand Protestants were much more inclined to call Catholic worship 'superstitious' (70.0 per cent versus 8.4 per cent of Catholics who selected this word for Protestant services).

The respondents were also asked to select the motive that, in their opinion, best described the other group's reason for practising religion. Each group gave as the most important reason 'Following of social custom', but Protestants (38 per cent) were more inclined than Catholics (8.4 per cent) to attribute 'Fear of Hell' as a motive for religious practice of the other party.

Father Smith concludes his account by saying that the problem seems to be a lack of 'truly friendly and trusting contact ... and

Table 2.3   Characterisations of Protestants by Catholics and of Catholics by Protestants

	Catholics consider Protestants to be	Protestants consider Catholics to be
	%	%
Friendly	40.6	32.0
Indifferent	45.7	32.0
Suspicious	12.9	14.0
Intolerant	0.8	12.0
Hostile	0.0	4.0
(Superior[a])		6.0

Note: [a]This word was not on the questionnaire but was written in by several persons

therefore lack of real experience of each other's intimate religious attitudes' (ibid.: 5).

The data from the Religion in Australia Survey did not shed much light on the anti-Catholicism or anti-Protestantism of relevant sections of the population. They did show however that Methodists (21 per cent, n = 172) and Presbyterians (23 per cent, n = 279) rather than Anglicans (14 per cent, n = 824) were inclined to exclude Catholics from a possible merger with their denomination.

Looking at the major Protestant denominations separately, the proportion of those who wanted to exclude Catholics was the same for regular and irregular church goers. The increased tendency of Methodists and Presbyterians, compared with Anglicans, to mention the Catholic Church as the denomination to be excluded, maintained itself for both regular and irregular church goers; of the 632 Anglicans who are irregular attendants, 14 per cent want to exclude Catholics from possible mergers; so do 14 per cent of the regular church goers (n = 101). Of all 111 irregular church going Methodists 21 per cent, and of the 61 regular ones 23 per cent wanted to exclude Catholics. Of the 189 irregular church going Presbyterians 23 per cent and of the 91 regular ones 22 per cent did not wish to merge with Catholics.

Those wishing to exclude Catholics exhibited some, but not all, characteristics of those who opposed any merger. They were more inclined to express negative feelings to out-groups but were equally represented in the educational categories. If excluding Catholics from mergers or feelings of being ill at ease with a Catholic can be taken as measures of anti-Catholicism, some of the speculations of the historical section were not confirmed: the younger generations, the educated or specific occupational groups were neither more nor less inclined to exclude Catholics from possible mergers, or to have negative feelings towards them. Although Nonconformists tended towards these attitudes more than others, those who had a high religious involvement were not inclined to exclude Catholics. If anything, anti-Catholic sentiments seemed to be expressed more by those in the secular–conservative corner. Anti-Catholics seemed less alienated than those who were against any merger. The anti-Catholics felt uneasy with other minorities as well. However, this is as far as the survey could go. To measure anti-Catholic sentiments in Australia adequately a whole battery of different questions would have been necessary.

Pringle's tendency to think that anti-Catholicism in Australia is stronger amongst evangelicals, is not borne out by the data, provided that we can use the experience of 'being saved by Christ' as a criterion of evangelicalism. On the other hand, the Nonconformists are more likely than the Anglicans to want to exclude Catholics from mergers; but there is no support for Donald Horne's suggestion that anti-Catholicism is an article of faith among many intellectuals. If we can equate intellectuals with people who have completed a tertiary education, 12 per cent want to exclude Catholics from mergers, compared with those with primary education (14 per cent), and those with secondary education (10 per cent). In all educational sub-groups there is an equal proportion of respondents (9 per cent) who feel 'friendly but somewhat uneasy with Catholics'. On the other hand, Horne (1964: 55) appeared correct when he located an 'anti-Catholic bias in a significant section of the Liberal Party'. Of those who want to exclude Catholics from mergers, 57 per cent hope to see the Liberal–Country parties win compared with 44 per cent of the sample as a whole.

McGregor's suggestion that there is an age and generation difference on anti-Catholic feelings, was not supported by the survey data. However, on other criteria than those used here to measure anti-Catholicism, these various authors may well be correct.

How much prejudice is there against Jews in Australia? The Jewish minority in Australia is small. The 1981 Census includes 62 126 persons of the Hebrew faith, 0.4 per cent of the total population. Almost half of these live in Melbourne and almost two-fifths in Sydney, showing that, as in other countries, Australian Jews are highly urbanised.

At least one author (McGregor, 1966: 86–7) has called existing anti-Semitism 'considerable'. He noted that there was only one Jew on the Melbourne Stock Exchange and that Jewish people who applied to become members had been blocked. However, there does not seem to be any discrimination at present. Charles Price (1964: 53), looking at the position of Australian Jewry in a world perspective, concluded that anti-Semitism in Australia had remained comparatively quiescent. Jews could move as ordinary individuals into all walks of society. The problem in this kind of society, says Price, is that the freedom to live anywhere, enter any occupation, mix equally with other citizens may result in loss of identity. Price also points out that Australian Jews are much overrepresented in professional, administrative, commercial and clerical occupations and that they have a 'very much higher proportion of employers—35.4 per cent compared with the Australian average of 8.2 per cent' (ibid.: 49). This was also true for the 1981 Census (18.3 per cent versus 5.7 per cent). They were similarly overrepresented in the professions (8.8 per cent versus 3.1 per cent for the population) and the semi-professions (4.1 per cent versus 2.9 per cent). Jews had four times more university graduates (12 per cent) than the Australian population (3 per cent). Although in 1981 only 20 per cent of Australians belonged to families with a combined income of $20 000 and over, 39 per cent of Jews lived in homes of this kind.

Professor Hammond of Melbourne University (1954: 85) investigated the problem of anti-Semitism in Melbourne. His Jewish sample was small (n = 60). Forty per cent felt that there was 'a good deal' of anti-Semitism in Australia, but only 11 per cent said that they had personally suffered 'a good deal' as a result of it. Hammond also published the results of responses of 370 citizens of Melbourne, randomly selected from electoral rolls, to fourteen statements about Jews. The project from which these data are taken was the 1948 Dyason Research project on social tensions carried out for UNESCO. We summarise the findings:

Social distance

Item

4 'A Jew is a Jew first and an Australian or Englishman a good last.' 72 per cent agree.

2 'When Jews are allowed to live in a district they spoil it for others.' 51 per cent agree.

13 'I would be willing to entertain Jews, as friends, in my own home.' 38 per cent disagree (13 per cent Jews against social interaction).

11 'There is no good reason against Jews marrying Australians.' 26 per cent disagree (72 per cent Jews against such marriages).

Economic

Item

7   'One big trouble with Jews is that they are never contented but always try for the best jobs and the best money.' 76 per cent agree.

3   'It is chiefly Jews who buy up flats and houses and let them out at very high rentals.' 62 per cent agree.

9   'It is mostly Jews who manufacture shoddy goods for sale at high prices.' 47 per cent agree.

14   'Jewish financiers control most of the world's money and are responsible for wars and depressions.' 45 per cent agree.

12   'Jews may have moral standards which they apply in their dealings with each other, but with Christians they are unscrupulous and ruthless.' 37 per cent agree.

8   'Jewish businessmen are just as honest as other businessmen.' 31 per cent disagree. (Jewish group overestimated gentile disagreement by 20 per cent).

Miscellaneous

Item

10   'Rich Jews often give money to charity to gain favour rather than to do good.' 33 per cent agree.

5   'There are a few exceptions but in general Jews have an unpleasant oily look about them.' 49 per cent agree.

4   'The true Christian can never forgive the Jews for crucifying Christ.' 29 per cent agree.

2   'Jews are said to have many faults but most of these are caused by the way people treat them.' 52 per cent disagree.

Table 2.4   Results of survey on voting to admit 'Jewish' (race) or 'Hebrew' immigrants (religion)

Group	Keep Out	Let only a few in	Allow them to come in	Try to get them to come
	%	%	%	%
Jews	58	25	15	3
Hebrews	43	18	33	6

Note: Figures are percentages (n = 370)
Source: *Dyason Research Project* (UNESCO, 1948:94–98)

Hammond concludes that Jews are ranked with Southern Europeans as far as 'distance' from the British heritage is concerned. The semi-skilled employees, the lowest occupational grouping, were more likely to endorse unfavourable replies than others, but Hammond felt that this could be due to 'a general view of the Jews as largely members of an employing class which is perceived as exploitative' (Hammond, 1954: 102). There was a slight tendency on the part of the older person and the Nonconformists to give more unfavourable responses with the opposite true for the better educated.

Medding found that 64.2 per cent of his Melbourne sample of 125 Jews believed that discrimination against Jews existed in Australia, whilst 38.8 per cent denied it. He says:

> Of the former 58.4 per cent thought that the problem was one of minor general discrimination against Jews and had encountered none personally, whereas 30.4 per cent claimed personal experience of it at some stage of their lives in Australia. Only 2.5 per cent saw it as a serious general problem, although none felt themselves to have been the victims of serious personal discrimination (Medding, 1968: 190).

In the Religion in Australia sample there were 1100 respondents (60 per cent) who said that they felt friendly and at ease with a Jew, 226 (13 per cent) who were friendly but uneasy, 59 (3 per cent) who felt uneasy and somewhat unfriendly, 37 (2 per cent) who felt quite unfriendly, 334 (18 per cent) who had no feelings either way and 69 (4 per cent) who did not answer the question. Table 2.5 gives a summary of the variables related to anti-Semitic feelings, provided that we can equate 'anti-Semitic' feelings with feelings of uneasiness and/or unfriendliness towards a Jew.

There are many more variables of this kind for anti-Semitism than for anti-Catholicism. Those who have uneasy or unfriendly feelings towards the Jews have similar feelings towards other minorities. The stronger their anti-Jewish feelings, for example, the more likely they are to admire the person who is against any Asian migration to Australia.

Anti-Semites tend to condone differential treatment according to the importance of a person, stress obedience rather than thinking for oneself, have less education and tend to have the majority of their closest friends inside the local church.

There are other differences not mentioned in Table 2.5. The percentage of people with negative feelings towards Jews is significantly larger for respondents residing in Victoria (21 per cent, n = 993) than in New South Wales (14 per cent, n = 781). Foreign born respondents appear to have more pronounced anti-Semitic feelings than others.

Table 2.5   Feelings of (un)easiness and (un)friendliness towards Jews by selected categories (1966)

Percentage of respondents who	Friendly and at ease (n = 1100)	Friendly but somewhat uneasy (n = 226)	Uneasy and somewhat unfriendly (n = 59)	Quite unfriendly (n = 37)
1 don't go to church regularly	62	72	81	70
2 have unskilled or semi-skilled occupations (process workers, labourers, etc.)	15	14	22	29
3 born in a non-English speaking country	9	11	17	32
4 have lived in a suburb less than 5 years	26	25	37	41
5 has completed a secondary education	33	28	32	19
6 are against any merger of their denomination	19	21	25	35
7 have most of their 5 closest friends in the local church	30	33	34	54
8 disapprove of the person who has a small job on the side and does not declare it for income tax purposes	37	36	39	19
9 disapprove of the person who has sex relations before marriage	65	72	58	38
10 believe in the existence of God without doubts	53	45	39	35
11 admires or approves of the person who treats people differently according to how important they are	19	25	36	46
12 admire the person who is against any Asians migrating to Australia	9	9	15	32
13 admire the person who is very patriotic	53	47	32	59
14 admire the person who is anxious to be an intellectual	42	44	39	30
15 definitely agree that the most important thing for a child to learn is to obey rather than to think for himself	25	30	22	46
16 agree that a person who has had a high social standing for many generations is therefore entitled to some respect	37	42	44	65

Table 2.5 **Feelings of (un)easiness and (un)friendliness towards Jews by selected categories (1966) (cont.)**

17 pray daily	36	30	20	27
18 would like to see Liberal/Country parties win	47	50	47	19
19 often act on the advice of their stars	2	0	0	19
20 have had (or think that they have had) an experience of being afraid of God	23	23	24	43
21 feel friendly and at ease with an Italian	90	61	64	49

Source: Religion in Australia Survey, 1966

In pursuit of the characteristics which distinguish the 'anti'-person, be it 'anti'-mergers, -Catholics, -sects or -Jews the Religion in Australia Survey came across a variety of religious variables associated with anti-Jewish feelings. Fewer respondents who feel unfriendly towards Jews believe in God without doubt, and more report being afraid of God, and say that they often act on the advice of their stars. They attend church irregularly, if at all, and do not pray regularly. There is a suggestion (see items 1 and 17) of a curvilinear relationship between anti-Semitic prejudice and religious involvement, in that those who feel unfriendly towards Jews are slightly more regular in public and private acts of worship than those who feel uneasy and somewhat unfriendly. In other words, those who are strongly and those who are not at all anti-Semitic show an upturn in religious involvement. The moderate anti-Semites seem to have also a moderate religious interest.

Another kind of curvilinear relationship between anti-Semitic feelings and religious involvement is suggested by Table 2.6. Here the concern is less with the gradations of negative feelings and more with the degree and kind of religious involvement. Table 2.5 suggests that all three indicators of religious involvement—church going, prayer and beliefs—were negatively correlated with anti-Semitism. This was unexpected not only because these indicators were not related to any other 'anti' attitudes, but because the variations in negative feelings towards minorities were uniformly spread through the Australian population and had nothing to do with religious involvement or lack of it. How precisely were these indicators, taken together and in isolation, associated with anti-Semitism? Table 2.6 shows that strong religious involvement is significantly associated with positive feelings, that is feeling friendly and at ease, and that the neutral responses, having no feelings either way, are largest when religious involvement is at a minimum. What is different is the slight but steady increase of negative feelings the further respondents move away from religious habits and beliefs of 'orthodox believers'. Yet the completely secular section of the sample shows a reversal of this trend.

Table 2.6   Feelings towards a Jew by religious involvement

	Percentage of respondents who have the following feelings for a Jew:		
	positive	negative	neutral
'Orthodox believers' (attend church regularly, pray daily and believe in God without doubts n = 311)	74	13	10·
'Public believers' (attend church regularly, and believe in God without doubts, but do not pray daily n = 146)	66	14	18
'Private believers' (do not attend church regularly, but pray daily and believe in God without doubts n = 177)	58	17	18
'Secular believers' (do not attend church regularly, nor pray daily, but believe in God without doubts n = 250)	60	18	20
'Vacilating secularists' (do not attend church regularly, nor pray daily, and believe in God some of the time n = 364)	57	23	19
'Consistent secularists' (do not attend church regularly, nor pray daily, and hold deistic, agnostic or atheistic beliefs n = 287)	55	17	25

Hammond's investigation of anti-Semitism was more detailed than the Religion in Australia project. The latter could add only that there seemed to be more anti-Semitic feeling in Melbourne than in Sydney and that religious involvement seemed to go together with more positive feelings towards Jews. Most data did corroborate Hammond's findings: the better educated were less likely to have negative feelings towards Jews, while the lower occupational categories were more likely to be anti-Jewish. Feelings toward Jews were similar to feelings for an Italian, confirming Hammond's ranking the Jews near the Southern Europeans in distance from the British heritage. The Nonconformist groups, mainly Methodists and Presbyterians, tended to have slightly more negative feelings towards the Jews (20 per cent, n = 540) than Anglicans (17 per cent, n = 738) and Catholics (16 per cent, n = 407).

How do these findings compare with overseas research? Glock and Stark (1966: 208) say that in the USA 'religion operates, under certain conditions, as a potent source of anti-Semitism' and that at least one-quarter of America's anti-Semites have a religious basis for their prejudices. The Australian data seem to contradict this conclusion, although having the majority of one's friends in the local church correlates with being unfriendly to a Jew. Yet, regular church going, praying and belief in God are more likely to predict positive rather than negative feelings.

Anti-Semitic feelings are at a minimum when the respondents have a high religious involvement. The virulent anti-Semite in Australia seems a shiftless, uneducated, superstitious, lower class person, alienated from the egalitarian value system of Australian society, prone to hate ethnic minorities. A picture comes to mind of the lower class Southern white in the USA, whose hatred of Negroes is often more virulent than that of middle and upper class whites.

Is all the research of the 1960s still relevant for the 1980s? If anything the trend to more cooperation between Catholics and Protestants has grown. Since the Vatican II Council (1962–1965) the boundaries around Australian Catholicism have been relaxed considerably. A decreasing hold by the Catholic Church on its membership and a lessening of anti-Catholic feeling by Protestants has been the result. The widespread tolerance and cooperation between the major denominations in the last quarter of the twentieth century contrasts sharply with the suspicions of the first. Yet below this level of permissiveness a number of militant, secular, and religious groupings seem to have emerged, and these are anything but tolerant. They draw strong boundaries around themselves and appear to make up in commitment and structure for what they feel is lacking in the culture: moral clarity, lack of direction and authority. The implication is that one can continue to expect closer cooperation between those religious denominations who fit in with the expectations of tolerance in Australian society, but an absence of meaningful relations between those sects and conservative groups who offer an antidote to cultural insipidness.

3   Religious Practices

We have seen how heterogeneous the 'membership' category is. As a scientific description it just will not do. It can mean far too many things. For the census members are those who happen to think of themselves as belonging to a particular denomination even when the link with that denomination is very tenuous indeed. On the other hand the churches generally regard only those who have made a confession of faith as bona fide members. Other hangers-on who sometimes make financial contributions or attend a service are often called adherents. The sects have even more stringent rules as to who belongs and who does not: the Jehovah's Witnesses insist that only those who witness to their faith by knocking on doors for a certain number of hours per month, are within the fold. Yet, however imprecise the concept, there is a difference, for instance, between Anglicans and Presbyterians who never enter a church, on such issues as mergers with other denominations.

Church going

Is church attendance then a more useful concept for those who want to describe the impact of religion on society and, vice versa, the effect society has on religion? Church going can be construed as an act of loyalty to a religious organisation and as such it may be a way to gauge the success of the churches in getting their messages, values and norms across. It is also a concrete act rather than a vague image of inclusion and therefore a useful indicator for 'religiousness'. There will be many instances where it will be shown that in Australian society those who go to church have sets of attitudes and norms which differ from those of the rest of society. Because it is such a concrete item, it is easier to use than very private religious convictions, although we will try to say something about these as well. Even so, 'church attendance' has its own limitations. The motives for going to church may differ from one person to another and may therefore have different effects. At any rate, let us begin to describe church attendance patterns in Australia from the early origins to the latest survey.

The Reverend Richard Johnson who arrived with the First Fleet in 1788 as first chaplain to the penal colony of New South Wales, had a captive audience. According to Collins (1798–1802) 'Divine service was performed every Sunday when the weather would permit, at which time the detachment of Marines under arms and the whole body of convicts attended' (Burton, 1840: 5). Yet even at the risk of reduced food rations many skipped church. The hardworking Mr Johnson blamed this on the absence of a building. He complained to Governor Phillip in 1792:

> ... We are wholly exposed to the weather ... On this account, sir, it cannot be wondered that persons, whether of higher or lower rank, come so seldom and so reluctantly to public worship ... (Bonwick, 1898: 75).

A year later there was still no church building. This astonished officers of a Spanish exploratory expedition visiting at the time who commented, 'It would be the first building constructed in a Spanish settlement' (Thompson, 1889: 18). Finally Johnson took the matter into his own hands and built a church from his own funds. It was opened on 25 August 1793 and could seat as many as 500. However, on Christmas Day that year fewer than 40 people attended (Grocott, 1980: 62). As there were approximately 1200 individuals living in Sydney at the time, this amounts to about 3 per cent of the population. Convicts and their guards alike spurned religion and certainly did not let it interfere with their gambling, drinking and whoring. In 1798 convicts actually burnt the church.

In the other convict colony, Van Diemen's Land, the situation was no different. At Port Arthur public worship was used by the felonry to carry on conversations while bawling hymns.

The religious situation could not get much worse; actually it improved under Governor Lachlan Macquarie (1810–1821). Commissioner Bigge (1823: vol. 3, 68) noted that church attendance was becoming more regular although there were still not enough churches. Yet the improvement he noted was only relative to an earlier era and Judge Burton, writing in 1840 was still not very impressed. He estimated that of a total population of about 102 000 only 11 000 Protestants attended Divine Worship (1840: 270). As approximately 28 per cent of the population was Catholic, one can estimate that average church attendance for Protestants in those days was about 15 per cent. Catholic attendance was not any better. In 1838 there were 21 898 Catholics of whom 2 880 or 12 per cent attended church regularly (O'Farrell, 1968: 52). One of the reasons for this low attendance rate was that a substantial part of the population (29 177 in 1836) was either working in road parties, ironed gangs or remote gaols or in the ten counties for which there was no minister of religion (Burton: 1840, 272).

The effect of a dispersed population on church attendance is shown graphically in the table, constructed by Pike, for South Australia in 1844. Of those in villages 12 per cent attended church and of those in the country 7 per cent. Pike estimates that in Adelaide, of Church of England adherents 18 per cent attended, of Church of Scotland 27 per cent, of Wesleyans 68 per cent and of Catholics 87 per cent.

A further reason for low attendance was the lack of church accommodation. In 1836 there was room in the churches of St James and St Phillip in Sydney for 2 300 persons, the number of Protestants for the area at that time being 14 391 (Burton: 274).

Still, none of these reasons could explain fully why the attendance rates were so low. Burton admits that 'the numbers of those who care for the church are perhaps in every community few in comparison with those for whom the church cares' (ibid.: 275).

As in England, the first half of the nineteenth century may be termed 'the bleak age of religion'. Barrett (1966: 185), comparing the 1890s with Australia today, points out that church going involved much the same proportion of the population. However, as in England, there is an interesting period when religious activity was higher. Already by 1850 in New South Wales the average number of worshippers on a typical Sunday had advanced considerably to approximately 41 000, about one fifth of the population. In the other colony of Van Diemen's Land in 1879 about one quarter of the population attended church on a Sunday (ibid.: 186). Still, in all colonies at that time church attendance was well below that in England and Wales. According to the religious census taken there in 1851, about 47 per cent of the adult population or 38 per cent of the total population attended church on a Sunday (Inglis, 1960: 74–86). This figure was never reached by the principal church in Australia, the Church of England, although later in the century many of the smaller denominations went beyond this figure.

In Victoria church attendance went up considerably in the last half of the nineteenth century as Table 3.1 shows.

The data are based on the attendance figures supplied by the churches and expressed as a proportion of the number of adherents to the denominations for the census of the same year. The figures should be treated with caution. 'Usual attendance' probably meant different things to the clergymen of the various denominations. The figures for 1881 in Victoria included those 'usually attending principal service', but those for 1891 included 'number of distinct individuals attending all services'. This explains at least partly the jump from 34.1 per cent (69 954: 203 863) to 49.60 per cent (123 499: 248 998) in Catholic attendance from 1881 to 1891. There was a similar increase for Anglican attendance from 16.44 per cent (49 261: 299 652) to 20.16 per cent (80 981: 401 604). In addition Wesleyans and Catholics included children, whereas Presbyterians only counted those over 16 years, although 'in the latter part of the century the statistician expected the returns to represent adult attendances' (Phillips, 1972–73: 387). It is still valid to conclude from the figures that during the third quarter of the nineteenth century Catholics and Presbyterians increased their church attendance substantially. Anglicans maintained their relatively low and Methodists their extremely high level of church activity. In the last quarter of the nineteenth century Catholics were the only ones who continued to increase their level of church attendance, but Presbyterian attendance decreased. Anglicans and Methodists again more or less maintained their respective low and high levels.

Table 3.1 Percentage of adherents of various denominations attending church in Victoria from 1861–1901

	1861[a]	1871[b]	1881[b]	1891[c]	1901[c]
Anglican	no returns	15.15	16.44	20.16	16.93
Catholic	20.08	23.13	34.31	49.60	54.30
Methodist	85.68[e]	89.25[f]	78.89[f]	87.65[g]	78.12[g]
Presbyterian	21.09[d]	39.52	56.33	41.81	49.27

Notes: [a]'usually attending' not defined
[b]usually attending principal service. This makes comparison between denominations difficult
[c]number of distinct individuals attending all services
[d]This is a slight underestimation as more Presbyterians are included in the census than in the attendance returns
[e]Wesleyan, Primitive Methodist and Bible Christians
[f]Wesleyan, Primitive Methodist, United Free Methodist, New Connection and Bible Christians
[g]Wesleyan, Primitive Methodist, United Free Methodist, Bible Christians
Source: Various editions of the *Victorian Statistical Register*, and Census data.

In that period church attendance in Victoria was considerably higher than in New South Wales. Dale, comparing the two states in 1886, calculated that in Victoria about 35 per cent of the total population attended the principal service on a Sunday, whereas in New South Wales the average attendance at the principal service was only about 24 per cent. He felt that a considerable addition must be made to the figures, if attendance at the other services is also considered (Dale, 1889: 228).

Table 3.2, although not strictly comparable with Table 3.1, shows that the observers in the colonies of Victoria and New South Wales were substantially correct. Apart from Anglicans who maintained their low level of church attendance, all denominations, especially Methodists and Presbyterians were far less active in New South Wales

Table 3.2   **Percentage of adherents of various denominations attending church in New South Wales from 1861–1901**

	1861[a]	1871[a]	1881[b]	1891[b]	1901[c]
Anglican	15.6	17.3	16.76	17.07	17.01
Catholic	22.9	35.7	30.22	38.12	31.42
Methodist	103.0[d]	88.5[d]	44.64[e]	41.14[e]	62.30[f]
Presbyterian	20.6[g]	22.4	22.15	26.79	20.49

Notes: [a] number of persons generally attending public worship
[b] attendance not defined
[c] estimated habitual adult attendance at Sunday and week-day services
[d] Wesleyan and Primitive Methodists only. Either the clergy over-estimated the attendance in 1861 or a proportion of people from other denominations attended Methodist services: only in this way can one account for the fact that there were more people attending Methodist churches than there were in the population at large
[e] Wesleyan Methodist only
[f] Methodist undefined
[g] Includes Presbyterians unattached

Sources: Various edition of the *New South Wales Statistical Register* (sometimes published as *Parliamentary Papers*) and Censuses

in the last quarter of the nineteenth century. Dale praises particularly the Methodists in Victoria and South Australia:

> It is very apparent that there is something in the organisation, the Creed and the characteristic spirit of Methodism that makes it a great religious force in a British colony (ibid.: 239–40).

However, he feels that those in New South Wales 'have shown less enterprise, but, perhaps, more prudence' (ibid.: 240). He bases these conclusions primarily on the Methodists' capacity to provide church accommodation. Speaking about 1886 he finds that Victorian Methodists number 124 060, but provide church accommodation for 160 880 and in South Australia there were 63 083 adherents with accommodation for 88 888 while in New South Wales the accommodation is less (78 459) than the number of adherents (85 968) (ibid.: 239).

For New South Wales in the last half of the nineteenth century W.W. Phillips (1969: 71) calculated church attendance from the annual returns and found a gradual increase from 22 per cent in 1850 to 38 per cent in 1870 (ibid.: 71). After this a decline set in until about 1886 when it rose again without ever attaining the 1870 peak. Expressing attendance in terms of the adult population alone, Phillips (1981: 87) estimates that in Sydney in 1880 around 50 per cent and in 1890 around 40 per cent went to church regularly. The problem with the 1880 figure is that it overestimates attendance as at least some children were included in the enumerator while excluded from the denominator.

How can one explain some of the nineteenth century church attendance variations from state to state and from decade to decade?

It is obviously wrong to follow Gregory's argument that new scientific and historical theories together with the social effects of the gold rushes diminished the influence of the churches around the later sixties. (Gregory, 1960: 58–59, 60). As measured by church going there was no such decline, in spite of the upheaval of the gold rushes. Instead there was a general increase in church activities both absolutely and, more importantly, relative to the number of adherents.

It is more sensible to see what happened in Britain at the time. Wickham speaks about the 'religious boom' in the second half of the nineteenth century. This seems an exaggeration but it is true that the large influx of migrants, almost exclusively from the British Isles, could not help but affect the religious climate of Australia. There was the same bustle of church building in both countries in the third quarter of the century.

However, the Australian scene had its own peculiarities. The pronounced increase in the third quarter of the century must have been affected by the increased habitability of both outback and cities; better housing, more females, the clearer shape of community life, the better provision of religious facilities and personnel (Trollope, 1873: 146). Once normality had been established there was no reason why religious involvement should increase further. The presence of the familiar institutions would be enough. To keep them somewhat on the periphery was more comfortable anyway. Denominational competition might be embarrassing for an emerging national spirit or for the sensitive integration of particular communities. Too much church influence might also upset the delicate tolerance of some of the favoured vices, such as drinking and gambling. On the other hand keeping them out of sight would not do either. After all they provided a nostalgic link with the English, Irish, Scottish or Welsh past. They alone provided both a moral and a transcendental frame of reference for the vicissitudes of life and guaranteed the moral integrity of community and family life.

There is little information available about church attendance in the first half of the twentieth century. Changes were taking place. Sunday evening services became much less popular in this period (Carruthers, 1901: 7) and certainly attendance was not increasing. Spurr, speaking about the earlier part of the century, estimates that only 25 per cent of the population attended church regularly, for which he blames the climate of hedonism (Spurr, 1918: 241).

Table 3.3   Church attendance for the major Australian denominations according to various Morgan Gallup polls

	1947[a]	1954[b]	1962[c]	1970[c]	1976[c]	1981[c]
Anglican	19	19	13	11	9	12
Catholic	63	75	55	51	42	37
Methodist	34	33	33	21	16	5
Presbyterian	31	21	19	20	11	8
Uniting	–	–	–	–	–	34

Notes: a Percentage of respondents who say that they attended a religious service on at least one of the two preceding Sundays
b Percentage attending weekly. The question was: 'How many times did you go to church in the last year' To make replies comparable, the figures were divided by 52
c Percentage of respondents saying that they had attended church in the last seven days

After World War II the various Morgan Gallup polls asked Australians twenty-one years and over (in the 1970s this changed to fourteen and over) questions about their church going habits. The percentage of those who had attended in the last seven days rose from 23 per cent in 1950 to 30 per cent in 1960 and 1966, but dropped from there to 25 per cent in 1970, 20 per cent in 1976, 19 per cent in 1980, to rise again to 22 per cent in 1981. As Table 3: 3 shows Catholics began the second half of the twentieth century with much higher church going rates than they began the second half of the nineteenth. Yet since the Vatican II council, attendance has been dropping in all Anglo-Saxon countries and Australia is not an exception. The opposite seems to be the case with Methodism: church going rates were the highest of all the major denominations in the second half of the nineteenth century, but its rates in the second half of the twentieth were much below those of one hundred years ago and have been dropping steadily over the past 30 years.

The 1981 figures are particularly interesting in that they support our argument in Chapter I that the active Methodists and Presbyterians who joined the Uniting Church appear to prefer to think of themselves as Uniting, whereas their more nominal brethren (and sisters) continue to adhere to the old designations. The drop from 16 per cent to 5 per cent for Methodist and from 11 per cent to 8 per cent for Presbyterian weekly attendance during the period 1976 to 1981 can only be explained as a tendency of the nominal members to swell disproportionately the old ranks, leaving the Uniting Church with a rather high 34 per cent of members who attend weekly.

Another interesting feature of Table 3.3 is that the percentage difference between Anglicans and Catholics who attend on an average Sunday has been more than halved since 1954: from a difference of 56 per cent in 1954 (75 per cent minus 19 per cent) it became 25 per cent in 1981 (37 per cent minus 12 per cent). Over the past twenty years Catholic attendance has dropped much more severely than Protestant church going although the Catholic rate is still amongst the highest in the country. Yet as Table 3.3 also shows, in 1981 it hardly differed from the Uniting Church. What of course is not shown in the table is the very high attendance rate of the sects, which represent too small a proportion of the population to appear in national surveys. Chant (1982: 112) mentions that Pentecostal attendance exceeds membership figures and that close to half of these church goers had no previous church attachments.

The large difference between Catholic and Protestant attendance round the 1950s also begins to appear less when one considers the casual church goers. A 1946 Gallup poll asked the question 'Are you a church goer?' Of the Anglicans 44 per cent, Catholics 68 per cent, Methodists 58 per cent and Presbyterians 50 per cent answered, yes.

The Religion in Australia survey (1966) confirmed that the percentage of casual church goers was larger amongst Australian Protestants than amongst Catholics. Table 3.4 shows that only 12 per cent of Catholics attended church occasionally, whereas more than a quarter of the Protestants did. These casual church goers do not differ much from those who say that they go 'hardly ever'. Only 7 per cent of the occasionals had been to church on the preceding Sunday (3 per cent of the 'hardly ever' ones) and it is for that reason that further tabulation included the occasional church goers in the 'irregular category'.

Although the percentages of the survey only applied to New South Wales, Victoria and Tasmania, they were roughly comparable to the Gallup poll results. In all instances Catholic attendance was by far the highest, followed at a distance by Methodists, Presbyterians and Anglicans, in that order.

An extensive range of questions on religion was contained in the Australian Values Study conducted in the second half of 1983 by Morgan Gallup polls. This study was synchronised with similar studies carried out in 24 countries (*the Bulletin*, 24 January, 1984: 28). The sample consisted of more than 1200 people aged fourteen years and over, living in Australia. The finding on church going was similar to the 1981 Morgan Gallup poll data: 21 per cent of the respondents attended church once a week (or actually 15 per cent did—another 6 per cent attended *more* than once a week). The Values Study had more details about those who were less regular: 7 per cent once a month, 7 per cent once every two or three months, 3 per cent Christmas or

Table 3.4   Church attendance of all respondents (including children) by denomination

Percentage of all respondents (including children) who went to church	Anglican	Catholic	Methodist	Presbyterian	Total (including others)
Never	32	11	18	21	23
Hardly ever (less than twice a year)	20	8	16	15	15
Occasionally (more than twice a year but less than once a month)	27	12	25	30	23
Usually (once a month, but less than 3 times a month)	9	10	14	17	12
Nearly always (3 times a month or more)	11	60	27	16	27
On preceding Sunday	14	61	26	19	30
Total number	1625	1114	379	551	4198

Source: Religion in Australia Survey, 1966

Easter, 1 per cent other holidays, 7 per cent twice a year, 6 per cent once a year, 11 per cent less often and 37 per cent who said quite decisively that they never attended any church.

How do Australians feel about church going? Is there a recognisable anti-church sentiment? In 1946 a Gallup poll asked 'What would be your main reason for not going?' and 'What do you think is the main reason why more people do not go to church regularly?' (1949 and 1961). The answers are almost never in terms of uselessness of religion or active hostility. In all three polls 'lack of interest' or 'apathy' is most often given as the main reason. The 1949 poll discovered that 58 per cent of the answers essentially blamed the people ('more interested in sport', 'too lazy', 'too busy', 'lack of religious training'), 27 per cent blamed the churches ('services too dull', 'too much hypocrisy') and 15 per cent had no opinions. This lack of hostility towards organised religion is also obvious in England. When in 1964 Gallup carried out a survey for ABC Television, the replies it received from the non-church goers, as to why they did not go to church, showed a similar, non-hostile, generally defensive attitude, such as 'lost the habit'. In 1949 the Anglican Diocese of Newcastle, New South Wales, commissioned a market research organisation to investigate what representative Anglicans throughout the diocese thought about church going. When the non-church going respondents of the sample (n = 423) were asked whether the church served any useful purpose in the world, only 2.6 per cent answered 'no'. Of the 94.1 per cent respondents who said 'yes', the replies to the next question 'why?' were primarily in such terms as 'good for children' (82.8 per cent), 'necessary for living' (18.6 per cent), 'sets standard of life' (18.3 per cent), etc.

Scott and U'Ren (1962: 55) in their Melbourne study remark that 'the high percentage who regard the church as important stands in apparent contrast to the low percentage who attend'.

More recently Kenneth Dempsey reported that in a small town in Western Victoria in which he and a team of interviewers did extensive field work, Protestants avoid church because they say it is irrelevant to them. Ninety per cent of the people regard themselves as Christians, yet less than 20 per cent go to church on an average Sunday. Other reasons for staying away from church (apart from the respondent not getting anything out of it) were 'lack of time, health problems, lack of faith, the hypocrisy of the church and its members, disagreements with views held by the clergy, and the church's preoccupation with money'. Dempsey comments that there is little enthusiasm about attending worship and that with the exception of some elderly widows living by themselves, the other inhabitants are plainly lukewarm about religion (Dempsey, 1983: 28–29).

Also recently Dorothy Harris muses that lack of allegiance is caused by increasing cosmopolitanism (differences in ethnic background), modernisation (increased urbanisation and mass media penetration), changing values (increasing individual autonomy and situational morality), cultural marginality (she quotes the Morgan Gallup poll of 20 August 1980, showing that 62 per cent of the respondents thought that religion was losing its influence on Australian life), and the fact that 'the new spiritual fervour is largely expressed outside the main denominations . . . She comments that decline in allegiance is inevitable unless denominations counterbalance these forces. Yet instead the churches 'remain tied to traditional territorial structures such as parish and diocese' rather than responding to 'the emergence of pluralistic partial communities (ethnic, professional and interest groups) . . .' (Harris, 1982a: 237–238).

What seems clear from all these reports and interpretations is that most Australians regard worship services as unexciting and uninspiring and that many of those who attend church regularly are not any less involved in, or motivated by, more secular sources. Yet on the other hand the Australian churches and sects have sometimes actually, and always potentially, been the source for greater integrity of individuals, families, communities and society at large, even when, or particularly when, these 'identities' were fragmented and dislocated.

How unique is the Australian pattern which has just been described? Not very, it seems. The New Zealand figures (Mol, 1982: 82–83) for the various denominations show that in the second half of the nineteenth century those who thought of themselves as Anglicans at census times had a similarly low record of attendance (about 16 per cent), Presbyterians and Catholics were in the 25–30 per cent range, whereas approximately 55 per cent of the Methodists attended church. In the middle of the twentieth century (as in Australia) Methodism and Catholicism had changed places (Catholic attendance was actually in the seventh decile). Again similarly, in the past quarter of the twentieth century Catholic attendance had dropped strongly. In Canada (Mol, 1985: Chapter 10) and England (Martin, 1972: 232) the same pattern occurs: Anglicans have the lowest attendance record, Nonconformists do somewhat better, but Catholic attendance is way up in the 60–70 per cent range until the 1960s after which the Church seems to slowly lose its hold on the membership.

In the USA church attendance has been much higher for all Protestant denominations, but the Catholic pattern is rather similar: very high until the early 1960s, then a severe drop right through the 1970s (Greeley, 1979: 10).

In Europe by contrast Catholic church attendance has always been much lower in the homogeneously Catholic countries, such as France, Italy, Portugal and Spain. Protestant attendance in Scandinavia (where Lutheranism forms the state chuch) is also much lower. However, in Europe the situation differs from region to region and global comparisons are therefore rather misleading (see the chapters on each of the countries of Europe in Mol et al., 1972).

All these observations and comparisons lead to the following generalisations in keeping with our emphasis on boundary maintenance, exclusivity and inclusivity. Wherever church organisations have, or had, a monopoly and therefore did not have to set themselves off against competing religious organisations, attendance is down. Where, on the other hand, boundaries had to be maintained (for ethnic or organisational reasons such as in Australia, Canada, New Zealand, USA) attendance is up. Yet the USA is different. Why?

Certainly Argyle is wrong (and it is unfortunate that he had been followed here by almost every English sociologist of religion who has directed himself to English–American differences) when he suggests that American religion is 'more liberal and more secularised, and is attuned to the values of the prosperous middle class' and that this explains different rates of church going, (Argyle, 1958: 38). The picture of American religion is distorted. The fastest growing denominations are precisely those that are not liberal, not secularised and if anything attuned to the lower classes (Wolf, 1959: 32–6). The differences between the USA on the one hand and Australia/England/New Zealand on the other are more likely to have something to do with the greater alacrity of Americans to join any organisation and to feel obliged to make it a lively success. Also Argyle and others overlook the possibility that resorting to religious gimmickry may be related to Americans taking religious faith seriously enough not to bury it in dignified but musty life styles. Of course, American religion is adjusted to the American life style, but this does not necessarily mean that it has become 'ideationally bankrupt' (Bryan Wilson, 1966: 114). Other important reasons for the greater vigour of religion in the USA may have to do with the fit between rapid social change in that country and the evangelical message (Mol, 1983: 24ff.).

Along similar lines we may speculate about the differences between Catholics and others in Australian and Anglo-Saxon countries. In England the 1964 Gallup poll on behalf of ABC Television asked the respondents why they thought people went to church. Catholics tended to emphasise a sense of duty, either self-felt or church-imposed. Protestants, however, were more likely to give non-religious reasons, such as 'it gives you a feeling of well-being' or 'the family has always gone to church'. This Catholic emphasis on duty stems from Catholic teaching but this teaching has also become internalised. Lawlor shows this in her projective tests of 364 children, aged eleven to seventeen years in which the latter had to fill in answers to cartoon characters' remarks. The first picture called for answers to 'I'm not going to Mass, why should I?' In order of frequency, answers fell into these: 'Obligation to God', 'Duty because you are a Catholic', 'Sin not to go', etc. (Lawlor, 1965: 81). In Protestantism, on the other hand, the needs of individuals seems to be the rationale rather than obligation. Protestant religious institutions therefore seem less capable of either adopting an independent stance or of implementing whatever norms they have.

Ultimately the Catholic/Protestant differences in church going are related to the priesthood of believers in Protestantism, and the resulting greater responsibility and role conflict for the Protestant layman who is to represent holiness in his own life. On the other hand, many Catholic laymen feel that they can pass this responsibility to the professional priest as long as they perform certain duties themselves, such as church going and making financial gifts. This greater role conflict for Protestants may have led to greater avoidance and withdrawal from the Protestant churches. The Catholic can resolve the role conflict between life style and religion by compartmentalisation. Protestants find this escape route blocked by the very doctrine of the 'priesthood of all believers' which gave them their freedom from the religious institution.

The Protestant lay persons, at least in the English speaking world, still hold the Church in reverence, but will be less inclined than their Catholic counterparts to become involved. The reason is not only that their 'theology' makes the institution less salient, but above all that involvement means separation and evokes images of personal responsibility for personal holiness. These impossible demands lead to the inevitable barrier which a Protestant clergyman feels is erected when he visits the non-church goer. It is similar to the polite hostility which an unwelcome sales person encounters, but the Catholic is spared the demand for this kind of holiness.

Secularisation is to some extent the logical outcome of the doctrine of salvation by faith of the individual—bypassing institution or works. The doctrine opts for the autonomy of the individual—rather than for the shelter of the community and the norms which sustain it. Secularisation may be seen as the result of the latent, but inevitable, dysfunction of this and other Protestant dogmas.

The severe drop in church attendance since Vatican II seems an apt illustration of our theorising. The essence of Vatican II was the opening of the windows of Catholicism to the modern world. Or to say it in our terms: the Catholic Church made a decisive move from exclusivity to inclusivity, thereby slackening its organisational boundaries. But the 'modern world' is strongly affected by the rational individualism so typical of secularisation. If individual thought and conscience begin to move to centre stage a religious organisation begins of necessity to be less cohesive, more divisive and pluriform. It may maintain all the trappings of the ancient theology (for instance 'no salvation outside the church') but in actual fact it has now opened its flank to an ideology in which individual autonomy is strong. And this means that institutional decision making has to compete more with individual opinion. Church going now becomes more optional.

The modern world with all its economic, political and scientific advances hinges on the by now almost 500 year old idea that certain forms of individualism are compatible with (and may even promote) the orderly complexity necessary for a higher standard of living. The relative freedom of the individual which until then had been regarded as a menace to order might have proved to be a boon in one respect (better mastery over nature), yet in another (increased alienation, meaninglessness and moral ambiguity) it was also an encumbrance. By letting the world in the Catholic Church also weakened the moral shelter it had provided for its flock.

The irony is that at the very moment that Catholicism is moving in the Protestant inclusive direction, the fastest growing Protestant sects are taking the opposite, exclusive course. Through separation from a diversified culture they create islands of specific commitment and moral clarity. They return to the old belief, that God is the epitome of order and Jesus the concrete manifestation of His saving (whole-making) design for the world. They are convinced that by restoring the traditional commitment link with God, snapped by secularism, a saner, regenerated form of existence can be restored. The fact that they seem to have both the fastest growth as well as the highest church going rate may foreshadow a twenty-first century culture in which islands of strong ideological commitment mop up the increasing number of refugees from a society in which complexity, tolerance and moral vagueness are necessary to guarantee man's independence from, and mastery over nature. At any rate it is only through speculations of this kind about the largest possible context that I can make sense of the very concrete data provided by research on church going in Australia. After all, the data seem to show that the more our religious organisations move towards the exclusive end of the continuum the higher their attendance rate and the more they go in the opposite direction the more tenuous, apparently, is the hold on their membership.

Bible reading and praying

Nine out of ten Australians have a bible in their homes, according to a 1960 Gallup poll. A cookery book shares the honour of being the type of book possessed by the largest percentage of Australians (91 per cent), closely followed by a dictionary (89 per cent) and an atlas (75 per cent). Further down come an encyclopaedia (59 per cent) and Shakespeare's works (42 per cent). An earlier (1954) poll found that Protestants (nine out of ten) are more likely to possess a bible than Catholics (7 out of 10).

However, possession does not necessarily mean that it is read. In many homes the bible is just gathering dust, apparently not being opened from one year to another. The 1960 Gallup poll investigated this as well, and found that 39 per cent of adults had not read the bible for at least a year. A similar percentage (38 per cent) had read it within the last fourteen days and the remaining 23 per cent had read it more than a fortnight but less than a year ago. There were denominational differences: Catholics (43 per cent) were more likely than Anglicans (34 per cent) or Presbyterians (24 per cent) or Methodists (20 per cent) not to have read it within the last five years.

Still, reading can mean a superficial glance or a concentrated effort. In 1954 Gallup therefore asked: 'How long is it since you read the bible for ten minutes or more?' Compared with the 38 per cent in 1960 who said that they had read the bible within the past fortnight, only 23 per cent in 1954 said that they had read it for ten minutes or more in the same period. This suggests that unless bible reading increased considerably between 1954 and 1960 (which is unlikely) a considerable number come in the 'superficial glance' category. Again Catholics (50 per cent) were less likely to have read the bible for at least ten minutes in the last ten years than Anglicans (63 per cent), Methodists (67 per cent), Presbyterians (71 per cent) and Baptists (80 per cent).

As possession does not necessarily mean reading, likewise reading does not necessarily mean knowing its contents. The 1966 Religion in Australia Survey was more interested in knowledge, so it included the question:

> The following statement has been made by some people here in Australia. Would you agree or disagree with it or don't you know? "The book of Acts of the Apostles gives an account of Jesus' life on earth."

It was a false statement (the Gospels provide this account, not the book of Acts), but it required more than a superficial knowledge of the New Testament to know this. Only 15 per cent of the sample (n = 1825) disagreed (correctly), 49 per cent did not know, and the rest gave no answer (6 per cent), or even agreed (30 per cent). As was to be expected, the percentage of irregular church goers who disagreed (10 per cent, n = 1218) was much smaller than the percentage of regular church goers (25 per cent, n = 604). As with the Gallup poll there were again denominational differences. The percentage disagreeing was smaller among Catholic (15 per cent, n = 270) than among Presbyterian (26 per cent, n = 91), Methodist (28 per cent, n = 61) or Anglican (36 per cent, n = 101) church goers.

It was not unexpected to find that Catholics showed the least interest in, and knowledge of, the bible for it was the Protestant Reformation which began to stress the scriptures, but it was surprising that so few regular church going Protestants had more than a superficial knowledge of its contents. All of them must have listened to scripture readings and sermons from the book of Acts, without being able to place them in their proper context.

The secularisation of the Australian public also shows in the comparatively small numbers saying grace before meals. In 1951 Gallup found that 52 per cent of Baptist families say grace, compared with 46 per cent of Methodist, 33 per cent of Presbyterian, 32 per cent of Catholic and 26 per cent of Anglican families. According to the same poll, a child normally says grace in 11 per cent of Australian

Table 3.5 Denomination by church attendance by other religious practices, experiences and opinions (1966)

Percentage of respondents who	Anglicans		Catholics		Methodists		Presbyterians	
	church attendance irregular	church attendance regular	church attendance irregular	church attendance regular	church attendance irregular	church attendance regular	church attendance irregular	church attendance regular
1 pray daily	20	55	29	61	16	54	15	50
2 pray occasionally	44	35	43	32	51	41	41	44
3 never pray	34	6	25	5	31	5	40	4
4 have had a feeling of being somehow in God's presence	36	68	42	70	32	89	36	71
5 have had a sense of being saved in Christ	23	53	29	47	28	71	20	44
6 have had a feeling of being afraid of God	19	18	23	39	20	31	14	19
7 have had a feeling of being punished by God for something they had done	23	37	27	38	23	28	23	36
8 know that God really exists and have no doubts about it	30	66	53	84	41	80	42	63
9 while having doubts, felt that they believed in God	27	17	15	9	32	13	24	21
10 did not believe in a personal God but in a higher power of some kind	17	6	8	4		3	14	6
11 defined the Church as appointed by God and as the home and refuge of all mankind	17	33	33	60	19	38	19	39
12 felt that the Church stood for the best in human life, in spite of short-comings found in all human institutions	43	42	29	17	44	36	40	32
13 regarded the usefulness of the Church as doubtful and thought that it might do as much harm as good	10	1	8	–	7	3	9	–
Total number of respondents	632	101	137	270	111	61	189	91

Source: Religion in Australia Survey, 1966

homes, father says it in 10 per cent, mother in 8 per cent and it is said together in 4 per cent. This means that there must be a fair proportion of Catholic homes where everyone goes to church regularly, but grace is not said (two-thirds go to church but only one-third says grace), and the reverse applies to Anglicans (less than 20 per cent go to church regularly, but 26 per cent say grace).

Table 3.5 shows that there are considerable numbers in all denominations who pray daily and do not go to church regularly. Vice versa, there are considerable numbers of people who go to church regularly, but do not pray daily. Naturally there is a strong relationship between church going and other religious practices, beliefs and experiences, but in no instance can one say that church attendance, daily prayer or belief in God are adequate and representative measures of religious life. The reason church attendance is used sometimes as the only measure is because it is the most observable index. It can be checked. On the other hand, daily prayer is so private, that one can only depend on the word of the respondent. Nevertheless, prayer is a good criterion of genuine religiousness as non-religious motives are less likely to interfere.

Table 3.5 has some other interesting features. It shows that Catholics who do not attend church regularly are more likely to pray daily than similar Nonconformists. It shows that more respondents report having had a feeling of being somehow in God's presence than a feeling of being afraid of God. Non-church going Anglicans and Presbyterians report this feeling almost as much as church going ones. Church going Catholics report this feeling most frequently.

The table also shows that church going Catholics are more likely to define the church as appointed by God, than church going Anglicans, Methodists and Presbyterians. Protestants are more likely than Catholics to choose the more secular definition of the church (as standing 'for the best in human life, in spite of shortcomings found in all human institutions'). It is interesting that so few non-church goers of any denomination doubt the usefulness of the church.

How do these findings and figures compare with other countries, and what do they mean?

Judging by the percentages which Argyle (1958: 35) quotes for Britain (46 per cent) and the USA (42.5 per cent), fewer Australian respondents (25 per cent) pray daily. On the other hand, more of the Australian respondents (30 per cent) had been to church on the preceding Sunday than in Great Britain, where 14.6 per cent were reported to attend weekly. However Australians were below Americans, 42.5 per cent of whom were reported as attending church every week.

It is interesting that more British respondents (61 per cent) than American ones (35 per cent) could name the four Gospels. Unfortunately there are no figures comparable to our finding that only 15 per cent of respondents could detect the falsity of a statement regarding the book of Acts. Argyle thinks that the difference in knowledge results from religious teaching in British but not in American schools.

Why is it that in both Britain and Australia more Anglicans pray daily than go to church? Argyle (ibid.: 159) suggests that Protestants are religious through inner motivations, Catholics through social pressure, and that therefore Protestants engage more in private than public prayer. However, our Table 3.5 shows that the percentage of non-church going Catholics who pray daily is higher than the percentage of non-church going Anglicans. Maybe the Protestant Church's hold over its membership is so much smaller than the Catholic one, that it is not difficult for the 'prayer rate' to surpass the 'church attendance rate'. However, the fact that the 'prayer rate' is much higher for those who attend church in all denominations suggests that public worship can reinforce and stimulate a private habit. There is a significant residue of those who pray daily without reinforcement or stimulation. They are presumably 'religious through inner motivations', even though this behaviour must have also been learnt. Catholics and Protestants may of course differ on the content of the prayer (formal? informal? routine? feeling-oriented?). But there is little or no information about this in Australia or elsewhere.

4 Sex and age

Sex

It has been said that if it had not been for women, Australia would be a much less 'religious' nation. Historians mentioned that in the outback Sunday was no different from any other day unless there were wives around (Kiddle, 1961: 143). They introduced family prayers to the stations and coaxed even 'the men in the hut' along by dispensing 'plum cake and a wee tot of rum ... after the evening service' (ibid.: 92–93).

Morven Brown says the same about Penrith, New South Wales in the first decade of this century; it was the mothers who insisted on religious practice and the girls especially were steered into church activities (Brown, 1957: 103, 107).

Many observers have noted that more women than men participate in church worship (Scott and U'Ren, 1962: 39) and others quote male licensed club members as saying that 'the club is my church', implying that they have no further need for churches.

The overrepresentation of women at Protestant church services has not escaped the attention of some wits. One made the following parody of a hymn:

In the world's great field of battle,
In the bivouac of life
You will find the Christian soldier
Represented by his wife.

After this, it is not surprising that a 1950 Australian Gallup poll found that more women (64 per cent) than men (49 per cent) regard religion as a greater influence on their own lives than politics. In the same year Gallup found that 28 per cent of women go to church every week compared with 18 per cent of men. Four years later, another poll stated that 30 per cent of women had been to a regular church service within a week compared with 24 per cent of men. Two years later Gallup found almost identical differences: 34 per cent of women had

68

been to church within a week compared with 24 per cent of men. The differences between men and women also show up in religious affiliation as reported in the census (see Table 4.1). In 1954 there were more than twice as many men than women in the 'no religion' category. The 1966 Census showed a sharp rise (from 37 550 in 1961 to 94 091 persons in 1966) in people of 'no religion', the rise being greater among women with the result that the sex ratio decreased.

This pattern has continued in subsequent censuses: in 1981 over one and a half million Australians chose the 'no religion' category, but because women now also joined the exodus in greater numbers, the sex ratio went down further to 130.14.

Table 4.1 Sex ratios (number of males per 100 females) for the major religious denominations according to the 1954, 1966 and 1981 Australian census

Religion	1954	1966	1981
Church of England	100.56	99.06	93.85
Catholic	103.68	101.54	96.77
Methodist	95.85	95.22	94.23
Presbyterian	98.03	96.31	91.65
Lutheran	107.94	103.10	95.27
Orthodox	146.17	113.12	105.10
Baptist	89.10	89.27	88.51
Church of Christ	89.17	88.71	83.56
Congregational	87.99	88.26	87.66
Salvation Army	90.01	92.00	85.52
Seventh Day Adventist	78.84	81.99	82.78
Brethren	84.46	91.98	90.34
Hebrew	102.77	97.91	95.50
Other Religion or Denomination	103.31	100.27	100.24
No religion	236.80	180.30	130.14
No reply	120.48	119.74	109.54

Table 4.1 also shows that in some denominations men were, or, are overrepresented. In 1954 this was particularly so for the Orthodox (146.17), the Lutherans (107.94) and to a lesser extent the Catholics (103.68) and Jews (102.77). Amost all of this was due to men migrating alone or ahead of their wives, leading to a temporary over-balance. In the 1981 Census only the Orthodox did not seem to have caught up as yet. However, new immigrant groups had entered by then and had started the process of male preponderance anew: the Muslim ratio (Islam was brought to Australia primarily by Turkish and Lebanese immigrants) was 202.7 in 1971 (n = 22 311) but dropped

to 123.4 (n = 45 205) in 1976 and 116.5 (n = 76792) in 1981. Similarly the Buddhist ratio (109.0 in 1981) was caused by an over-representation of males from Vietnam, Malaysia and the rest of Asia.

Table 4.1 has some unexpected features. The major denominations used to represent the nation at large. And so one would expect Anglicans and Catholics (together comprising 60 per cent of the population in 1947 and still forming a majority in 1981) to have a balanced ratio of approximately 100 males per 100 females. This was indeed the case more or less in 1954 and 1961, but since then the ratio has gone down considerably for Anglicans to 99.1 in 1966, 96.5 in 1971, 95.1 in 1976 and 93.8 in 1981. For Catholics the corresponding ratios were 101.5, 99.7, 98.2 and 96.8. Since this decrease coincided with a steep increase (from 37 550 individuals in 1961 to 1 567 718 in 1981) in the 'no religion' category, it seems natural to suggest that the nominal Anglican and Catholic men were spearheading the outflow from their respective denominations, nominal women following at a respectful distance. At first sight this argument does not seem valid in that the ratio has been dropping severely over the past twenty years,suggesting that more women than men changed to 'no religion'. However this is not so: women may have increased their component of the category relative to 1954 and 1966, but they have not done so in absolute terms. For instance, in 1981 240 570 more men had joined the 'no religion' category (891 591–651 021) as compared with 1976, but only 207 845 women (685 126–477 281). If one adds the surplus 32 725 men to Anglican men of the 1981 census, the ratio is more than restored to the 1976 level (95.5 as against the actual Anglican ratio of 95.1 for 1976). Similarly for Catholics (98.5 as against the actual ratio of 98.2). Of course these 32 725 should not be distributed arbitrarily over just one denomination but over all those whose ratio has been dropping. And then it is obvious that the male flow to 'no religion' provides anything but an exhaustive account. There are two other likely possibilities that might attempt to explain the decrease. One, males are also overrepresented in the 'not stated' category. The ratio is 109.54. However, there are only 3 097 surplus if one calculates the excess additions over 1976 and this does not take us very far. More important seems a general decrease of the sex ratio in the population at large from one census to another: it dropped from 102.2 in 1961 to 101.4 in 1966, to 101.1 in 1971 to 100.0 in 1976 to 99.4 in 1981. Yet this does not help us very much either, as one can expect this decrease to be affected by the belated joining of wives of immigrants, few of whom are likely to be either Anglican or Catholic. If on the other hand, the ageing of the population (males have a shorter life expectancy) is a factor in the decrease, then one might also expect a flow on to the Anglican and Catholic sex ratio.

A third cluster of data from Table 4.1 which deserves comment is the generally low sex ratio of all the sects. The lowest of all (the Jehovah's Witnesses 81.54 in 1981) is actually not on the table, as I had to adjust the 1981 categories to the existing categories of the older table in the Religion in Australia Survey. They are closely followed by the Seventh Day Adventists who have a long history of low sex ratios, the Church of Christ and the Salvation Army. As the sects and the smaller denominations often require strong commitments and intense religious feeling (of which women seem to be more capable) one might expect the lower ratios.

At first it seems strange to see a major denomination (the Uniting Church) in the same category as the sects as far as sex ratio is concerned (84.9). As we have already discovered in the previous chapter, the Uniting Church has a much higher percentage of church goers than the participating denominations (Congregational, Methodist and Presbyterian). And as women are much the better church goers one may expect this preponderance to be also reflected in the larger number of women putting 'Uniting' on the census form. After all, active rather than nominal Christians seem to be involved in the Uniting Church. This argument is complementary to the argument we have advanced above, that the flow on to the 'no religion' category is spearheaded by men who, in Anglo-Saxon societies, are traditionally less involved in religion.

However, before getting involved in a discussion as to why this is so, let us look at the data from the Religion in Australia Survey which show not only that more women go to church regularly, but also pray daily and have orthodox beliefs regarding God and the Church. More of them report experiences of God's presence and being saved in Christ, although interestingly enough, more men than women report having been afraid of God. Women are slightly more interested in religious services on radio and television. However, more of them say that five years ago they went to church more often than they do now. Women are also more likely to disapprove of premarital sex and adultery. On other values, such as the priority of obedience and respect for social standing, they do not appear to differ much from men.

It would be interesting to compare some of these data with the April 1980 national poll carried out for the *Age*. This poll asked approximately 2100 individuals on the electoral rolls what their denomination was and whether or not they were regular or irregular church goers. Of those who said they were Anglicans 11 per cent of the males and 14 per cent of the females were regular attenders. The corresponding percentages for those belonging to Uniting/

Table 4.2 Sex by religious and other categories (1966)

Percentage of respondents who	Men (over 20)	Women (over 20)
1 are Anglican and attend church regularly	17	23
	(n = 793)	(n = 813)
2 are Catholic and attend church regularly	66	73
	(n = 545)	(n = 569)
3 are Methodist and attend church regularly	37	44
	(n = 175)	(n = 203)
4 are Presbyterian and attend church regularly	26	41
	(n = 266)	(n = 282)
5 prayed daily	25	40
6 knew that God really existed and had no doubt about it	43	55
7 did not know whether there was a God and did not believe there was a way to find out	9	4
8 were of the opinion that the Church was appointed by God and that it was the home and refuge of all mankind	25	32
9 regarded the usefulness of the Church as doubtful and felt that it might do as much harm as good	9	6
10 reported that they had had an experience of God's presence since childhood	41	55
11 reported that they had had an experience of being saved by Christ since childhood	29	38
12 reported that they had had an experience of being afraid of God since childhood	23	22
13 disagreed that the book of the Acts of the Apostles gave an account of Jesus' life on earth	16	14
14 regularly listened to or watched religious services in radio or television	15	20
15 went to church more often five years ago	13	19
16 attended meetings and activities of other organisations (not church) once a week or more	13	10
17 disapproved of people who had sex relations before marriage	52	73
18 disapproved of people who had sex relations after marriage with someone other than husband or wife	82	91
19 disagreed that the most important thing for a child to learn was to obey rather than to think for itself	52	53
20 disagreed that a person whose family had had a high social standing for many generations was therefore entitled to more respect	57	53
Total number of respondents (items 14, 15, 16)	1279	1327
Total number of respondents (items 5–13, 17–20)	877	959

Source: Religion in Australia Survey, 1966

Methodist/Presbyterian Churches were 14 and 22, for other Protestants, 32 and 43 and for Catholics 36 and 47. The 1980 percentages
are considerably below those of 1966: Anglican men dropped from 17

to 11 per cent, women from 23 to 14 per cent; Uniting/Methodist/ Presbyterians on average seem to have halved their percentages; Catholic men dropped from 66 to 36 and women from 73 to 47. Yet the differences between men and women were sustained. Why are women more religious? Surveys in other countries report the same phenomenon (Mol et al. 1972).

Attempts to explain the variations have been made by Argyle (1958: 78–79) and by Glock, Ringer and Babbie (1967: 43). Argyle suggests that women have more guilt feelings. The reason why the ratio of women rises on the continuum from Catholicism to extreme Protestantism is because of the greater emphasis on sin and salvation in the latter groups. Argyle's argument is weak; there are proportionately more Catholic than Protestant women participating in religious ritual. The difference between Catholic and Protestant frequency of attendance is more likely to be related to social structure factors than personal needs. Argyle who, to his credit, is not very happy about his explanation, has another suggestion borrowed from Freud. God is a projected father figure and because girls prefer their fathers, they are more attracted to a deity presented as a fatherly male. Nevertheless, as Argyle says, parental preferences may be independent of sex.

Glock and his colleagues follow a more promising line of explanation. Men and women have different roles. The family role of the mother and the occupational role of the father have contrasting effects. As the bonds between family and church are still relatively strong, and those connecting church and the economy have weakened extensively, one can expect females who are involved heavily in the family role to be more church oriented (Glock et al. 1979: 44). Another suggestion made by them is that women simply have more time to devote to church than men (ibid.: 45)

The suggestions have a number of weaknesses. There is no evidence that either occupational or marital status can explain sex differences. If the availability of time is a factor, then there should also be a link between church attendance and other organisational involvement; there is no Australian evidence for this. Australian males or females do not seem to look upon the churches as primarily a social outlet. Related to this is another weakness: an adequate explanation has to cover greater religiousness in general and not just organisational involvement. None of the arguments explain why women engage more in private prayer.

The following seems a more reasonable explanation. In a fragmented world where different orientations either help or hinder the attainment of specific goals, religious orientations aid conflict resolving, emotionally healing, integrating functions. It is with these integrative areas that both religion and women are traditionally preoccupied. Martin (1967: 126) comes close to this view. On the other hand, males of all classes in modern western society are socialised into thinking and believing that drive and aggressiveness are positive orientations. They learn how to cope with conflict and play it often as an institutionalised game. Specific goals are primary and conflict resolution secondary, even though for both social and personal reasons, conflicts will be minimised by institutionalisation and by rule restrictions. Both the emphasis on accomplishment and the consequent playing of the rough conflict game need legitimation. The source of this legitimation of the male ethos in our culture is secular rather than religious because steely neutrality rather than emotional surrender (love) serves its purposes better.

Religion is associated with the latter and though the values of Christianity such as acceptance, forgiveness, moral uprightness, etc. can be distinctive assets in the male game, they can also become a liability when more than skin deep. Private prayers rather than church attendance, which after all can be defined and tolerated as a desirable convention, seem to go more than skin deep in this respect. This suggested explanation has the advantage of providing a link with culturally defined sex roles, but even more importantly with basic sexual expectations, love by the female and satisfaction by the male.

Additional support for our argument comes from comparative religion. All religions, from the most ancient to the most advanced, contrast feminity with masculinity; femaleness usually stands for whatever includes and holds together, receptivity, softness, whereas maleness symbolises the opposite: intrusion, fragmentation, aggression, bestowal, hardness. This is as true for the ancient Chinese distinctions between Yin (female) and Yang (male) as for the Maori myths which as Biggs (1960: 12) observes 'divides all of nature into male and female' (Mol 1976: 236; 1982: 22; 1983: 62ff.). The point I am trying to make is not that this distinction is uncompromisingly sharp, but that there are elements of integration (to which religion and art are partial) and differentiation (to which mastery over nature and efficiency are partial) which can still be detected (in spite of thousands of years of dynamic interaction and their resolutions) in such present day phenomena as differences between male and female religious behaviour in Australia in 1984.

Age

Many Australian clergy have complained that modern youth is a slippery entity. 'You think that you finally have a few interested in the church' I heard one minister say, 'but then they slip away to join other teenagers in some less serious pursuits'. His opinion is confirmed by W.F. Connell who, in a large study of 8 705 teenagers conducted in the early 1950s, found that the number of hours spent in church activity for one hundred adolescents was small compared with such activities as sport, pictures and dancing (Connell, 1957: 127). One of his tables shows that the hours spent on church decrease from 72 for 13-year-old boys to 50 for 18-year-olds and the corresponding hours spent on dancing increase from 25 to 215 for boys over the same age group. Girls are definitely more religious, but their hours spent on church drop from 92 (13 years old) to 76 (18 years old) and the hours spent on dancing rise from 57 to 195. Upper class teenage boys spent more time (76 hours per 100 boys) on church activities than the middle class (70) or lower class (63) boys, but all of them spent more time on pictures (185 hours for upper class, 268 for middle and 358 hours for lower class boys). It was the same with girls: per 100 upper class girls 99 hours were spent in church activities (95 hours for middle and 81 hours for lower class girls), but 164 hours on films (234 hours for middle and 309 hours for lower class girls).

Connell's findings are supported by the 1951 report on church going in the diocese (Church of England) of Newcastle (p. 33) which says: 'There is abundant evidence that, once they reach adolescence, few young people exhibit any desire to maintain their association with church or Sunday School'. The authors of the study regard this drift as the very crux of the church's problem.

Young men in particular are underrepresented in some Protestant congregations, (Oeser and Hammond, 1954: 20) and they are virtually not represented at all, as Henderson mentioned, in Synods and their committees (Henderson, 1923: 41). Fifty years later the situation does not seem to have changed much in the major denominations. Dempsey writes that in Smalltown only a quarter of the worshippers are men, that the majority of those are either retired or close to retirement but that they hold the balance of power in church affairs (Dempsey, 1983: 40). His enquiries showed that these men were generally not motivated by a great zeal for the Gospel, but accepted these church responsibilities 'because of the store they placed by family and community life'.

Some observers have spoken about the 'age gap' by which they mean the absence not so much of adolescents but of the young married couples in the churches. John Roberts, introducing the Australian Broadcasting Commission programme 'Encounter' on this subject in October 1965, said:

How many of us have watched televised church services, and how many of us have noticed the composition of the congregations? If you think about it you will probably recall seeing children and teenagers and mature or middle-aged people and old people, but there seems to be an age gap, a conspicuous absence of people in the age group from about twenty to about forty-five. Yet there are three and a half million people in this group, more than a quarter of the total population of the Commonwealth of Australia. These are the young professionals, the junior executives, the young men making their way in the world. These are the people who must necessarily have drive and enthusiasm to build their careers and make their homes, yet somewhere, somehow, the church seems to be losing them.

In desperation some of the churches are 'trying to sort of pep themselves up, to get in touch with the modern generation by jazz masses and gimmicks of all sorts', but as the Rev. Hayward who made this observation on the above mentioned programme said, 'This is something that makes one curl up inside'. Obviously the problem is too deep to be solved by gimmickry.

However, the earlier Australian data do not show a large 'age gap'. The gap certainly is not as definite as the one between men and women. In the 1951 Report on the Decline of Church-going (p. 47) 27 per cent of the respondents over 35 (n = 467) were regular church goers (at least once a fortnight) compared with 22 per cent of the respondents between 18 and 35, and even this difference would have been smaller had the report calculated separate urban–rural figures (there was a slight overrepresentation in the sample of older people in the country where church attendance was much higher). Gallup poll data of the 1940s and 1950s are not very conclusive either. True, a 1947 poll found that the numbers of church goers (attendance on at least one of the two preceding Sundays) increased with age, from 29 per cent among those in their 20s to 38 per cent for the 50s age group. A 1957 poll found also that only 19 per cent of those 21–29 had read the bible in the last week, compared with 24 per cent of the 30–39 group, and 34 per cent of those over 40. However, a 1960 poll found no marked difference in church going in the age groups except for a slight tendency to cease church going with advancing years (this poll did not back its conclusion with figures).

In the Australian denominations and sects age groups are not equally distributed. About one third of the population is in the 0–19 age cohort, according to the 1981 census. Yet the Muslims (the religion of relatively young and recent immigrants from the Middle East) has as many as 46.2 per cent below the age of 20. The sectarian groups also have generally more than their share of young people: 43.1 per cent of the Latter Day Saints (Mormons), 40.6 per cent of the Pentecostals and 39.7 per cent of the Jehovah's Witnesses are in the 0–19 age bracket. On the basis of their age distribution alone (and not even considering the evangelising power of these sects) one can therefore expect these groups to grow faster than others.

By contrast particularly the older Protestant denominations and the Jews present an ageing profile: 24.5 per cent of those who thought of themselves as Methodists at the 1981 census, 24.6 per cent of Jews, 26.1 per cent Presbyterians and 30.5 per cent of Anglicans were in the 0–19 age group and were therefore underrepresented in their denominations as compared with the nation at large. Of course in these denominations the older (non-reproductive) age groups are correspondingly overrepresented. Catholics in Australia are somewhere in the middle: 37.8 per cent of their (census) membership is below 20 years of age.

Much detail about religious beliefs, experiences and attitudes of the various age groups was provided in the 1966 Religion in Australia Survey. Table 4.3 summarises the findings. It showed, as in the 1960 poll, that there was little difference in church going between the age categories. The replies to the question 'Did you go to a church service or Mass last Sunday?' similarly showed little difference: 27 per cent (20–24 year old respondents), 25 per cent (25–39), 26 per cent (40–59) and 24 per cent (60 and over) had attended church on the preceding Sabbath.

There was more variation in the age categories of children and adolescents. Of the 0–4-year-old children (n = 429) 31 per cent attended church regularly, of the 5–9 category (n = 435) 57 per cent did, of the 10–14 (n = 374) 60 per cent did, and of the 15–19-year-olds (n = 353) 46 per cent attended once a month or more (the definition of 'regular'). Corresponding percentages for those who had attended the previous Sunday were 21, 43, 48 and 40. The figures showed clearly that the children of the sample went to church more regularly than adults. Adolescence appeared to be a period of adjustment to the less frequent attendance of adults.

This applied also to attendance at other church meetings including committees, study groups, and Sunday Schools. Complementing the percentage of item 2 of Table 4.3 for the younger age categories, 9 per cent of the 0–4-year-old children, 27 per cent of the 5–9-year-olds, 21 per cent of the 10–14-year-olds and 15 per cent of the 15–19-year-olds attended these meetings at least once a week. Again the peak of attendance was in the 5–14-year-old group, showing that during this period a remarkably high percentage of parents, primarily Anglican sent their children to Sunday School, although they themselves did not attend church or other church meetings.

Although there was no difference in church going between the various age categories of adults, there was some variation within the denominations. Schreuder generalised that 'the lower the level of religious practice, the more children and old people will be

Table 4.3　Age by religious behaviour, beliefs, experiences and other attitudes (1966)

Percentage of respondents who	Age			
	20–24	25–39	40–59	60+
1 went to church regularly (once a month or more)	34	32	33	33
2 attend other church meetings at least once a week	9	4	4	4
3 prayed daily	22	26	36	46
4 knew that God really existed and had no doubts about it	40	47	50	57
5 while they had doubts, felt that they believed in God	28	23	18	17
6 did not believe in God	3	2	2	1
7 were of the opinion that the Church was appointed by God and that it was the home and refuge of all mankind	30	31	27	28
8 thought that the usefulness of the Church was doubtful and that it might do as much harm as good	10	9	5	5
9 reported to have experienced God's presence since childhood	46	47	49	52
10 reported having had an experience of being saved by Christ since childhood	27	28	37	40
11 reported having had an experience of being afraid of God since childhood	30	25	21	15
12 disagreed that the Acts of the Apostles gave an account of Jesus' life on earth	14	16	16	10
13 regularly listened to or watched religious programmes on radio or TV	10	11	20	29
14 during the time they grew up had fathers who attended church regularly	30	38	43	47
15 during the time they grew up had mothers who attended church regularly	41	50	55	59
16 said that they attended church more often five years ago	21	19	12	15
17 disagreed that the most important thing for a child to learn was to obey rather than to think for itself	61	62	52	31
18 disagreed that a person whose family had had a high social standing for many generations was therefore entitled to some respect	61	66	54	33
19 disapproved of people who had sex relations before marriage	49	56	66	78
20 disapproved of people who had sex relations after marriage with someone other than husband or wife	91	83	87	89
21 had negative feelings towards Jews	23	19	16	14
22 had negative feelings towards Atheists	29	24	33	41
Total respondents, items 1–2 and 13–16	336	785	970	504
Total respondents, all other items	235	580	659	345

Source: Religion in Australia Survey, 1966

overrepresented in the church' (Schreuder 1964: 118), and this is shown when Anglicans in the Religion in Australia Survey are compared with Catholics. Of all Catholics over 20, (n = 628), 65 per cent attended church regularly; of all Catholics under 20, (n = 479), 75 per cent did so. Of all Anglicans over 20 (n = 1026), 14 per cent attended church regularly; of all Anglicans under 20 (n = 575), 31 per cent did so. Although Catholic children and adolescents under 20 attended church more regularly than Catholics over 20, the gap is smaller than between Anglicans under and over 20 years of age. The percentage of Anglicans over 20 attending regularly is less than half that of those under 20. There was also a slight difference between the percentage of regular worshippers (12 per cent) of Anglicans in the 20–39 age groups (n = 421) and the corresponding percentage (16 per cent) of Anglican respondents over the age of 40 (n = 605). (There was no difference between similar Catholic age groups). However, this difference was too small to warrant speaking about a considerable age gap as was done in the 1965 ABC programme.

It would make more sense to speak about considerable age differences in prayer habits. Item 3 of Table 4.3 showed that more of the older respondents pray daily than the younger ones.

Items 4, 5 and 6 are interesting as they showed that the percentage of younger respondents who do not believe in God hardly differs from the corresponding percentage of older respondents. However, more younger respondents have doubts, although they believe in God.

The finding could mean either that this kind of religious belief begins to crystallise with advancing age or that more of the younger generation are scrutinising convention. Whatever the answer, it should be remembered that the contents of religious beliefs are generally vague and unstructured and the social influence on them can be correspondingly great.

On religious experiences, it is interesting that more of the older respondents reported the experience of 'being saved in Christ', (item 10), but that more of the younger ones reported the experience of 'being afraid of God', (item 11).

Although the younger generation is better educated than the older, their biblical knowledge did not seem any greater: the percentage disagreeing with the faulty statement that the book of the Acts of the Apostles gave an account of Jesus' life on earth is small in all age categories.

The numbers listening to or watching religious services on radio or television accorded with American findings and are understandable: older respondents are more likely to have the time and the interest to listen to and watch these programmes (Moberg: 1965).

Items 14 and 15 are of considerable interest. They showed that the younger the respondent, the less his parents are reported to have attended church. If we can trust the respondents' recollections, church attendance had been decreasing for several generations.

Items 17 to 22 were put in the table for more general interest. Item 17 showed that more of the younger respondents disagree that the most important thing for a child to learn is to obey rather than to think for itself. Many more disagreed that a person whose family has had a high social standing for many generations is entitled to some respect. Although the percentage of younger respondents disapproving of adultery is as high as the corresponding percentage of the older respondents, fewer of them disapproved of the person who had sex relations before marriage.

Unexpected are the percentage differences between the age categories on negative feelings towards a Jew. As the younger generations are better educated one would have expected fewer rather than more of them to have negative feelings towards Jews, as is the case with the atheist.

Since the Religion in Australia Survey was carried out in 1966 important changes have taken place, as Mason (1983: 32) and Wilson (1983: 18) noted and as Harris (1982a: 259) documented. A Morgan Gallup poll of 1976 found that regular church attendance in Australia dropped severely from 26.2 per cent in the 14–19 year age bracket to 11.5 per cent for those 20–29 years of age. It rose again to 21.3 per cent for those 30–49 years old and to 20.2 per cent for those 50–69 years of age to rise further to 32 per cent for anyone over 70. This fits with Dempsey's observation that adolescents and people in the 26–50 year age bracket were underrepresented in the churches (Dempsey, 1983: 39). Wilson uses a 1979 *Herald–Age* poll showing that at the time the percentage of the population attending church weekly began at a low 9 per cent for those 21–24 years of age, moved up to 12 per cent for those in the 25–34 to 20 per cent for those in the 35–59 age bracket and to 28 per cent for those 68 years and over (Wilson, 1983: 18).

Unfortunately national church attendance figures are rather meaningless as the differences between the denominations are considerable. Table 4.4 is the result of a reanalysis of data from the April 1980 age poll providing church attendance data separately for the major denominations or denominational groups.

The various age polls did not distinguish between Uniting, Methodist and Presbyterian because the cells would have been too small for meaningful analysis. For the same reason (to keep the cells as large as possible) I combined the six age groups of the poll (18–20; 21–24; 25–34; 35–44; 45–59; 60 +) into three. Table 4.4 shows that with the exception of Other Protestants (Baptists, Lutherans, Church

Table 4.4 Percentage of regular church goers (self-definition) for major denominations in Australia by selected age categories

	Age		
	18–34	35–59	60 +
Anglican	9 (n = 232)	12 (n = 289)	19 (n = 140)
Catholic	35 (n = 209)	45 (n = 211)	54 (n = 61)
Uniting/Methodist/Presbyterian	17 (n = 126)	22 (n = 151)	26(n = 105)
Other Protestant	39 (n = 33)	40 (n = 42)	32 (n = 34)

Source: Age poll, April 1980

of Christ, Pentecostals, Jehovah's Witnesses, etc.) church attendance increases with age for all denominations. This seems to suggest that since the 1960s the exodus from the churches has not only been spearheaded by the men, but also by the young.

What do all these figures mean and how do they compare with overseas findings?

A peak of church and Sunday School attendance in the 5–14 age bracket was observed in a 1962 study of 998 randomly selected inhabitants of Christchurch, New Zealand (Mol: 1962). It was concluded from this survey that for large numbers of Protestants at the time adult behaviour and church attendance were dissociated, and that it would be inevitable, seeing that father or mother models would be much stronger determinants of a child's aspirations than sermons and Sunday School lessons, for most of these children to lapse at a later age. This conclusion appeared to apply to the Australian data as well. The New Zealand study also showed that the gap between child and adult attendance was smaller for Catholics.

For England, Argyle similarly reported that many irreligious parents did send their children to Sunday School (Argyle, 1958: 59). Attempting to explain the decline in church attendance in adolescence he was inclined to emphasise personal decision (ibid.: 65) rather than parental example as the cause. Australian evidence is that teenage children of Anglican parents both of whom attend church regularly, were almost without exception regular themselves, and that the drop was entirely due to Anglican teenagers of families where at least one parent is irregular. Argyle seemed to underrate the effect of the immediate family on religious behaviour. Also the large difference between Anglicans and Catholics was very difficult to explain in terms of a psychological variable, but much easier in terms of a social one (e.g. the cohesion of a Catholic sub-culture). Of course from 1961–76 Sunday School attendance decreased by about 50 per cent (Harris, 1982a: 255) probably showing that irregular church goers removed themselves further from their religious sub-culture through abandoning a felt obligation for religious upbringing.

Both Argyle and Glock go into considerable detail in explaining the varying rates of church attendance of adults according to age. I have my doubts about the Argyle/Glock assumption that differences are due to general psychological processes or to role changes in the life cycle. (Argyle, 1958: 65, Glock, 1967: 47).

Lazerwitz looking at American survey data, came to the conclusion that there was no 'meaningful change in church attendance among Protestants 21–24 years old (Lazerwitz, 1964: 432). Moberg's summary of American studies points in the same direction. He singles out the study of Orbach, who found that age *per se* was unrelated to changes in church attendance (the analysis was based on 6911 adults aged 20 and over in five probability samples) (Moberg, 1965: 83).

Orbach suggests that other studies which came to a different conclusion were weak on the levels of both sampling and the analysis of relevant sociological variables other than sex. Still there is strong evidence that in other parts of the world, age has a significant effect. Houtart and Pin mention that in Cuba indifference to religion is much greater in the 18–25 age bracket than in the 50+ category. In Central Chile they say the practice of religion drops from 50 per cent for young people aged 11–18 to 10 per cent for people aged 21–30 (Houtart and Pin, 1965: 171).

Köster who did his research in 1956 in a typical urban Lutheran congregation near Hamburg, Germany, reported that only 22 per cent of practising adult Lutherans were in the 20–44 age group, whereas 49.7 per cent of all adults in the town were in this age category (Köster, 1959: 90–91). There are many more examples of differential rates according to religious practice of youth, middle and old age (Mol et al., 1972).

To summarise our data and to put them in a larger frame of reference: the decrease in Catholic church attendance in general and amongst Catholic youth in particular is part of a world wide phenomenon. When Vatican II opened the windows of the Catholic Church much fresh air was let in. Yet much also was let out. Youth is least impressed with tradition and therefore the first to take advantage of relaxation of boundaries. It dispensed with existing loyalties all the more easily because old loyalties (to one's family of origin for instance) are on the decline anyway and new loyalties are still being formed. In addition older people are more likely to appreciate cosmic interpretations of the fragile situations in which they are involved and visions of integrity which counterbalance them. They are, or feel, responsible for their families, communities, religious organisations, nation and do not easily defect.

This argument can also be used to account for the differences we found in Protestantism over the past twenty years or so. After all, the difference in roles according to the life cycle remains, even when defection for Protestants has always been easier because of Protestant individualism and the corresponding looser boundary around Protestant religious organisations. The latter can, -everything else remaining the same, account for the generally lower level of church attendance at all age levels when compared with Catholicism in pre-Vatican II days.

This brings us to the various data (Australian and otherwise) showing that there are situations where there are *no* differences between the age groups. Again there is no problem with pre-Vatican II Catholicism; the boundary was rigid enough to contain anyone of any age. Sacralised conformity reigned supreme particularly in those countries (such as Australia) where the Catholic Church did not have the aura of a state church and where it had to compete with other denominations. Nor is there an accounting problem for the lack of age differences in the sects; here too the boundaries are firmly drawn and sects have a similar appeal to persons of any age who feel on the outer.

It becomes more difficult to interpret the earlier data for the major Protestant denominations. Here one would expect the religious organisation to lose out easily in the battle for loyalty of young people. Why were there exceptions? First, there may not have been so many exceptions after all. There were persistent reports in the 1950s and 1960s of youth abandoning the churches. Even the Religion in Australia Survey found that 31 per cent of Anglicans under 20, only 12 per cent of those 20–39 and 16 per cent of those over 40 attended church regularly.

Also, the American figures are likely to refer both to the smaller sect type organisations *and* to the major Protestant denominations who, like the Catholic Church in pre-Vatican II days, were and are very vital organisations with high attendance figures for all age groups and, as we have seen, the larger the church going rates in general, the lesser the age differences.

Thirdly, there may be a parallel (or even correlation) between the much more pronounced age differences in Church attendance of the early 1980s as compared with the early 1960s on the one hand, and the increasingly looser weave of Australian society in the intervening period. If this is so the pronounced age differentials in church attendance may say a great deal not, as is usually imagined, about the increasing secularisation of Australian society, but about the predicament of those religious organisations who in contrast to the sects and pre-Vatican II Catholicism have leaned too heavily toward an increasingly heterogeneous or pluralistic culture.

5 Religion and education

In days gone by religion and education were regarded as inseparable. To our ancestors living in the first half of the nineteenth century both religion and education were powerful means of making responsible adults, reliable citizens, and morally upstanding parents out of children. And so schools and churches were generally on the same premises. Pupils were taught by ministers and priests or at least by individuals who had had similar training and were paid from similar funds.

In Australia the separation in function was much more readily endorsed by Protestants than by Catholics. Protestants happily assumed that reading, writing and arithmetic were technical accomplishments which had little, if anything, to do with morals or with more cosmic interpretations of existence. Catholics by contrast were much less sure that the pursuit of techniques for their own sake did not have implications for other aspects of life. However much rational thinking and individual accomplishment were rewarded within the Catholic universities in Europe and within the erudite orders, they were also felt to be potential emasculators of the moral cohesion of families, communities, convents and monasteries. And so obedience, humility and self denial were stressed, whereas Protestants tended to be confident that a reasonable degree of independent thinking and acting on the part of all people would not necessarily jeopardise order to the breaking point. Catholic hesitancy regarding the latter, and Protestant confidence, affected the flourishing of democracy, entrepreneurship and scientific investigation in the nations in which either the one or the other predominated. However, in Australia both were present and in this chapter I hope to show that different ideas as to how much protection was required by units of social organisation against a hell bent ego indirectly shaped such items as literacy rates, educational accomplishments, the religious behaviour of the educated and emphasis on thinking for oneself rather than on obedience.

In a separate chapter (6) I will discuss how these ideas also had an effect on denominational schools.

Literacy

Historians of nineteenth century Australia agree that Protestants were better educated. Michael Roe, speaking about Eastern Australia toward the middle of the nineteenth century, characterises the Catholic 'Austral–Irish' as 'unschooled' (Roe, 1965: 104). Towards the end of that century another Catholic observer called his fellow believers 'uneducated' in relation to Protestants (Fogarty, 1957: 334–335). Similar characterisations were made within Protestantism, where at least in one instance Presbyterians were described as 'well educated' (by French, in his review of T.L. Suttor's book *Hierarchy and Democracy in Australia 1780–1870* (*Dialogue*, 1 (1), Spring 1966: 44).

Colonial censuses tabulated literacy according to religion in order to estimate the efficacy of denominational and state schools. These figures support the historical impressions. However much the rates varied from colony to colony, from 1861 to 1901 Catholics always had more illiteracy than any other in the rank order of denominations. The further back in history one goes, the greater the differences are between Catholics and Anglicans, who remained equally solid in third place throughout the period in all colonies.

The Church of England represented the population at large more than any other denomination. It was the largest denomination and on this account was more likely to cover a range from lower to middle class. Thus the literacy rate of Anglicans was more representative for the colonies as a whole than any of the other denominations. Presbyterians and Methodists had the highest literacy rate of the four major denominations. In the population over fifteen years of age Presbyterians were ahead of Methodists, but the Methodist children of 5–15 years of age were ahead of the Presbyterians, according to the census figures for 1861, 1871 and 1881 in Victoria and 1891 in New South Wales (see Table 5.1). The figures in the table show rapidly decreasing illiteracy in the second half of the nineteenth century, indicating a surprisingly large difference between the colonies.

In 1891 the New South Wales rate of illiteracy for children was still much higher than in Victoria in 1881. One factor which may explain the differences is that in 1872 Victoria was the first to pass an act which made education free and compulsory. New South Wales followed eight years later in 1880. Victoria also took the compulsory clauses seriously enough to appoint truant officers within two years of passing the act (UNESCO, *Compulsory Education in Australia*, 1951: 19). Another possible factor is the lesser concentration of the New South Wales population in urban areas. As was pointed out by the Registrar–General, who introduced the section on Education of the

1861 Census in Victoria, the literacy rates of the rural areas were much lower than those of the urban and gold field areas. Both *Wealth and Progress of NSW 1890–1891* and the *Victorian Yearbook 1890–1891* mention that the metropolitan population in Victoria was larger than in New South Wales. At the same time the total population in each state was almost identical (1 132 234 inhabitants in New South Wales and 1 140 405 in Victoria). The difference applied to all denominations. Not without some glee the Registrar-General, William Henry Archer, in his statistical report on education (p. 7) pointed out that according to the 1861 Census, of all persons over five years of age '205 in every 1000 were unable to read in New South Wales, against 120 in 1000 in South Australia, as against 93 in 1000 in Victoria'. Probably he thought this could be expected in a colony where the depressed segments of Irish and English society had played a prominent part, but he was wise enough not say so.

Table 5.1   Percentage of children between 5 and 15 years of age who could not read by denomination in Victoria for the years 1861, 1871 and 1881 and in New South Wales for 1891[a]

	Victoria 1861	Victoria 1871	Victoria 1881	NSW 1891
Church of England	22.97	15.54	9.05	18.59
Catholic	30.77	20.91	11.19	19.56
Methodist	12.23	10.28	7.19	16.13
Presbyterian	17.98	13.50	7.55	16.34

Percentage of adherents over 15 years of age of each denomination who could not read[b]

	Tasmania Census of 1901	NSW Census of 1901	WA Census of 1901
Church of England	5.68	3.36	2.27
Catholic	8.93	5.18	5.23
Methodist	2.73	1.96	1.42
Presbyterian	1.79	1.53	0.67

Notes: [a]See 1881 *Census for Victoria*, p. 172 and 1891 *Census of New South Wales*, pp. 211–212
[b]The absolute figures from which these percentages were computed can be found on p. 162 of the 1891 *Census of Tasmania*, pp. 250–251 of the 1901 *Census of Tasmania*, p. 138 of the *Statistician's Report of the 1901 Western-Australian Census*, pp. 236–7 of the 1901 *Census of New South Wales*

The number of illiterate immigrants coming to Australia in the nineteenth century has as much to do with the literacy rates as the inadequate educational facilities existing at the time. In 1861 less than half the population of New South Wales was born in Australia and the reports of the New South Wales Immigration Agent show that of all adults (persons over twelve years) who entered the colony as assisted migrants, only 58 per cent of Catholics could read or write, compared with 79 per cent of Wesleyans, 80 per cent of Anglicans, 85 per cent of Presbyterians and 80 per cent of all other denominations (Barcan, 1962: 50).

There were significant differences between the literacy figures of the smaller denominations. In the census figures of 1861 to 1901 in Victoria and New South Wales, the percentage of Jews who could read and write was always higher than that of any of the major denominations (Price, 1964: Appendix XIII). The rates of Baptists and more particularly Congregationalists was also generally above those of the major denominations (Barcan, 1962: 52).

The Bible reading denominations, such as Baptists, Congregationalists, Methodists and Presbyterians were more literate than Anglicans and particularly Catholics in the last century. A concern for education, together with economic success seems to have given these denominations an advantage. Is this still visible in the census figures on education by denomination?

Educational accomplishments

In early Australian history the problem of literacy was paramount, but the accent soon shifted from whether a person could read and write to how much education he had completed. On amount of education, there were significant denominational differences. Barcan writes of the second half of the nineteenth century:

> Not only were many Catholic parents unconcerned regarding denominational education; the Catholic working class community was less concerned with education as such. Presbyterians and Methodists, largely in middle class occupations, were relatively highly educated. The free selector, Catholic and non-Catholic, often preferred to keep his child at home for his labour rather then send him to school (Barcan, 1962: 51).

This showed in the lack of Catholic concern for higher education. In 1868 there was a preponderance of Presbyterians amongst students at Sydney University. The Presbyterian College usually had the largest enrolment throughout the nineteenth century, 'closely followed by the Anglican College and then the Catholic' (ibid.: 52).

In 1900 the number of teachers in non-Catholic private schools in New South Wales with a university degree (178 out of 1 735) was much higher than in corresponding Catholic schools (12 out of 1 617) (ibid.: 53). This was partly because the former concentrated on secondary education, but then there was less demand for secondary education among Catholics. One observer wrote:

Our people have been, and still remain, relatively poor, and in secular matters uneducated. On account of their limited means, they are unable to leave their sons as long at school as do the wealthy Protestants (Fogarty, 1957: 331).

Catholics continued to lag in the twentieth century. In 1916 Archbishop Mannix maintained that Catholics were kept at the bottom of the social ladder, because they did not make as much use of higher education as others (ibid.: 334). However, the 1921 census showed that Catholics were not very far behind. Although they comprised 21.6 per cent of the total population, 18.7 per cent of undergraduates were Catholic. Anglicans were proportionately further behind (34.7 per cent of undergraduates, but 43.7 per cent of population), whereas Methodists (13.7 per cent of undergraduates and 11.6 per cent of population) and particularly Presbyterians (18 per cent of undergraduates and 11.7 per cent of population) were over-represented. According to Barcan the depression years affected Catholics more severely.

At the time of the 1933 Census Catholics made up 15.7% of the student body, but 19.4% of the total population. Anglicans were now found in almost exact proportion to their weight (38.7%) of the population, while the smaller denominations continued to have undue representation in the student body (Barcan, 1962: 55)

At the time of the 1966 census 11 in every 1000 Catholics males had a university degree as compared with 14 per 1000 Anglican men. According to the 1 per cent sample of the 1981 census 21 in every 1000 Catholics (both men and women) as compared with 23 for Anglicans had a university degree. And even this small difference disappears altogether if one looks only at those Australians who were born here of native born parents, eliminating the influence of the heavy Catholic migration since World War II. The number of university graduates in this category is 22 per 1000 for both Catholics and Anglicans.

The 1981 figures show some interesting discrepancies between the various denominations. Per 1000, adherent Jews (123), those stating to have no religion (66), and Uniting (40), have far more than their share of university graduates than the population at large (30). Those of the Hebrew faith have traditionally stressed the importance of a university education. In Europe in previous centuries Jews often did not have the same advantages as the native population and so it became a tradition wherever they went to become more secure through using all available educational opportunities. The 'no religion' category seems to represent those who have consciously and rationally broken with the Australian convention that one must belong to some denomination even if one does not practise one's religion in any way whatsoever. The overrepresentation of university graduates among those belonging to the Uniting Church may similarly be attributed to the fact that the more educated have consciously and rationally made the step of transition to this new denomination. By contrast those who stated on the census form that they regarded themselves as Methodists and who had obviously not made that step, comprised only 12 university graduates per 1000. The individual rationalism which universities instil in their products also makes them more prone to accept change.

As in previous censuses, the 1981 one per cent sample of the population showed that both the denominations of recent immigrants and the sects had less than their share of university graduates. For instance the Orthodox had only 13 graduates per 1000 adherents. The Muslims had 22, but all of these were born overseas of foreign parentage, suggesting that at least some of them had come to academic appointments in Australia.

As I have already noted, there were no university graduates amongst the 500 Jehovah's Witnesses who were randomly selected for the one per cent sample. In the 1976 census there were three Witnesses with a university degree for every one thousand adherents as compared with 28 in the population at large. The Salvation Army did only slightly better; in 1976 there were six, in 1981 seven graduates per 1000 census members. The Pentecostals were less heavily under-represented: in 1976 there were 15 graduates per 1000 adherents, in 1981 there were 22. This is not unexpected. As we have seen in the first chapter, the sects do not appeal to those 'who have arrived', irrespective of whether this refers to educational, financial, occupational or other socially desirable accomplishments.

As would be expected there are more university graduates in the Australian capitals than in the country areas. Yet in both areas the inter-denominational differences are sustained. For example the number of graduates per 1000 in the Australian Capital and Northern Territories is much higher (72) than in the population at large (30). The number of graduates in the 'no religion' category rises in roughly the same proportion to 143 per thousand as compared with 66 in the 'no religion' segment of the population at large. So does the proportion of Anglican (47) and Catholic (43) graduates as compared with 23 and 21 respectively in Australia generally.

Religious practices

What effect does education have on religious practices? Do the educated go to church less, pray less and believe less? The most detailed answers to these questions were given in the now dated Religion in Australian Survey. The general impression of these 1966 data was that amount of education had an effect on prejudices and political views rather than on religious practices and beliefs. The more education respondents had received, the more likely they were to feel friendly and at ease with the kinds of people about whom the population as a whole had ambivalent feelings. A good example was the generally unfavourable attitude towards atheists. Only 36 per cent of those who had never completed a secondary education (n = 1215), 46 per cent of those who had only completed a secondary education (n = 458), and 59 per cent of those who had completed a post-secondary diploma or degree (n = 120) felt friendly and at ease in their company. The sample as a whole expressed either neutral, 'nothing either way' or negative feelings, 'friendly but somewhat uneasy' to 'quite unfriendly'.

Similar differences came to light in responses towards the presence of an Italian or a Japanese. Forty-five per cent of those with primary education, 61 per cent of those with secondary education and 68 per cent of those with tertiary education felt friendly and at ease with Italians. Similarly 43 per cent with primary education, 50 per cent with secondary and 56 per cent with tertiary education felt that way towards Japanese. More education presumably means greater familiarity with a variety of people, thought, forms and cultures. It results in greater tolerance of divergent views and less sense of threat in the face of diversity. Even if an educated person feels uncomfortable with people whose beliefs, reactions, habits and language are different, his longer education may have made him more conscious that these feelings are inappropriate and that he should be more broad minded. Differences as to what is regarded as a proper response may explain the above figures equally as well as differences in actual behaviour patterns. Both educated and uneducated seem to have a similar sense of uneasiness with people who speak and think on a different wavelength from one's own, but the former seem to have more guilt feelings about it.

Education also seemed to make an important difference to political preference. The question in the 1966 survey was: 'What party would you like to see win if there were an election today?' The more education respondents had, the less they favoured the Australian Labor Party and the more they favoured the Liberal/Country Parties. Of those who had a primary education only, 30 per cent hoped to see Labor win, 39 per cent the Liberal/Country Parties. Of those who had completed secondary education only 19 per cent hoped to see Labor win and 53 per cent the Liberal/Country Parties. Of those who had completed a tertiary degree or diploma, only 15 per cent hoped to see

Labor win and 61 per cent the Liberal/Country Parties. One would expect more educated Catholics to gravitate to the Australian Labor Party than Protestants, but this is not so. Of Catholic respondents who had only completed a primary education (n = 278) 30 per cent preferred the Australian Labor Party; for corresponding non-Catholics (n = 937) the percentage was 31. Similarly 17 per cent (n = 121) of Catholics who had completed a secondary education preferred the Australian Labor Party compared with 18 per cent of non-Catholics (n = 450) with the same qualification.

Turning to the mutual effect of education and religious practices, experiences and beliefs, education makes a difference even if it is slight. In Europe 'higher levels of education are not particularly conducive to religious faith' (Stoetzel, 1983: 85). Yet in Australia in 1966 the educated were, if anything, more religious.

Looking first at church going, in the survey 38 per cent of the respondents who had completed some kind of tertiary education said that they were regular church goers, compared with 33 per cent of those who had only completed secondary education and 33 per cent of those with primary education. The rank order remains the same but becomes more pronounced and statistically more significant when we look at what the respondents said they actually did on the preceding Sunday. Thirty-three per cent of those with tertiary education, 26 per cent with secondary education and 24 per cent with primary education had been to Divine Service or Mass. That these figures are lower than the preceding ones can be explained by the fact that in the survey 'regular' meant those people who went to church at least once a month. Those who went less than once a month, hardly ever, or never, were designated as 'irregular'. One can expect that the percentage of so-called 'regulars' is higher than the percentage of respondents who had actually been to church on the preceding Sunday.

Does the denomination to which one belongs make a difference? As Table 5.2 shows, the educated Catholics and to a lesser extent Presbyterians and Anglicans are more regular church goers than those who have never finished a secondary education. The reverse seems to be true for the Methodists, who traditionally have a greater membership among the lower classes. The lower class sectarian groups increase the average church attendance for those with primary education only, in the rest of the sample. The well educated group of people with 'no religion', however, decreases the average church attendance of those who have finished secondary education.

Men and women continue to differ when we look at both education and church going. The percentage of regularly attending males who have completed only primary education (n = 834) is 28, secondary education (n = 312) is 29 and tertiary education or diploma (n = 106) is

Table 5.2   Percentage of regular church goers (once a month or more) by denomination and education (1966)

Denomination	Primary education only	Have completed a secondary or tertiary education
Anglicans	12	17
	(n = 708)	(n = 290)
Catholics	62	73
	(n = 444)	(n = 176)
Methodists	36	27
	(n = 173)	(n = 63)
Presbyterians	27	35
	(n = 241)	(n = 116)
Rest of sample	41	22
(including 'no religion')	(n = 222)	(n = 123)

Source: Religion in Australia Survey, 1966

33. The corresponding percentages for females is significantly higher in all instances: for those with primary education (n = 954) it is 37, secondary education (n = 303) it is 38, tertiary education (n = 47) it is 51.

With regard to prayer, education has neither a strong negative nor positive association. For the sample as a whole 33 per cent claimed to pray daily, 40 per cent occasionally and 25 per cent never or hardly ever. The variation from this average was never more than 2 per cent for any of the education categories. As the educated are slightly better church goers, this suggests that the educated regular church goers are less likely to pray daily. Of regular church goers with primary education (n = 384) 64 per cent pray daily while of those with secondary education or more (n = 198) only 53 per cent pray daily.

There is no difference in how educated and others respond to whether they have had or think that they have had a 'feeling of being somehow in the presence of God' since childhood, 48 per cent of the sample claim this experience and it makes no difference whether one has had tertiary or primary school education. There is a slight difference on the experience of 'being saved in Christ'. Here 36 per cent of those with primary education (n = 1215) and 28 per cent (n = 578) of those with secondary education or more claim the experience. The difference is not very great but the chance that the variation is random is almost negligible (1 in a 1000). There may be a faint suggestion that the more educated are less inclined to claim the least neutral, least rational and most emotionally charged religious experience.

There is a greater difference between the educational groups on attendance at meetings of various kinds. Those who have completed secondary education and particularly those who have completed tertiary education are more likely to be involved in other church meetings apart from the worship service, and more involved in meetings which have no relation to the church such as Rotary and the Parents and Citizens Association. However, there are denominational differences. Catholics with secondary or more education tend to be more involved than Catholics with primary education in other church meetings. Of the former 25 per cent (n = 173) attend sometimes, but less than once a week, while the percentages for the others are 15 per cent (n = 440) and 16 per cent (n = 581) respectively. Protestants with at least secondary education tend to be more involved in secular meetings with 34 per cent attending sometimes. The corresponding percentage for Catholics with at least secondary education is 23 per cent, for Catholics with primary education only 20 per cent and for Protestants with primary education only 22 per cent. These figures suggest that Catholic intellectuals centre more of their social life around their church than Protestants, who in turn are more involved in secular organisations than the former.

As was to be expected, those with tertiary education are more knowledgeable about the content of the bible, or to be more accurate, they are the least ignorant. Only 13 per cent of those with primary education, 15 per cent with secondary education and 36 per cent with tertiary education disagreed with the faulty statement that 'the book of Acts of the Apostles gives an account of Jesus' life on earth'. All the others either said they did not know (the vast majority) or that they agreed.

On ecumenical matters the educated are less opposed to the merging of their denomination with any other. Of the respondents with primary education 24 per cent oppose mergers, but the percentages drop to 16 per cent and 9 per cent for those with secondary and tertiary education.

As expected, those who have finished at least a secondary school education are more mobile than those who have not, with 56 per cent of the former having lived less than ten years in the area where they are now living as against 42 per cent of the latter. This is likely to be one of the reasons why fewer educated people have the majority of their friends (25 per cent) in the local church compared with the less educated group with 34 per cent.

The surprises in the 1966 tabulations of religious beliefs and education are again that there are so few differences. Almost half (48 per cent) the sample believes that God really exists and has no doubts about it. All educational categories come very close to this average. The percentage of respondents who don't believe in God

(2 per cent) is very small and again education makes no difference. It is only when the 'agnostic' category, 'I don't know whether there is a God, and I don't believe there is any way to find out', is combined with those respondents who say that they don't believe in a personal God, but do believe in a higher power of some kind, that we find a significant difference. One of these two categories was selected by 29 per cent of those with tertiary education, 19 per cent with secondary education and 16 per cent with primary education. Both categories can be regarded as consistent with a rational or natural rather than supernatural orientation. It appears that those with tertiary education are more likely to adhere to this view than the others.

Opinions regarding the Church are less unanimous. The educated are no more likely to prefer a theological definition that 'the Church is appointed by God' or a negative one that 'the usefulness of the Church is doubtful' than those who have less education. However, they are more inclined to select the most popular definition that 'On the whole the Church stands for the best in human life, in spite of shortcomings found in all human institutions'. (41 per cent of those who have completed secondary education and 32 per cent of those who have not completed secondary education are in this category.)

Finally, the difference between specific levels of education and opinion questions occurred with respect to the statement that 'It does not matter what one believes as long as one leads a moral life'. More of those with a tertiary education (34 per cent) disagreed than those with secondary education (26 per cent) and those with primary education (19 per cent). It would be interesting to speculate at this point that the 'commitment' or 'integrative' elements of beliefs are apparently precious to the very people who more than others are rewarded for scepticism and tolerance of diversity.

How has the picture changed since 1966? Unfortunately detailed comparisons cannot be made until surveys in the stage of execution at the present time (The Australian Values Study and the National Social Science Survey) are available for analysis. In the meantime, however, a reanalysis of polls asking questions about both church attendance and denomination can help us to understand what has remained the same and what has changed over the past fifteen years.

Tabel 5.3 is the result of a reanalysis of the last of eight national polls carried out for the Melbourne *Age* (1981) in which religious data can be crosstabulated with information about level of education. Comparing this table with Table 5.2 (in so far as that is possible) it appears at first sight that little has changed. Certainly the respondents with more education of the main denominations (Anglican and Catholic) tended to be more regular in their church going. If anything,

Table 5.3 **Percentage of regular church goers (self-definition) for selected denominations by education**

	University and other tertiary	Completed Secondary	Trade Quali-fication or some Secondary	Primary	Total
Anglican	21 (n = 111)	14 (n = 169)	9 (n = 270)	17 (n = 71)	13 (n = 621)
Catholic	56 (n = 107)	41 (n = 148)	40 (n = 199)	43 (n = 54)	44 (n = 508)
Other	31 (n = 156)	21 (n = 171)	23 (n = 246)	38 (n = 86)	26 (n = 659)
Total	35 (n = 374)	24 (n = 488)	22 (n = 715)	31 (n = 211)	27 (n = 1788)

Source: Age poll, November 1981

the Anglican attendance seems to have gone up slightly in that period. However, in the intervening period large numbers of those who in 1966 regarded themselves as Anglican now identify themselves as having 'no religion'. In both the 1981 census and the November 1981 *Age* poll the percentage of individuals with 'no religion' had grown to 11 per cent of the population. Also in both those with tertiary qualifications were heavily overrepresented in the 'no religion' column (in the 1 per cent sample of the 1981 census 24 per cent of those with a university degree, in the 1981 *Age* poll 21 per cent of those with tertiary qualifications thought of themselves as having no religion). All this means that it is only to be expected that with this significant exodus of the tertiary educated from the denominations those remaining are likely to include a larger number of regular church goers.

As we have already seen in a previous chapter Catholic attendance has dropped substantially in the intervening period and it has affected all groups equally. Even so, Catholics still attend church more regularly than Protestants at all educational levels. What seems to have changed slightly since 1966 is that now the differences between those who have completed a secondary education or who have some trade qualification on the one hand, and those with either tertiary or only primary education on the other, are more pronounced. Not only in the *Age* poll of November 1981, but also in that of April 1980, the middle group seems to be less active, at least in Protestant denominations. In that particular poll 18 per cent (n = 122) of Anglicans with tertiary qualifications, 10 per cent (n = 452) of those with at least some secondary schooling or trade diploma and 14 per cent (n = 85) of those with primary education regarded themselves as regular church goers. For those who were Uniting, Methodist or Presbyterians, the corresponding percentages were 34 (n = 76), 15 (n = 253) and 33 (n = 52). In the April 1980 poll Catholic differences were insignificant.

What conclusions can be drawn from this information?

First, the data provide no comfort for those who believe that the more education people have the more they must discover the significance of religious truth. Neither do the findings back the secularists for whom Christianity is just another form of superstition which will wither 'like a leaf before a flame when the scientific attitude is brought to bear on it' (Davis, 1964: 536).

If we accept the idea that the scientific attitude is most thoroughly inculcated in people who have more extensive school or university education the scientific attitude seems to have only a moderate effect on religious orientations. The data suggest that religious practices and attitudes neither flow naturally from more education nor stand in sharp contrast to it, but that the effect of one upon the other is limited, in spite of religious alarmists or atheistic confidence. If there had been strong links, we would have found far more and far stronger negative or positive correlations.

Even if we accept that the scientific ethos and religious ideology have some contradictory traits, that still should not lead us to presume that human beings must have a logically consistent view of life or that all educated people make scientific method into a system of meaning embracing all phenomena. Religion has important integrative functions in the non-rational realm of human existence.

Whatever is the case, the more educated seem to be slightly over-represented in the public or social sector of religion; they attended both services of worship and other church meetings more frequently, although this was not true for all denominations. In the private sector of prayer or general religious experiences they differed in no way whatsoever. On the other hand they were significantly under-represented in the group who claimed or thought that they had had 'a sense of being saved in Christ', an experience which the educated presumably associate with an emotionally charged conversion experience.

It would be wrong to conclude that the differences are consequences of different needs. The more educated may attend church because the aesthetics of liturgy or church music appeal to their sensitive ear; or they may like the status conferral of the church community; they may feel an obligation to back the social institutions which reinforce moral standards or, they may feel the need for a religious answer to problems of integration. But then this may not be, and so they may attend church more frequently because the clergy or other church members have applied more pressure on them than on people with lower status in the community who are therefore less eligible for informal or formal leadership. Or again, the well-educated clergy may almost unwittingly speak and converse on a level closer to that of the educated than that of those who have primary education only. Similarly the clergy may effectively avoid or rationalise the areas where the scientific and religious attitudes are in contrast. One sometimes gets the impression that the clergy go further with this compromise than is institutionally necessary, as an unconscious response to and affirmation of the status system which rewards the highly educated more than the religious functionary.

The relatively high status of the educated in Australian society and their power of knowing more may also help us to understand better an anomaly in the findings, that the educated as a group seem to be simultaneously more liberal and more conservative. They are more tolerant of people of different backgrounds and opinion, and are better able to cope with diversity of any kind. As they seem to have absorbed the values of the scientific ethos better, they are able to accept the change and conflict brought about by rational scrutiny and independent thought.

But simultaneously their political hopes are decidedly more conservative and their religious beliefs and practices do not substantially deviate from the traditional patterns. There may be some deviation here and there, but the differences are insignificant when random variation is taken into account. Those with tertiary education are likely to admire the person who is patriotic, but they don't admire the person who is very ambitious any more than those in other educational categories. They are just as likely to agree with statements prizing high social standing or express satisfaction with what one has, as the less educated categories.

Maybe we can resolve the anomaly by suggesting that the educated in Australia tend to differ from the less educated only in so far as they adhere to values, such as independent and unbiased judgment, which are at the core of scientific advance and enterprise, but that on other issues they conform to the expectations of a society which rewards them well enough to discourage social innovation.

Taking into consideration the relative independence of education and religion in Australian society, the stress on the importance of beliefs by the educated respondents of the 1966 survey, and the observation that the educated are just as much committed to something, be it modern art, nuclear disarmament, ecology, football or Christianity, as the less educated, we could ask ourselves why competitive secular sources of commitment are as viable as they are, relative to the religious forces which historically filled this function. It is obviously incorrect to blame intellectual dishonesty or deadening institutionalisation exclusively for the plight of the churches, as is done so often. All movements have to institutionalise themselves, and the churches have not suffered unduly in the past from this necessity.

Nor does lack of intellectual sophistication in the churches, granted that there is little, worry the educated to the extent that it causes them to stay away. Religious observance seems to be rather independent of this issue.

Why does the Christian religion serve less as an actual focus for commitment? The word 'Christian' is introduced purposely here, as a good case can be made out for calling 'religion' anything that functions to integrate persons or societies meaningfully.

It can be presumed that this need for commitment as an emotional mechanism of integration is undiminishable. Integration is bound up with man's basic security and on the social level it is justifiably taken as a functional prerequisite.

The answer to the question is not easy. Man's freedom of choice, running parallel to the comparative lack of constraint of industrial societies, has made Christian commitment as optional as any other. The Christian religious institutions were not prepared for this competition in the past. Most of them seem to have made room for alternative forms of commitment without taking on the challenge. However, in the more militant sects or Catholicism in Australia in the last quarter of the nineteenth century organisational strength and influence have certainly not diminished as they have in the churches where the goals were accommodated to suit the pressures of members who want to have many cakes and eat them all.

At any rate, the pressures of the educated for greater tolerance of diversity and greater openness for other beliefs and views have paradoxically not meant that the educated are above a single-minded religious commitment. A failure to recognise this paradox may be an important reason for the loss of function of some of the Christian religious institutions.

However, it is this area which deserves far more attention. It may quite well be that the loss of function of Christian religious institutions has come about because other forms of commitment on the psychological level are better rewarded. The dedicated worker may soon be promoted, or the patron of *avant-garde* music may now move in upper status circles. This competition for the commitment of their members may be the basic reason why many American churches now offer the reward of fraternisation with high status individuals. This may be the reason why these very churches flourish, not so much because they are snobbish (they may be so inevitably but not explicitly), but because they need to offer a better reward system in a heavily competitive pluralistic society and provide it by facilitating social intercourse between like-minded people. Conversely, at the core of both religious apathy and increasing anomie may be the decrease of commitment to general religious values (that are not rewarded highly compared with, for instance, occupational success and possession of its symbols), and an increase in commitment to specific ones, the rewards for which are more visible and obtainable. It may be that the integrative function of religion, stressed so much by anthropologists, does operate less on the social level because modern societies are pluralistic and not very conducive to integration. Therefore it pays religious institutions to integrate personalities through counselling, or to emulate successful subsystems which bring together individuals of like mind or like status. This does not mean that there are not sufficient pressures to reinforce the more general social values, but these pressures are not as strong as those arising from occupational and other subsystems where humans have face-to-face contacts. The response to the 1966 survey statement relativising beliefs suggests the existence of these pressures and a need for a kind of integration transcending the more direct and concrete ones.

However, it is time to leave this speculative plane without abandoning some of the theoretical purposes of this conclusion. While there is strong evidence that educational and religious subsystems are largely independent of one another, we are not entitled to overlook areas of interaction and mutual effect. I suggest that there are at least four such areas.

Firstly, although religious institutions have never been notable for their tolerance of those with different views, the scientific ethos inculcated in individuals through secular learning has had a sufficiently strong impact to make intolerance definitely a thing of the past, particularly in the major denominations. In Australia and other Anglo-Saxon countries it is assumed that the major Protestant churches indoctrinate their pupils in Sunday and public schools into a specific theological commitment peculiar to their particular denomination. It is clear to anyone who has ever attended these classes that this presupposition is unrealistic and that much of this teaching is not only innocuous, but concentrates heavily on the acceptable standard of brotherly love and antagonism to prejudices. Of course, even if a specific theological commitment is the goal, 'the present supremacy of bread and butter values will not be seriously challenged by another forty minutes Scripture a week' as Kenneth Henderson correctly observed more than 60 years ago (Henderson, 1923: 21).

Secondly, although the concern of religious institutions with moral order has previously tended to stress common obedience rather than individual scrutiny, the individualistic criteria of an increasingly better educated church membership seem to increase the democratisation of Catholic institutions in particular. The popularity of a theology of the laity in all the major churches of Christendom is symptomatic of this change in the democratic direction.

Thirdly, the basic elements of the scientific ethos which encourage both scepticism and independent, individual, rational scrutiny, are functional for social and cultural change but seem to be dysfunctional for emotional integration. It is generally the reverse with religion which has often facilitated integration both for society and personality, but has retarded change. The extent to which both subsystems are complementary is therefore not any more academic than their conflict. The relation between the scientific ethos and religion will tend to converge to the point where dysfunctions for each are minimised and functions maximised. This in itself will militate against the absorption of one by the other, as the very separation guarantees a better division of labour.

Fourthly, both subsystems are concerned with socialisation. Public education can only inculcate those norms which are nationally regarded as important. However, a minority denomination such as Catholicism will increase its institutional strength in a pluralistic society when it can shield its membership from competing ideologies. The relativisation of religious belief is one of the latter. Control over the educational process by the religious institution will not only facilitate this shielding, but will also allow more positively for the inculcation of loyalty norms. This point will be discussed in the section on the effect of Catholic schools.

Obedience and thinking for oneself

The incompatibility of individual rationalism (thinking for oneself) and loyalty to units of social organisation (obedience) is a phenomenon touched on in both the introduction and the preceding section and requiring further elucidation.

Some observers of the Australian religious scene claim to have detected a submissiveness on the part of the average Catholic which contrasts with Protestant independence:

> Catholic schools ... produce few men and women who are highly individualistic. Of those who do fall into this latter category, many are 'failed Catholics', their independence turning them to question the beliefs and discipline of the Church itself (Solomon, 1967: 2).

Others observed that Catholics in Australia differ from others in that they obey the Church's dictates in matters ranging from voting to family planning to censorship; in short that they are more loyal to their Church and therefore obey the norms better.

A 1955 Gallup poll found that more Catholics (72 per cent) than Methodists (68 per cent), Anglicans (65 per cent), Presbyterians

Table 5.4   Percentage of respondents, by education and denomination, who agree with the statement that 'the most important thing for a child to learn is to obey rather than think for himself' (1966)

Religion	Primary or some secondary	Completed secondary education only	Completed post-secondary diploma or degree
Catholic	62	50	37
	(n = 264)	(n = 96)	(n = 19)
Non-Catholic	47	29	23
	(n = 880)	(n = 328)	(n = 96)
Total	50	34	25
	(n = 11440)	(n = 424)	(n = 115)

Note: The 6% of respondents who did not know or did not answer have been eliminated from the calculations, so that the percentage disagreeing is the reciprocal of those agreeing
Source: Religion in Australia Survey, 1966

(60 per cent) and Baptists (55 per cent) were opposed to permitting speakers on the radio to criticise religious beliefs.

On the other hand there are many prominent Catholics whose spirit is more indomitable. A good example is the former leader of the Australian Labor Party, Arthur Calwell, a Papal Knight, who told a Melbourne meeting on 11 May 1969 that certain Irish bishops who had no idea of the living conditions of their flock should be sacked. When a man in the audience protested 'We look to the priest for guidance', Mr Calwell replied:

> The sooner you stop doing that, the better. On matters of theology, on doctrinal matters, I am as good a Catholic as anyone ... but on matters of the institutional church, I do what I think is right by the community.

One question in the 1966 Religion in Australia Survey had some bearing on this issue. Respondents were asked to agree or disagree with the statement 'that the most important thing for a child to learn is to obey rather than to think for himself'. Twenty-five per cent of those who had completed some tertiary education, 34 per cent of those who had only completed secondary education and 50 per cent of those who had completed primary education only, agreed with this statement. As Table 5.4 shows there is an interesting difference between Catholics and non-Catholics; for each educational level Catholics were more inclined to agree than non-Catholics.

Could these differences be explained by the kind of training Catholics received in their denominational schools? If Catholic schools, rather than Catholicism instilled such attitudes, we should find that Australian Catholics who never attended a Catholic school would differ from those who have, and be more similar to Protestants. However Table 5.5 shows clearly that this is not the case; whether or not the Catholic respondents of the survey had gone to a Catholic school makes little difference. All Catholics, irrespective of kind of schooling, continue to differ from Protestants.

How do these findings compare with overseas research? One American observer, Thomas O'Dea, asks:

> Is it true that students in the Catholic school tend to feel that because they are taught all or most subjects by a religious authority they must accept passively what is given to them? Passive learning, passive acceptance and memorization appear to play a much larger part than they should in Catholic education in religious matters. Is this carried over into the instruction methods for other subjects? Does our Catholic teaching so combine authoritarianism and the verbal formula as to discourage active inquiry on the part of the students? (O'Dea, 1958: 135).

Table 5.5   Percentage of respondents, by parochial and state school education and by level of education, who agree with the statement that 'the most important thing for a child to learn is to obey rather than to think for himself'. (1966)

	Denominational school education		State school education	
	Primary education	Secondary or tertiary education	Primary education	Secondary or tertiary education
Catholic	63	42	60	70
	(n = 187)	(n = 92)	(n = 77)	(n = 23)
Non-Catholic	47	27	47	28
	(n = 75)	(n = 122)	(n = 805)	(n = 296)

Source: Religion in Australia Survey, 1966

Another American, Gerhard Lenski, asked a question similar to the 1966 survey in his sample of 656 adult persons in Detroit. Although he held class rather than education constant, he found that the higher the class the more the subject was inclined to value intellectual autonomy (thinking for oneself) above heteronomy (that is, obedience to the dictates of others) and that within 'all of the class levels, Jews and white Protestants are more likely than Catholics to do this' (Lenski, 1961: 200).

Similarly, Broom and Glenn in discussing the findings of their secondary analysis of seven national polls from 1953–1961 in the USA found that

When non-Southern urban Protestants and Catholics with twelve years of school are compared, 63 per cent of the Catholics, but only 50.5 per cent of the Protestants agreed that the most important thing to teach children is absolute obedience to their parents (Broom and Glenn, 1966: 206).

On the other hand another large scale American study suggests that there is no evidence that Catholic school graduates are more reluctant to argue that thinking for oneself is more important than obedience. The authors of this study conclude:

> If more rigid emphases on obedience were stressed in their education, the passage of time and the general American consensus on how children ought to be reared has erased any differences between Catholic school Catholics and other Americans, whatever their faith or education (Greeley and Rossi, 1966: 129).

However the question on obedience in the National Opinion Research Center's Survey was expressed differently from the question in the 1966 Religion in Australia Survey. Instead of asking respondents to agree or disagree with a statement in which a child's learning of obedience was ranked above learning to think for itself, as in the 1966 survey, or a statement in which the one value was to be ranked over the other (explicitly in Lenski's, implicitly in the 1953 NORC sample as reported by Broom and Glenn), the Greeley and Rossi survey asked them to agree or not agree with the statement that 'it is as important for a child to think for himself as to be obedient to his parents'.

Although the difference is subtle, it is possible that respondents for whom the issue was not particularly urgent would agree with the statement and make a choice one way or the other only if asked to do so. This presumes that only in the latter instance do the Catholic/non-Catholic differences become visible. If the presumption is correct and applies to Australia we should find that respondents would 'tend to agree or disagree', rather than 'definitely agree or disagree'. However this is not what is found: Catholics (37 per cent) are more likely to agree definitely with the statement than non-Catholics (22 per cent). On the other hand, non-Catholics (32 per cent) are more likely to disagree definitely than Catholics (17 per cent). The percentages of those who tended to agree or disagree were about the same for both groups.

Is age an intervening variable? Although more of the young people disagreed with the obedience statement than older ones, the differences between Catholics and non-Catholics in the younger age bracket are even greater than in the older one. The percentage of Catholics agreeing in the 20–39 age bracket is 51, from 40–59 it is 58 and at 60 + it is 79; the percentage of non-Catholics agreeing in the 20–39 age bracket is 30, from 40–59 it is 42 and at 60 + it is 62. Whatever the merits of the Greeley–Rossi research for the USA, in Australia it is clear that the differences between Catholics and non-Catholics on the obedience statement is not due to different levels of education, nor of age or denominational schooling.

What could these findings and comparisons mean? Unfortunately I have not come across comparable research since 1966. However, I feel that the conclusions based on the Religion in Australia Survey are still relevant in 1984.

For one, whether one agrees or disagrees with the statement that 'the most important thing for a child to learn is to obey rather than to think for himself', the answer may depend on whether order and the capacity to fit in with the demands of society or the family are preferred to individual independence and rational scrutiny. The values inculcated by the secular institutions of learning in the western world come down on the autonomous side—the values of the Catholic Church more on the heteronomous one. A concern with the moral order, for which obedience to norms and beliefs is a prerequisite, seems to have priority for Catholics. A concern for the rational processes which reward scepticism of premises and independent scrutiny seems to have priority for the educated, although both concerns are intertwined in religious and educational institutions. Our findings then may reflect the long standing historical capacity of the Catholic Church to inculcate a concern for moral order in its members. On the other hand, the non-Catholic emphasis on individualism, via a historical concern with personal salvation and a relativisation of good works and consequently the moral order, appears to converge rather than contrast with the increasingly successful inculcation of the scientific ethos among the highly educated.

In the literature the moral order/individualism dichotomy as a central explanatory device is little used nowadays, in spite of the fact that one of the fathers of sociology, Emile Durkheim, employed it to account for the variation in suicide rates. I feel that these two concepts are still the best fit not only for the findings of this section, but also for related observations, such as the 'anti-intellectualism' or the 'authoritarianism' of Catholics. The dichotomy has also the advantage of being the most sociological and the least value-laden of explanations. Many authors have naively condemned the anti-intellectualism of Catholics in particular and Australians in general without realising that this might be the outcome of a basic concern for an agreed-upon moral order, for the maintenance of which individual scrutiny and sceptism could not be given limitless free rein. The 'authoritarianism' of Catholics has been noted, but as Knöpfelmacher correctly observed:

> . . . it is not surprising that Catholics score highly on the scale with its strong loading on family virtues, respect for parents, sexual morality, and so on, since by and large these are articles of Catholic belief, but who declares them to be 'authoritarian'? (Knöpfelmacher, 1961: 155).

The very tendency of Catholics to be more dominating or dominated may well be the outcome of the priority given to the security of the moral order and a corresponding downstaging of 'thinking for oneself'.

Although younger Catholics continued to differ from younger Protestants, the fact that the former are more ready to disagree than older Catholics may indicate that we are witnessing a further loosening of the cohesion of the Catholic Church in Anglo-Saxon countries. The Church may find it increasingly difficult to assign a permanent and unquestioning character to those moral and institutional areas in which the sacred is embedded. Thinking for oneself as a cherished or even sacred value is likely to conflict with the sacredness of institutional teaching. The Church's past suspicion of 'individuals who dared to think independently in certain fields' (Lecomte du Noüy, 1948: 207–8) is now inexorably making room for the autonomy of the individual conscience. There seems to be little choice.

The effect of increased education on the value priority of independent thinking is also likely to produce an increased democratisation of both religious and political structures. It is interesting to watch the USSR in this regard. The priority of the value can only be maintained when the precarious balance of influence of institution over individual, and of individual over institution, is shifted away considerably from institutional autocracy.

Strangely enough, the autocratic religious institutions foster this democratisation process themselves when like other social institutions they show, as they do in Australia, a preference for the educated on their councils and in church meetings. By doing so they bestow, like the secular culture, relatively high status on the educated. In return for the accompanying prestige the church will be under greater pressure to live up to the value priorities of the educated. An illustration of this point is the pressure felt by the Catholic Church to liberalise and innovate in the more highly educated areas like Anglo-Saxon and Western European countries. The increasing influence of the educated laity in the Catholic Church will no doubt lead to a further democratisation and it may diminish the few value differences still existing between the Catholic and the non-Catholic in Australia.

6   Denominational schools

We have seen that religion and socialisation have been strongly intertwined and that religious institutions have put great store on the young perpetuating those values and beliefs needed for the shielding of community, family and nation. In Australian history Protestants have generally trusted the state to look after itself, whereas Catholics have been much less sure that civil authorities would safeguard what it felt to be essential attitudes and ways of perceiving the world. The Catholic Church has therefore built a costly and elaborate system of denominational schools to protect both its pupils and its organisation from the inroad of unwanted ideas, beliefs and norms. With exceptions (the Reformed Churches, the Seventh Day Adventists and an increasing number of fundamentalist organisations) Protestants have generally established denominational schools less for the protection of their theology than for the safeguarding of more class based values and achievements, such as leadership.

During the first half century after the 1788 landing, denominational schooling was the assumed mode of educating the young. The Church of England, regarded as the established church, received the lion's share of aid 'for the erection of churches, the payment of clergy and the establishment of schools' (Black, 1883a: 2). However the public gradually became dissatisfied with the poor quality of these schools and in 1847 a separate national school system was established (Bollen, 1973: 39). The general boards of education in the colonies did their work so well that by 1869:

> ... in name, curriculum, methods of teaching, textbooks and tone, there was little to distinguish one type of school from another, and the ignorant and the simple among the bishops' flocks could well be forgiven for failing to see the difference between the government-assisted Catholic schools and any other government school. Throughout the country Catholic children made up eighteen per cent of the pupils attending non-Catholic schools— a proportion nearly as great as the proportion of Catholics in the population as a whole (Austin, 1961: 195).

However, in 1864 Pope Pius IX published the encyclical *Quanta Cura* with its attached Syllabus of Errors. It unambiguously condemned liberalism and the belief that education should be subjected to civil and political power. After the colonies successively passed legislation establishing a universal secular system of education and abolishing all state aid to church schools, this document began to have its effects. The Catholic bishops initiated a programme to establish more Catholic schools, and to warn the many Catholic parents who persisted in sending their children to other schools that they had committed a serious moral offence and were to be regarded 'as habitually and deliberately living in a state of sin and, therefore, to have excluded themselves from the Sacraments' (Fogarty, 1957: 215). The problem facing the hierarchy seemed insurmountable. Money had to be raised from the membership, religious orders had to be galvanised into providing staff and, above all, the ignorant and apathetic faithful had to be convinced that this immense effort was worth the trouble. The Joint Pastoral letter of the Catholic bishops in 1879 fiercely denounced the public schools and resulted in a considerable withdrawal of Catholic children from these schools.

> ... in the diocese of Melbourne alone, enrolments at Catholic primary schools increased between 1885 and 1905 almost ten times as fast as enrolments at State schools. It was becoming normal for Catholic and non-Catholic children to be strangers. In 1890, possibly half the children of Catholics were attending State schools. The proportion dropped to one third by 1933, and by 1950 to about one-fifth, of whom almost half were in country areas far from Church schools and the rest were in urban areas (Inglis, 1961: 11–12).

Both Fogarty and Inglis suggest that at the time of their writing, the proportion of Catholic children in state schools was much higher 'owing to the fact that Catholic schools were unable to keep pace with the increased population' (Fogarty 1957: 453), or 'largely on account of European immigration' (Inglis 1961: 12). This estimation was corroborated by two journalists who suggested that in 1967 only 65 per cent of Catholic children were in Catholic schools (Moffitt and Williams, 1967: 9). Michael Mason estimated that in 1976 'barely half of Catholic school-age children were attending Catholic schools' (Mason, 1983: 33).

The plight of the Catholic Church in having to provide facilities for its rapidly increasing number of children is well illustrated by the decrease of students attending Catholic schools, from 19 per cent in 1966 to 18 in 1969 and 16.8 in 1977 (Hally, 1982: 81). However the percentage has risen since then, so that in 1981 almost 18 per cent of Australian students attended Catholic schools.

One reason for the belated flourishing of the denominational school system (the percentage of students attending Catholic and other private schools climbed from 21.3 per cent in 1975 to 24.4 per cent in

1983, according to *Schools for the A.C.T.* (1983: 17) was the gradual increase in state aid to non-governmental schools. In 1963 the federal government began to finance new science laboratories and other facilities in private schools. In the 1970s it provided a grant of '20 per cent of the standard public school cost for each child attending a private school' (ibid.: 13). At present the Labor government recognises the needs of the private schools and subsidises the poorer schools more substantially than the 41 wealthy schools. The result is that about 13 per cent of the Commonwealth education budget goes to private schools and since these schools provide for close to 25 per cent of Australian children, it pays in actual fact 'about half what is paid by the Federal Government to educate a child at a government school' (*The Australian*, 12–13 November 1983: 14).

The effect of Catholic schools

Are the pupils of Catholic schools more religious? Ever since their establishment Catholic and Protestant protagonists have claimed that their schools had a favourable effect on the Christian quality of their pupils. In the Joint Pastoral Letter of the Catholic Archbishops and Bishops in 1879, secular education was deemed to lead to 'practical paganism ... to corruption and loss of faith, to national effeminacy and to national dishonour' (Clark, 1955: 722). By implication Catholic schools were judged to avoid all these evils.

Even if the bishops had to eat some of their own intemperate words, they soon discovered that the crisis in Australian Catholic education in the last quarter of the nineteenth century was a boon for the morale of the Church. In 1880 Bishop Quinn wrote to the Minister of Education in Queensland that in spite of gross injury 'nothing could happen which would conduce more to the prosperity of the Catholic Church in this colony' (Fogarty 1957: 303). Only fifteen years later in 1895 Archbishop Carr could speak of an accomplished fact when he said 'the Catholic Church [was that] day substantially stronger, more united, and better equipped than if the old school system had been permitted to continue'. (ibid.). Another twenty years later Archbishop Mannix called the Catholic School the 'ante-chamber of the Church', indicating that without it the churches would have been empty (ibid.: 305). Other Catholics have claimed that Catholic schools instil qualities of citizenship, community service, patriotism and respect for authority (Solomon 1967: 2).

Catholic schools have always differed from most other denominational schools in that they provided for the less affluent. Catholics provided only a few schools for the children of the

Table 6.1 Percentage of Catholic respondents according to type of schooling (1966)

Percentage of respondents who	No parochial school education	Some parochial school education
1 were regular church goers	48	80
2 had been to church on the previous Sunday	39	72
3 had fathers who were regular church goers when they grew up	50	66
4 had mothers who were regular church goers when they grew up	64	78
5 had at least three of their five closest friends in the local congregation	33	43
6 know that God really exists and had no doubts about it	59	80
7 disagree with the statement that it is not necessary to go to church to be a Christian	27	43
8 disagree with the statement that the book of Acts of the Apostles gives an accurate account of Jesus' life on earth	5	15
9 disagree with the statement that it does not matter what one believes as long as one leads a moral life	16	33
10 pray daily	40	55
11 are sure that since childhood they have had (or at least think that they have had) a feeling that they were somehow in God's presence	49	65
12 are sure that since childhood they have had (or at least think that they have had) a sense of being saved in Christ	35	44
13 are sure that since childhood they have had (or at least think that they have had) a feeling of being tempted by the Devil	39	52
14 are of the opinion that the Church is appointed by God and that it is the home and refuge of all mankind	34	58
15 are of the opinion that on the whole the Church stands for the best in human life, in spite of shortcomings found in all human institutions	33	18
Total sample A (children and adolescents included) items 1 & 2	368	668
Total sample B (adults over 20 only) items 3 and 4	188	427
Total sample C (adults over 20 from whom attitudinal material was available) all other items	109	290

bourgeoisie, the squatters, and the professional classes because their numbers came from the *petit bourgeoisie* and the working class' (Clark, 1963: 149). Yet others have suggested that regardless of denomination, 'the child from the economically poorer home is more likely to be in a State school' (O'Donnell, 1967: 33). The Religion in Australia Survey tried to verify some of these hypotheses in 1966.

It found that of those Catholics who had had some denominational school education, 80 per cent went to church regularly (n = 668). Of those who had never been to such a school, only 48 per cent went regularly (n = 368). This difference sustained itself in almost all the diverse religious items. In only items 5, 8 and 12 of Table 6.1 is there a 10 per cent chance that the difference is caused by chance. Without exception, more of the Catholic school Catholics give 'religious' responses, more go to church regularly, pray regularly, more have had religious experiences, fewer have doubts about God's existence, more prefer the theological rather than the institutional definition of the Church, more are likely to have most of their friends in the local congregation, and more say that their parents were good church goers. In most instances the government school Catholics take a position somewhere between the Catholic school Catholics and the non-Catholics. More go to church regularly, more pray regularly, more of their parents were or are church goers, fewer have doubts about God's existence, more have had religious experiences, the Church is sacred to more of them than to non-Catholics, but on all these items they are less 'religious' than Catholic school Catholics.

Table 6.2 shows that Catholic school Catholics differ also from state school Catholics on various non-religious variables. On the level of permissiveness, Catholic school Catholics differ from both state school Catholics and particularly non-Catholics. More of the former frown on the person who has sex relations before marriage. Many more disapprove (far more than the Catholics who have not been to Catholic schools) of fellow Catholics who use the contraceptive pill. One gets the impression that the Catholic school Catholics are less permissive and more middle class, than the Protestant school upper middle class Protestants. They are not any less inclined to admire those who are very ambitious, or more inclined to be satisfied with what they have. Faint traces of scepticism of people who are 'anxious to be an intellectual', 'very patriotic', or who entertain anti-egalitarian notions 'treating people according to how important they are', are more visible amongst other categories than among those who have a Catholic school education. The Catholic school Catholic has more education than the state school Catholic and is slightly more mobile. All of which is consistent with the middle class image emerging from the data.

Table 6.2 Catholic respondents in selected attitudinal and other categories according to type of schooling (1966)

Percentage of respondents who	No parochial school education	Some parochial school education
1 had fathers who were professionals, managers, graziers or self-employed shop owners[a]	19	25
2 have lived in their present suburb or town longer than ten years	53	48
3 earned more than $4000 before deductions in the year 1964–1965[b]	6	5
4 have at least completed a secondary education	21	30
5 have completed a tertiary education	2	6
6 attend meetings or activities of a non-religious nature once a month or more	21	21
7 disapprove of the person who has sex relations before marriage	60	74
8 disapprove of the Catholic who uses the contraceptive pill	38	52
9 admire the very patriotic person	36	50
10 admire the person who is anxious to be an intellectual	34	41
11 disagree that the most important thing for a child to learn is to obey rather than to think for himself	36	42
12 agree that a person whose family has had a high social standing for many generations is therefore entitled to some respect	38	46
13 agree that it is more important to try to get ahead than to be satisfied with what one has	69	70
14 would like to see the Australian Labor Party win if there were an election	29	24
15 would like to see the Democratic Labor Party win if there were an election	7	14
16 would like to see the Liberal/Country Parties win if there were an election	31	35
17 would feel friendly and at ease with a Communist	10	15
18 would feel friendly and at ease with an atheist	31	40
19 would feel friendly and at ease with a Jew	58	64
20 would feel friendly and at ease with an Italian	60	66
Total sample B (adults over 20) items 2–6	188	427
Total sample C (adults over 20 from whom attitudinal material was available) items 7–20	109	290

Notes: [a]The percentages are based only on those fathers of respondents who were in the workforce (i.e. 158 in the first and 383 in the second column)

[b]As this question was made optional approximately one third of all respondents did not answer it. This lowered the percentages in all other categories considerably

Although the patterns were clear, it is premature to claim that Catholic school education is solely responsible for the greater religiousness and moral conservatism of its pupils. For it is very likely that more religiously involved Catholics sent their children to Catholic schools than lethargic ones. It would be wrong to attribute to a school system what may be a matter of family background. The independent effect of parental church going and respondent's school attendance can be investigated by Table 6.3 which eliminates these factors in turn. The disadvantage of this kind of analysis is that the cells become

Table 6.3   **Percentage of Catholic respondents who regularly attend church, according to parental church going and denominational schooling**

Both parents of respondents were			Catholic school education	
			Yes	No
regular	church	goers	83 (n = 273)	53 (n = 92)
irregular	church	goers	48 (n = 71)	39 (n = 51)

small, particularly if one concentrates on the polar situation, eliminating the in-between cases where, for instance, one parent is regular but another is not. The smallest percentage of regular Catholics (39 per cent) is in the cell in which respondents neither went to a denominational school nor had parents who were regular church goers, and the largest (83 per cent) is in the cell where both conditions were present. It is clear that both the church going habits of the parents and Catholic school education have a significant bearing on the church going of the respondent. It is interesting that there are still 20 out of 51 respondents (39 per cent) who were regular church goers in spite of the absence of both conditions. Who are these people? Eleven were converts to Catholicism and married to Catholic partners who usually had a Catholic school education and came from church going homes. Five were married to partners with an active Catholic background. One can only make guesses about the remaining four. An active priest woke them out of a dormant state? Pressure from the Catholic subculture made them behave like good rather than bad Catholics? A crisis experience? Conversely we can ask, who are the forty-five irregular church going Catholics, whose parents were regular church goers and who had attended Catholic schools? Thirteen of them were immigrants, Italian, Polish, Hungarian and Maltese, nine were married to persons of a different faith, six were elderly, five were married to inactive partners and the rest seem to have just drifted away for reasons not obvious from the survey.

Table 6.4 looks at additional religious variables and shows the expected trends. When both parents were reported as regular church goers and the respondents had been to denominational schools, more prayed regularly, more believed strongly in God, and more were likely to report the experience of a divine presence. When any of the two

Table 6.4 Catholic respondents in selected categories according to parental church going and denominational schooling

Percentage of respondents who	Parents both regular church goers		Parents both irregular church goers	
	Resp. has parochial school education	Resp. has no parochial school education	Resp. has parochial school education	Resp. has no parochial school education
	(a) n = 185	(b) n = 50	(c) n = 47	(d) n = 34
Pray daily	55	44	45	35
Believe that God really exists and have no doubts about it	82	56	70	59
Have had (or at least think that they have had) an experience of being somehow in the presence of God	71	50	51	50
Who would like to see their own denomination join or merge with any other and would not want to exclude any	51	46	36	29[a]
Who would feel friendly and at ease with atheists	44	38	30	29

Note: [a]There was an equal number of respondents in this category who had no opinion on the subject. In other words, the conclusion should not be drawn that the reciprocals of the percentages are against unqualified mergers.

factors or both were missing, the respondent's score was considerably lower. In all instances, regular church going of parents reinforces the pattern considerably but in no instance is it a sufficient substitute for Catholic schooling. In at least one instance, the belief that God really exists, Catholic school education seems to have a stronger effect than parental church going. The opposite appeared to be true in the case of respondents' church going in Table 6.3. In Table 6.4 the percentages in column (c) were smaller than in column (b). However, the cells are too small to observe a trend with any degree of confidence. Also no information is available about parental beliefs and experiences, and these factors may well exert a stronger influence than either Catholic school education or parental church going. It would be reasonable to think that those Catholics who were brought up by church going Catholic parents and who had attended Catholic schools would be more inclined to be on the defensive against those who do not belong to the fold. Still the 'in-group' feeling is weaker amongst those with an active rather than an inactive background. The relationship is not very strong, but those children of regular church goers who have been to Catholic schools are more likely to say that they feel at ease and friendly with atheists than those whose parents were irregular church goers. They are more inclined to favour an unqualified merger with other denominations than Catholics who have not been to Catholic schools and whose parents were irregular church goers. How can this finding be explained? Those in column (d) who are inactive Catholics are more likely to give neutral answers, that is, they don't care or don't identify sufficiently with the church. The active ones in this column are more likely to be converts who traditionally over-conform and ardently defend their new religious commitment. On the other hand, those in column (a) may well be more effectively plugged into the Catholic 'communication network', from which the ecumenical message could be heard loudly and clearly in 1966. Also, and this applies to 'plugged-in' Protestants as well, the understanding of, and even empathy with the atheistic position is not altogether foreign to both scriptural and ecclesiastical traditions in Christianity. Quite apart from these considerations, there is sufficient evidence from other sources to dispute the suggestion that bigotry is positively correlated with religious activity. At the same time, this finding should warn us not to carry our conclusions regarding the 'cohesion' of the Catholic Church too far, however much the loyalty of the average Australian Catholic to the Church is beyond any doubt.

As some age groups have had less denominational schooling than others, age should be watched as a variable which might explain the variations we found between the differently educated Catholics. If those under and over 40 are separately analysed, the independent effect of Catholic school education is maintained, although the cells are small. In other words, if respondents under 40 are compared with one another, those with a Catholic school education give the more 'religious' response. The same applies to those who are over 40. Yet age proves to be a factor which should not be neglected. For comparing Catholics of the two different age groups with one another, holding type of education constant, interesting differences come to light, as shown in Table 6.5. Age strengthens the pattern considerably: there is a greater difference between Catholics under 40 who have gone to state schools and Catholics over 40 who have gone to Catholic schools, than there is between Catholics of all ages who have gone to Catholic schools and Catholics of all ages who have not. On the other hand, the two middle columns of Table 6.5 indicate that

Table 6.5 Catholic respondents in selected categories by type of education and age (1966)

Percentage of respondents who	Catholics without parochial schooling		Catholics with parochial schooling	
	under 40	over 40	under 40	over 40
	(a) n = 40	(b) n = 63	(c) n = 154	(d) n = 134
1 had at least three of their five closest friends in the local congregation	24	40	42	45
2 disapprove of a person who has sex relations before marriage	43	73	69	79
3 disapprove of Catholics who use the contraceptive pill	28	44	44	61
4 pray daily	28	49	49	63
5 are sure that since childhood they have had (or at least think that they have had) a sense of being saved in Christ	28	40	40	49
6 agree that a person whose family has had a high social standing for many generations is therefore entitled to some respect	30	44	43	50

Source: Religion in Australia Survey, 1966

the independent effect of age and Catholic schooling cancel one another out. On the whole, the very significant differences are between columns (a) and (d), less significant are the differences between columns (b) and (c). This multiplier effect of age and Catholic school education is understandable. The younger, more mobile Catholics who went to school with non-Catholics can be expected to have more of their friends outside the local parish. Age and Catholic school education are likely to have a conservative influence on some of the ethical issues raised. But are regular prayer habits and the experience of being saved in Christ subject to similar conservative influences? One would expect these to be more independent of age, as indeed some of the other items are.

The 1966 research on the association between Catholic schooling and Catholic church attendance became controversial around the time (1971) that the entire survey was published. Don Anderson (1971: 66) wrote that the relation between schooling and attendance held only for respondents whose parents were regular church goers, but not for the lower row of Table 6.3, as the difference was not statistically significant. Therefore, he said, the possibility remains 'that attendance at Catholic school is incidental to religious socialisation in the family or that schooling is effective only in association with parental religion'. In the rejoinder (Mol, 1971a: 68) this was not denied, but it was also pointed out that associations may very well exist even if the difference is not statistically significant, and that exploratory surveys have many advantages over the controlled experiment technique favoured by Anderson, particularly when the field 'is almost entirely unexplored' as the sociological study of religion in Australia was in 1966.

Other research had a bearing on the attempt to find out more about the effect of Catholic schools. Yvonne Robertson (1968: 28) in her survey of 250 post-school Catholic adolescents in Sydney found that 56.1 per cent of her respondents who had 'all Catholic' education rated high on religious practices, (mass and communion weekly or more, confession sometimes or more) compared with 19.1 per cent of those who had part of their education in Catholic schools and 11.4 per cent of those who had been to state schools. Unfortunately Robertson does not hold parental religiousness constant, so there is no way of telling how far Catholic schooling has an independent effect. However, her other data agree with the 1966 findings.

Scott and Orr (1967: 131) compared 753 students in Grades 9–11 in seven independent (five of which were Anglican) and two state high schools in Queensland. They found that the state school pupils were more likely to read the Bible and to like going to church or chapel services voluntarily during the week. The state school students also outscored the independent school students on the first factor of a values inventory, identified as a general factor 'religious zeal'.

Ian Hansen (1969: 16–8), comparing sixth form boys of various independent schools, found that 68.3 per cent of the boys in the Protestant schools considered the influence of Christianity to be weak or almost nonexistent. However he found that 84.3 per cent of the boys in the Catholic school testified to the strength of the Christian factor in their school. In the Anglican schools in particular Hansen found a low incidence of orthodox faith and church going; only 12.6 and 11.8 per cent of the boys in the two Anglican schools were regular.

Both surveys appeared to confirm the evidence of the Religion in Australia Survey that on a number of significant religious items Protestant school pupils did not score more highly than the state school pupils.

Other observations about the independent effect of the Catholic schools come from Leavey (1972: 340). She studied sixth form students from nine Catholic girls' schools and concluded that there was some evidence that the schools were 'making a contribution independent of the home, and that students take on something of the general religious culture of the school'. Flynn (1975: 286) puts it much more forcefully when he concludes from his study of sixth form students in 21 Catholic Boys' High Schools that 'there were very strong indicators that schools in which there existed a supportive religious climate were having a influence on students' religious development independently of the home influence'.

More recently De Vaus (1981: 48 ff.) shows that the religious behaviour of teenagers (his sample consisted of 1735 year eleven and twelve students in six Catholic and six state schools in Victoria) continued to differ according to whether or not they attended a denominational school. Unfortunately he did not ask questions about home background, but his figures show that close to 80 per cent of pupils in Catholic schools but only around 51 per cent in state schools were regular church goers. There was no difference between boys and girls on attendance, but boys tended to be more highly orthodox in their beliefs (63 per cent versus 42 per cent) and more highly devotional (41 versus 20 per cent) if they attended a Catholic rather than a state school. Girls by contrast were much more likely to be highly orthodox or highly devotional irrespective of the school they attended. De Vaus concludes (ibid: 51) that girls have probably 'learnt from other sources that it is quite acceptable to be both feminine and religious', whereas boys needed the Catholic school to assure them that one could be both masculine and religious.

How do the findings compare with overseas data? There are differences, but also many similarities in the study undertaken by the National Opinion Research Center in Chicago, USA by Greeley and Rossi (1966).

Unlike Australia only a minority of Catholic children in the USA attend Catholic schools. On the other hand, Australia does not have any Catholic liberal arts colleges of which there are many in the USA. It is possible for an American Catholic to have all his education, including tertiary levels, in a Catholic institution, and the NORC study found the association between Catholic education and adult religious behaviour was strongest among those who went to Catholic colleges, especially the males (Greeley and Rossi 1966: 158). However, the major finding of the American study was similar to the 1966 Religion in Australia Survey that the association between Catholic education and adult religious behaviour is strongest amongst those who come from church going families.

We can speculate about the possible meaning of the data for a current problem. In Australia as elsewhere, Catholics have for some time now been debating the merits of their school system.

What are these arguments? One runs that the Catholic school system has not achieved what it set out to do. Another one is that the Church's resources could be used more fruitfully in other areas and that the ghetto mentality of Catholic schools will prevent Catholics from participating fully in the problems of a secular society. Still another one runs that Catholic schools are merely duplicating what the state schools are already doing.

As is often the case with sociological research, it cannot solve the problem, but it can clarify some of the issues and lift them out of deadlocked value-based positions. The independent and cumulative contribution of a parochial school system as measured by increased church attendance, more regular prayer and stronger beliefs in God, seems beyond any doubt. Is this increase in loyalty to their Church, their faith and their traditions worth the considerable expenditure of both finance and manpower? If the author were a Catholic (he is not) he would probably make a value judgement at this point and say, 'These orientations and loyalties are crucial and therefore no amount of effort should be spared to strengthen them, for the survey shows that Catholic school Catholics are better Catholics'. If the author were a secular humanist, which he is not, he would make the opposite value judgement and say: 'Catholic school education makes only a slight impact, if at all, on such important values as tolerance and thinking for oneself. To make such enormous efforts for such a small return is simply not good economics'.

The research has measured some effects of parochial school education. The value attached to what is measured is clearly a matter which lies beyond the competence of the sociologist. It is a matter for the 'decision makers' in the Catholic hierarchy. It may well be that they feel that the Catholic schools have not achieved what they set out to do, and that the kind of Catholic or Christian which the parochial school produces is not sufficiently superior to warrant the monopolisation of vast amounts of labour and financial resources of the Church. The goals of Catholic education may be 'saintliness' rather than 'loyalty' to the institution, 'quality of prayer' rather than a routine 'Hail Mary', 'loving one's neighbour actually', rather than saying that in a hypothetical case 'one would feel friendly and at ease with the Japanese'.

The 'ghetto mentality' argument also merits some consideration. From the data, it did not appear that Catholic school Catholics with Catholic schooling tended to have more of their closest friends in the local parish than others. Yet loyalty to the Catholic subculture is not necessarily incompatible with loyalty to the society at large. In this kind of argument the inescapable fact that a cohesive community of fellow believers is a prerequisite to maintain and carry out a religious orientation is almost always overlooked. The problem of Catholicism in the countries where it is not a minority is that it is too amorphous rather than too cohesive. If the goal of the Catholic Church in general and Catholic schools in particular is the formation of apostles, then the Church will have to provide a home base from which these apostles can operate. A loose assemblage of individuals is not likely to meet the sociological requirements.

We can be short on the argument that Catholic schools are merely duplicating what the state schools are already doing. Plainly, in Australia the state schools are more likely to relativise implicity rather than reinforce a host of religious beliefs and orientations by the very necessity for neutral aloofness. Apparently, many Australians feel that secular learning is all that matters and that if religious knowledge is at all necessary, it can be dispensed quite adequately in Sunday schools and scripture classes. Yet the Catholic Church seems to have realised early that the priority of a religious framework of meaning in a secular age cannot be maintained by separating the two kinds of knowledge institutionally. Its decision to increase its influence over the entire process of education has certainly proved to be a redoubtable barrier to the secularisation of its membership. The institutional strength of the Catholic Church compared with the Protestant Churches even in 1984 is to an important extent attributable to this institutional coordination rather than separation. However, the underlying worry of those Catholics who argue against the Catholic school system seems to be that this institutional strength does not necessarily lead to the formation of actual, intrinsic, Christians.

The major findings of this section are as follows:

1   Those who have attended Catholic schools score more highly on the religious variables than the others. More go to church regularly, more pray regularly, more believe strongly in God, more are of the opinion that the Church is appointed by God and more are likely to have had religious experiences.

2   Those who have no Catholic school education score not as high, yet higher than Protestants.

3   Fewer Catholics with at least some Catholic school education admired the very patriotic person, and more agreed that trying to get ahead was more important than being satisfied with what on has.

4   Irrespective of type of education, significantly fewer Catholics disagreed with the statement that the most important thing for a child to learn was to obey rather than to think for itself.

5   Catholics with at least some parochial school education tended to be more puritanical than Catholics who had been to state schools or Protestants. More disapproved of the person who had sex relations before marriage. Many more disapproved of the Catholic who used the contraceptive pill.

6   Catholics who had been to Catholic schools were slightly better educated than Catholics who had gone to state schools.

7   More Catholics than Protestants, and more Catholic school Catholics than state Catholics, had the majority of their closest friends in the local parish.

8   Age (being over 40) strengthened the correlation of Catholic education and other factors such as friendships in the local church, disapproval of the person who has sex relations before marriage, etc. Being under 40 would weaken the pattern. Age had no effect on the correlation between Catholic school education and church going. However it did have an effect on prayer, for about as many of the younger people with Catholic school education prayed daily as older people who had not had the benefit of a Catholic school education. This suggests that private devotional habits and experiences are more common among older people, but that public religious practices are largely independent of age.

Some further speculations:

1   The arguments against parochial school education in the Catholic Church underrate the importance of coordination rather than separation of educational and religious institutions for the strength of the latter. This is particularly so in a secular age when the priority of a religious framework of meaning is difficult to maintain, and when religious institutions are relegated to the periphery. Without its enormous and costly effort in education the Catholic Church in Australia would be much weaker and would have decidedly less hold on its membership. The success of the schools may also be due to the teaching orders. One gains the impression that not the lay teachers, but the Brothers and Sisters are vitally concerned with behaviour in general, rather than just behaviour at school. Yet Catholic schools are more and more staffed by lay people. The number of Sisters fell by almost the same percentage (15) with which the Catholic population increased from 1966–1976 (Hally, 1982: 83).

2   Still the previous paragraph should not lead to an overestimation of the cohesion of Catholicism in Australia. The ties with the values of the population as a whole, the relatively accepting responses to such diverse people as atheists and Japanese, the desire for mergers with other denominations, should warn us not to take the ghetto mentality

of Catholics too seriously. Catholic in-group feeling is not as strong as it used to be. Conversely the decreasing hostility of non-Catholics makes the defence of an imperilled and therefore cohesive subculture less necessary.

3   Although the Catholic school system has had a positive effect on the loyalty of Catholics to their Church, it should not be regarded as the only factor. After all, the Protestant schools in Australia have had no such effect. Maybe the crucial distinction is between the reinforcing of old loyalties and the creation of new ones, and a parochial school system is capable of doing the former but not the latter. After all, those Protestant denominations which unlike the big non-Catholic institutions in Australia, have been able to increase the loyalty of their membership through a school system could build on an already existing committed membership. If this is so, it means that in the last quarter of the nineteenth century Catholics in Australia must have possessed a general and relatively strong allegiance to their religion for the reinforcing effect of a school system to be at all a success. This initial allegiance was probably based on common Irishness, common social economic deprivation, or, more likely, on a common traditional awe for religious authority which was missing in Protestantism.

The effect of Protestant schools

Are people who went to Protestant schools more 'religious' than those who went to state schools? Protestant schools have always been thought to cater for the more wealthy, and the child from the poorer home could rarely, if ever, get to such a school. In the nineteenth century, these schools served the wealthy squatters and the upper middle class,

> together with a few talented children whom they bought with scholarships. Their schools were modelled on the English public schools and designed for the education of boys and girls to serve God in Church, State and the professions—to produce that upright man who feared God and eschewed evil and at the same time was dedicated to the service of the wordly aspirations of the British people (Clark, 1963: 148).

Usually Protestant schools deny that they are elite schools, and headmasters go out of their way to defend their schools in terms of the contribution they make to Christian leadership.

Do pupils of Protestant schools differ from pupils of state schools? Table 6.6 shows that in 1966 they varied little on religious items. The existing differences seem to point to slightly less religiousness among

Table 6.6   Percentage of Protestant respondents according to type of schooling (1966)

Percentage of respondents who	No private school education	Some private school education
1 were regular church goers	27	29
2 had been to church on previous Sunday	18	20
3 had fathers who were regular church goers when they grew up	34	41
4 had mothers who were regular church goers when they grew up	46	48
5 had at least three of their five closest friends in the local congregation	30	24
6 know that God really exists and have no doubts about it	42	44
7 disagree with the statement that it is not necessary to go to church to be a Christian	19	15
8 disagree with the statement that the book of Acts of the Apostles gives an account of Jesus' life on earth	15	17
9 disagree with the statement that it does not matter what one believes as long as one leads a moral life	19	26
10 pray daily	28	29
11 are sure that since childhood they have had (or at least think so) a feeling that they were somehow in God's presence	45	45
12 are sure that since childhood they have had (or at least think that they have had) a sense of being saved in Christ	33	24
13 are sure that since childhood they have had (or at least think that they have had) a feeling of being tempted by the devil	32	25
14 are of the opinion that the Church is appointed by God and that it is the home and refuge of all mankind	23	17
15 are of the opinion that on the whole the Church stands for the best in human life, in spite of shortcomings found in all human institutions	37	45
Total sample A (children and adolescents included) items 1 and 2	2621	330
Total sample B (adults over 20 only) items 3 and 4	1661	260
Total sample C (adults over 20 from whom attitudinal material was available) all other items	1194	195

Source: Religion in Australia Survey, 1966

Protestant school educated Protestants. Regularity of church attendance, regularity of prayer, experience of God's presence and belief in God are all approximately the same. The chuch going habits of the mothers of both groups of respondents are all very similar, although the fathers of those who had private school education tended to be more regular than the fathers of the others. Those with Protestant school education tend to have fewer of their closest friends in the local congregation, are not so inclined to relativise beliefs, or to claim the experience of being saved in Christ, or of being tempted by the devil. This, together with their preference for the institutional rather than the theological definition of the Church, makes it appear that amount of education or class position could better explain some of these differences. Indeed the outstanding differences between the two categories are father's occupation and amount of education. (see Table 6.7).

A Protestant with private school education is far more likely to have a father with an upper class occupation, to have had more education and to prefer the Liberal/Country Parties to win. Otherwise there are few differences: like the better educated, more are involved in meetings and activities of a non-religious nature, and more admire the person who is anxious to be an intellectual. More disagree that the most important thing for a child to learn is to obey rather than to think for himself, and feel relatively friendly and at ease with such controversial people as communists and atheists. They are also more mobile (tend to have lived for less time in their suburb) and earn more. Not surprisingly, they tend to prefer the *status quo*: fewer are inclined to agree that it is more important to try to get ahead than to be satisfied with what one has, and more admire the very patriotic person. Slightly more are libertarian and fewer disapprove of the person who has sex relations before marriage.

The introduction of age in no way alters the Protestant pattern of schooling. The few differences such as the higher percentage of private school respondents with fathers in the upper class occupations or the higher percentage of private school respondents favouring the Liberal/Country Parties, are maintained irrespective of age.

Previously it was mentioned that the slight differences found in the 'religious' responses of Protestants with or without denominational schooling might disappear when amount of education is held constant, for the syndrome of responses was reminiscent of the responses of the educated.

This is indeed what Table 6.8 shows. Yet there are two interesting exceptions; those who have not completed a secondary education still tend to have had more active fathers. They are also more likely to claim the experience of being 'saved in Christ'. The data suggest that

Table 6.7   Non-Catholic respondents in selected attitudinal and other categories according to type of schooling (1966)

Percentage of respondents who	No private school education	Some private school education
1 had fathers who were professionals, managers, graziers or self-employed shop owners[a]	17	44
2 have lived in their present suburb or town longer than ten years	55	50
3 earned more than $4,000 before deductions in the year 1964–1965[b]	5	13
4 have at least completed secondary education	25	59
5 have completed a tertiary education	5	15
6 attend meetings or activities of a non-religious nature	26	35
7 disapprove of the person who has sex relations before marriage	61	56
8 disapprove of the Catholic who uses the contraceptive pill	49	54
9 admire the very patriotic person	49	54
10 admire the person who is anxious to be an intellectual	39	47
11 disagree that the most important thing for a child to learn is to obey rather than to think for himself	55	60
12 agree that a person whose family has had a high social standing for many generations is therefore entitled to some respect	35	37
13 agree that it is more important to try to get ahead than to be satisfied with what one has	68	59
14 would like to see the Australian Labor Party win if there were an election	29	15
15 would like to see the Democratic Labor Party win if there were an election	2	1
16 would like to see the Liberal/Country Parties win if there were an election	45	63
17 would feel friendly and at ease with a Communist	18	23
18 would feel friendly and at ease with an atheist	40	49
19 would feel friendly and at ease with a Jew	59	64
20 would feel friendly and at ease with an Italian	55	61
Total sample B (adults over 20) items 1–5	1661	260
Total sample C (adults over 20 from whom attitudinal material was available) items 6–19	1194	195

Notes: [a]The percentages are based only on those fathers of respondents who were in the workforce (1475 in the first and 250 in the second column).
[b]As this question was made optional approximately one third of all respondents did not answer. This lowered the percentages in all other categories considerably.
Source: Religion in Australia Survey, 1966

in Protestantism there are two kinds of homes from which the pupils of denominational schools come. The first kind consists of people in the professions, management and grazing. They are not in any way more 'religious' than people in the same occupational bracket who sent their children to state schools.

As a matter of fact, the fathers in these homes tend to be slightly

Table 6.8 **Non-Catholic respondents in selected categories by type and amount of education (1966)**

| Percentage of respondents who | Non-Catholic with state school education | | Non-Catholic with private school education | |
	Primary education or some only	At least completed secondary education	Primary education or some only	At least completed secondary education
1 had fathers who were regular church goers when they grew up	33	36	48	37
2 had at least three of their five closest friends in the local congregation	31	25	29	21
3 disagree with the statement that it does not matter what one believes as long as one leads a moral life	17	23	19	28
4 are sure that since childhood they have had (or at least think that they have had) a sense of being saved in Christ	22	28	30	20
Total sample (item 1)	1201	414	102	156
Total sample (items 2–4)	855	314	70	122

Source: Religion in Australia Survey, 1966

less regular church goers—38 per cent (n = 112) are regular compared with 47 per cent (n = 251) in the other category. Their children end up in the same way, for the Protestant school has no effect on their religious habits, views and beliefs. They are indistinguishable from children who have fathers in similar occupations and who have not gone to such a school, with the exception that the former are even less prepared to claim the experience of being 'saved in Christ'—23 per cent against 38 per cent who went to state schools. The second kind of home from which Protestant school pupils come consists of people with clerical and skilled occupations. They seemed to be more 'religious' than other people in the same occupational bracket. Here 51 per cent (n = 88) of the fathers are regular church goers compared with 38 per cent (n = 251) of fathers whose children have gone to state schools. The children are no more likely to attend church regularly, but more of them pray daily, 42 per cent (n = 66) versus 28 per cent (n = 496). However, these children do not differ otherwise. This contrasts with children from similar Catholic homes.

There is reason to believe that this category of pupils, sent to independent schools for religious rather than class reasons, has been on the increase since 1966. In 1981 forty-five Christian schools were using the USA based Accelerated Christian Education curriculum. The materials are fundamentalist, stress individual progress of pupils and are used particularly by the charismatic churches and some Baptists. None of these schools existed in 1976. Another group of Protestant Christian schools are those controlled by parents. They have a basis in Dutch Calvinism, and grew from only 3 in 1967 to 31 in 1982. Yet currently only slightly more than one third of the pupils is of Reformed origin (Jones, 1983: 38). A third group consists of the Christian Community schools. They are much more geared to Australian culture, but are also decidedly bible-based. They grew from 1 school in 1976 to 26 in 1983. By contrast the Christian Community colleges originated in the main line denominations; there are 4 in Victoria at present, some of which began as Catholic/Protestant endeavours (ibid.: 70ff.).

Are there important differences between Protestant and Catholics who send their children to Church schools? In the upper occupations, 76 per cent of Catholic fathers sent their children to Catholic schools. These percentages are 70 per cent for the middle and 67 per cent for the lower occupations. Although fathers in the lower occupations have been less inclined to send their children to Catholic schools than fathers in the middle and particularly the upper occupations, the differences are hardly significant. There is an entirely different pattern for the Protestants. Of the fathers in the upper occupational categories 31 per cent have sent their offspring to denominational schools. The figures for fathers in the middle and lower occupational categories are 11 per cent and 8 per cent respectively. The upper classes are indeed overrepresented in the Protestant schools. It is to these schools rather than to the Catholic ones, that the following observation of Jean Martin seems to apply:

> ... the most important purpose served by the non-government schools is seldom officially acknowledged: this is the task of preparing the child to take his place among the higher status members of the society by teaching him their customs, imbuing him with their values, and by providing him with friends and contacts within this section of the society (Martin, 1957: 28–29).

Although there are Protestant denominational schools to which this observation would not altogether apply (those not belonging to the 41 wealthy schools which saw their federal aid cut in 1983) it is certainly true that a disproportionate number of alumni from Protestant denominational schools can be found in sections of the Melbourne business world or in the Department of External Affairs in Canberra. A Canberra journalist (*Canberra Times*, 12 Sept 1968: 3) made the following observation:

> The Geelong Grammar syndrome continues to hold sway in the Department of External Affairs. An analysis of the educational background of Australian career diplomats shows that 158 are products of private and church schools. Only eighty-three have a State school background. A further breakdown of the figures reveals some startling differences from State to State.
>
> Almost ninety per cent of those diplomats educated in Victorian secondary schools was drawn from the 'private and church' category (sixty-five as opposed to ten) whereas those from New South Wales were almost evenly divided in school background (fifty-two 'private and church', forty-eight 'State'). Only in the Australian Capital Territory were the State school people in the majority (five to two).

That the pattern described by the 1966 Religion in Australia Survey has not fundamentally changed over the past 20 years is clear from a 1984 controversy in Melbourne over the reappointment of the popular head (Joan Montgomery) of the Presbyterian Ladies College. She was closely associated with what was characterised by members of its Council as the liberal humanist tradition with a strong dose of feminism thrown in. The Continuing Presbyterians who acquired the school after the 1977 formation of the Uniting Church wanted a much more bible centred education and therefore decided not to reappoint Miss Montgomery (see *National Times*, 8–15 March 1984: 8). This was strongly resented by the alumnae of the school. Obviously the latter represented the broad spectrum of well-to-do Australian Protestant and private school pupils, whereas the Continuing Presbyterians favoured those in the survey whose Christian practices and beliefs had been advanced by attending a Protestant school.

What can we conclude?

The important difference between the non-Catholics who had been to denominational schools and those who had not were generally unrelated to religious factors. The differences were either political, (more preferred the Liberal/Country Parties) or educational (more than twice as many had completed at least a secondary education) or occupational (twice as many had fathers in professional, managerial or grazing circles). However this should not be interpreted to mean that the religious and social effect of the Protestant denominational schools is negligible. It may well be that there are significant differences in leadership qualities of pupils, or any of a host of other factors, for which there are no data in Australia as yet.

Sunday schools

When in the second half of the nineteenth century, Protestants generally acquiesced in separating religious and educational functions, they did not in any way abandon the role they saw for themselves as teachers of religious beliefs and moral values for the young. The vehicles for this task were the Sundays schools. Originally they had been intended primarily for the poor outside the church, but soon many other Protestant families took advantage of the new service offered by the churches. Catholics continued to stress the importance of Catholic day schools, but nevertheless made provision for other children who went to state schools. Yet the expansion of the Sunday School system was in the Protestant corner of the denominational spectrum. In NSW the Catholic share of attendance in the system actually dropped from 25 per cent in 1870 to 21 per cent in 1890.

Walter Phillips (1972–73: 397) estimates from the official returns regarding the numbers of children 5–14 years attending, that in NSW in 1860 27 per cent of all children in that age group went to Sunday school. His calculations show that this percentage rose steeply to 41 per cent in 1870, 39 per cent in 1880 and 46 per cent in 1890 to drop to 40 again in 1900. There were also figures for enrolments in 1880 and 1890 and these showed that in those years 52 per cent and 55 per cent respectively of children in that age group appeared on the rolls, suggesting that approximately three-quarters of children actually attended.

Phillips also calculated the denominational distributions of attending pupils. At the peak in 1890, of all children in Sunday schools, 30 per cent were Anglican, 21 per cent Catholic, 11 per cent Presbyterian and 25 per cent Methodist, the remaining 13 per cent being distributed over Congregationalists (6 per cent), Baptists (2 per cent) and Salvation Army (5 per cent).

For most of the twentieth century the Sunday schools remained venerable institutions. Even parents (particularly Anglican parents) who did not go to church themselves felt obligated to send their children. However, the fashion of paying lip-service to a long standing cultural tradition seems to have come to a somewhat abrupt end in the 1960s and 1970s. The Commission on Christian Education of the Australian Council of Churches published a study (Stewart, 1976: 62) showing that from 1963 to 1974 the number of children attending Sunday School in the major Protestant denominations (Anglican, Methodist, Presbyterian) appeared to have halved in that relatively short period. By contrast Sunday School attendance in the Salvation Army dropped by only 20 per cent, whereas the Baptists even gained 8 per cent over the period.

The report on the decline has been corroborated by research done by David Hilliard (1979). He showed that from 1954 to 1976 Anglican Sunday school enrolments in South Australia dropped from 103 per 1000 children (aged five to fourteen) to 21. These data show that now large numbers of nominal Anglican, Methodists and Presbyterians feel under no constraint to maintain the last tender link with their denomination (as compared with earlier periods of Australian history), and fill in 'no religion' on the census form and have no qualms of keeping their children from those Sunday schools that they themselves rather reluctantly attended when they were children.

7   Beliefs and morals

I have been trying to understand the phenomenon of religion in Australia from a variety of angles—all of them with their own inadequacies. Yet hopefully together they present as comprehensive a picture as possible. In this array of indicators of religion, belief is one that should not be overlooked. After all, beliefs are supposed to sum up how individuals view reality. They are known to sustain patterns of behaviour and moral convictions. First then I will describe the beliefs of Australians, after which I will embark upon an analysis of the effect these beliefs have on morality. Implied in the description will be my interest in the effect beliefs have on the integrity of individuals and the various units of social organisations in which they find themselves. Morality will be judged in terms of the contribution it makes to the integration not just of Australian society, but also of families, communities and other 'identities'.

Beliefs

Do Australians believe in God? Can we assume they don't because they do not attend church or pray?

Opinions differ as to how meaningful questions about belief in God really are. For one thing, what people mean by God differs from one person to another. For another, stating that one believes in God does not indicate how strong these beliefs are and what these beliefs entail. This does not mean that questions such as 'Do you believe in God?' are meaningless, particularly when the answers are related to other data. People who believe in God without doubt may differ from others by having different moral convictions, for instance.

Gallup Poll International asked a representative sample of people in at least a dozen countries whether they believed in God. One of these polls was published in February/March 1948, another in April 1969, and yet another in 1983. In 1949, 95 percent of Australians said 'yes'; in 1969 this percentage had dropped to 87 percent and in 1983 to 79 percent. There was a similar drop in the United Kingdom (from 84 to 77 to 70 per cent). In other countries, again, the percentage rose and fell from 94 per cent to 98 to 95 in the USA and from 66 per cent to 73 to 62 in France. These polls show that only a small minority wants to go on record as not believing in God and that this is true for almost all western countries.

In Australia in 1969, men (82 per cent) were significantly less prepared to affirm their beliefs in God than were women (93 per cent). The same was true for other questions, such as beliefs in heaven (men 57 percent, women 73 per cent) in life after death (men 41 per cent, women 53 per cent), in hell (men 31 percent, women 38 per cent) and in the devil (men 30 per cent, women 37 per cent). There were also significant differences between the various Australian denominations, as Table 7.1 shows.

Table 7.1   Percentage of believers by major denominations

Percentage of respondents believing in:	Anglican	Catholic	Methodist	Presbyterian
God	88	94	90	91
Heaven	60	82	70	60
Life after death	40	65	46	40
Hell	26	64	28	17
The devil	23	59	26	21

Source: Gallup poll, 1969

These differences between Catholics and non-Catholics had existed for some time. In another Gallup poll, carried out in October 1959 as many as 62 per cent of Catholic respondents said that they believed in a 'fiery hell' in contrast with only 17 per cent of non-Catholics.

More recently the Australian Values Study showed that in Australia in 1983, 49 per cent believe in life after death, 34 per cent in hell, and 57 per cent in heaven. Unfortunately the breakdown of the 1983 poll for denomination and sex was not available at the time of writing.

It is obvious that these beliefs do not intertwine to a great extent. If the respondents had thought about God primarily as the One with whom they were to be united in heaven after death there would have been far fewer differences. Obviously there is a considerable percentage of Australians, particularly Protestants, for whom belief in God does not include belief in heaven and much less belief in an after-life or hell. Is this perhaps because the concept of God evokes a far less specific imagery than a mediaeval devil torturing the condemned? It would be too simple to say that in our consumer oriented world, bleak images of judgement and hell are rejected, but that more hopeful symbols of acceptance and heaven are still part of people's beliefs. There are probably more complex factors operating such as, for instance, the concept of God being for many a focus of moral values or a crystallisation of social sentiment or the memory of a stable past or the hope of a meaningful future or abstracted order. It is clear that the concepts of God and devil, heaven and hell do not belong to a well integrated, interdependent and interacting belief system where one element depends on the other, and where the whole structure disintegrates because belief in one item has become obsolete. The presumption that there is such a general integrated belief system on the part of some churches may be just as unreliable as the assumption that people do not believe in God anymore. The predicament of religious institutions and theologians may consist of the dislocation of what was a coherent belief system, rather than of modern societies being immune to religious or even 'supernatural' interpretations. Secularisation may consist of this dislocation rather than man's increasing espousal of the rational. The fact that the 1969 Gallup poll on beliefs showed less divergence within Catholic rather than Protestant ranks may be related to the greater capacity of Catholic religious authority at the time to impose the internal rationale of its belief system on its members. Yet the percentage differences within the Catholic column of Table 7.1 suggest that Catholicism too has undergone a crisis of authority which has, if anything, grown worse in the 1970s.

It seems certain that there are different shades and kinds of believers and unbelievers. Yet the kind of question which Gallup poll asked did not allow for subtle distinctions. By contrast the Religion in Australia Survey probed more deeply. The answers it received on its belief question were as follows: of all 1825 adults over 20 years old, 49 per cent said that they knew God existed and that they had no doubts about it. Another 20 per cent said that while they had doubts, they felt that they did believe in God. Seven per cent found themselves believing in God some of the time but not at other times. Twelve per cent said they did not believe in a personal God, but in a higher power of some kind. Six per cent gave the agnostic answer: they did not know whether there was a God and they did not believe that there was any way to find out. Two per cent gave an atheistic answer: they did not believe in God. A further 2 per cent gave other replies.

Comparing these figures with those of the 1969 Gallup poll it is clear that the 87 per cent of Australians who then claimed to 'believe in God' covered a mixed bag of people: those who have no doubts about God's existence, others who have their occasional doubts and again others who are only prepared to believe in some kind of higher power. Also the 7 per cent of Gallup poll respondents who said that they did not believe in God (a further 6 per cent could not say) is likely to consist of both atheists and agnostics.

In spite of the finer lines of distinction within the category of those who believed in God, there was still a much larger percentage of people who believed in God without doubt than those who attended church regularly or who prayed daily. What clusters arise when all three variables, beliefs, public and private worship are combined?

Disregarding some of the smaller cells, (that is, for instance, those respondents who go to church regularly, or pray daily, but have their occasional doubts of God's existence), the sample of the Religion in Australia Survey seemed to fall into six groups named as follows for easier reference:

orthodox believer	respondent who goes to church regularly, prays daily and knows without doubt that God exists (17 per cent of sample)
private believer	respondent who does not go to church regularly but prays daily and knows without doubt that God exists (8 per cent of sample)
public believer	respondent who does not pray daily, but goes to church regularly and knows without a doubt that God exists (10 per cent of sample)
believing secularist	respondent who does not go to church regularly and does not pray daily, but knows without a doubt that God exists (16 percent of sample)
vacillating secularist	respondent who does not go to church regularly and does pray daily, but although he has doubts, still believes in God or finds himself believing in God some of the time (20 per cent of sample)
consistent secularist	respondent who does not go to church regularly, does not pray daily, and who either does not believe in God, or does not know whether there is a God, or does not believe in a personal God, but in a higher power of some kind (16 per cent of sample)

One wonders what 'belief in God' actually means for the 'believing secularists'. It is not likely to mean anything like fervent commitment to a specific biblical God demanding loyalty and worship. If this were the case one would imagine that they would want to structure their faith in specific contexts of public and private worship. One would also imagine that they would find this belief somewhat at variance with hedonistic commitment of one kind of another. More likely than not they are typical of the adolescents whom Connell (1957: 55–6) and his co-workers described as disliking both 'someone who does not believe in God' and 'someone who is very religious'. Either of these disliked categories in our sample would be on opposite ends of the continuum: the 'consistent secularist' whose specific anti-religious commitment is rather well characterised in the pages of the Australian Humanist (Fairbanks, 1968: 40), and the 'orthodox believer', on the other hand; both seem to be equally outside the approved norm of the middle category for similar reasons: they are committed too emotionally to a specific stance.

Since the Religion in Australia Survey was published, Hogan analysed data on secularism in Australia from the Roy Morgan Australian Social Barometer Survey of 1977. In this survey two questions were asked: 'What religion were you brought up in?' and 'What religion do you follow now?'. Hogan (1979: 397) compared the answers to these questions and discovered that there was what he called considerable 'seepage'. Of the 36 per cent of respondents who were brought up as Anglicans, only 22 per cent said that they now 'follow this religion'. For Catholics, the corresponding figures were 25 and 18 per cent; for Uniting Church 23 and 14 per cent, presumably including all Methodists and Presbyterians. Apparently the respondents who were brought up in a particular denomination no longer felt any allegiance and yet continued to believe in God, were put into a separate category of 'secularists'. Apart from 'those who believed in God only' (12 per cent), also those with 'no religion' (20 per cent) and those who did not answer the questions were put in this 'secular' category. Unfortunately, these three items were neither mutually exclusive, nor well described and are therefore not comparable with those of the Religion in Australia Survey. Yet the reason for mentioning the survey is the association which Hogan found between these secular beliefs and values of liberalism and permissiveness. We will return to this issse later, in the section on morality.

Probing further in the literature on secular beliefs in Australia, Black (1983c: 155) describes the New South Wales Humanist Society, which regarded 'superstition and dogmatic religious beliefs as barriers to human progress and unity'. It had 937 members in 1974 but they fell to 401 in 1977, partly because some of the causes in which it strongly believed (such as abolition of government aid to denominational schools and the withdrawal of troops from Vietnam) were either lost or won. Obviously its adamant stand against supernatural beliefs did not attract a large following.

Numerically stronger in the Australian population are those who believe in astrology. The Religion in Australia Survey asked its adult respondents: 'Do you ever act on the advice of your stars?' Eighty per cent said that they never did, 11 per cent did sometimes, 2 per cent often and another 2 per cent did not answer the question. Women (16 per cent) were slightly more inclined than men (13 per cent) to act on the advice of their stars at least sometimes; so were people with no religion (19 per cent, n = 54) compared with Catholics (9 per cent, n = 407), or irregular church goers (16 per cent, n = 1218), compared with regular ones (9 per cent, n = 603), or people who thought that the church is a stronghold of much that may be unwholesome and dangerous to human welfare (24 per cent, n = 21) compared with people who thought that the church was appointed by God (12 per cent, n = 527). Other categories in which the percentages of those who acted at least sometimes on the advice of their stars were overrepresented were: those who had had, since they grew up, a feeling of being punished by God (22 per cent, n = 500) or those afraid of God (19 per cent, n = 176) or those who admired the person who was against Asian migration to Australia (18 per cent, n = 174). One notices that to some of these people the horoscope takes the place of Christianity, and that the need for guidance by one's stars is greater amongst the insecure and the frightened. Understandably, the churches strongly reject these secular beliefs and practices. The Anglican Archbishop of Sydney called occultism 'faked, shallow and diversionary' (Loane, 1975: 3) Yet the newspapers continue to publish horoscopes, obviously because people read them, and clairvoyants continue to attract followers. One of these, Trudy Lucas in Fremantle, Western Australia, had to move premises in order to accommodate 'up to 120 people who could cram into the former store for Sunday services' (Locke, 1983: 116).

Yet the implicit hedonistic views of Australians are much more influential than the secular beliefs promulgated by esoteric organisations. As is often the case, these beliefs are a mixture of self assertion and conformity, with the former prevailing. It is the conforming side which makes these respondents affirm a belief in God (the Religion in Australia Survey therefore called them 'believing secularists'), but in actual fact the attitudes are guided by what maximises individual pleasure and minimises stress and pain. The belief in God is somewhat residual and certainly not central enough to consistently make for self denial and for altruism and Christian love, which church going and private prayer seem to reinforce. Belief in God, if it is more than a weak, vaguely held sentiment, has an implicit effect on restraint and on sensitivity for those values which bolster family, community and society. This theme will be documented in the following sections.

Morality

Ever since the establishment of the first convict settlement in Australia in 1788, rulers and ruled alike have tended to look on religion in terms of its social utility. This is not surprising, since around the turn of the century this was the English view of religion. In England in 1818 a Bill was introduced to build more churches in the industrial cities. The Prime Minister, Lord Liverpool, agreed with others in strongly defending the need for them, because the people in those areas were exposed to 'vicious and corrupting influences dangerous to the public security as well as to private morality' (MacIntyre, 1967: 18–19).

Church of England clergymen in the convict colonies were primarily regarded as moral policemen, and as such they were hated by the convicts and used by the rulers. Their religion had 'an obvious social usefulness in a convict society, for it preached in favour of subordination and against drunkenness, whoring and gambling' (Clark, 1963: 22). This did not mean that the clergy thought of themselves in this way. However,

> their work as moral policemen so identified them in the eyes of the world with a particular social order that their charge to all who receive the gifts of divine love seemed arrant hypocrisy. The price they paid for serving the material interests of the English governing classes was to be branded as civil servants in cassocks by all who did not share their faith (ibid.: 23).

One of these 'civil servants in cassocks' was Samuel Marsden, colleague and successor to Johnson, the first chaplain to the colony. In a letter to Governor Hunter he wrote,

> ... I cannot but attribute to the neglect of public worship as a chief cause that idleness and prodigality, and excess and ruin, which have raged among the Settlers and prisoners ... (Bonwick, 1898: 194)

Similarly, when in 1820 Catholic priests were reluctantly introduced into the colony of New South Wales, the prime motive for their appointment was to keep Catholics under control. It was only natural that their salaries were paid from the Police Fund (Farrell, 1968: 16).

About the same time Governor Macquarie encouraged the British and Foreign Bible Society as well as the Sunday School Movement because, like its founders, he was convinced that bible knowledge could correct the most ferocious manners and would promote worldly comfort (Clark, 1963: 48).

In Victoria in the middle of the nineteenth century the situation was apparently no different. A Bill in 1853 began with the words:

> Whereas for the advancement of the Christian religion and the promotion of good morals in the colony of Victoria it is expedient to encourage the observance of Public Worship ... (Gregory, 1960: 33).

About the same time in the Lachlan, the Lower Murrumbidgee and Moulamein areas of New South Wales the urgent need was felt for a number of Anglican clergymen, the rationale for their coming being as follows:

> The way in which Sunday is usually spent in these parts is far from being conducive to the promotion of morality, and nothing but the presence amongst us of faithful ministers will even have any effect in counteracting such proceedings (Clark, 1955: 186-7).

The conviction that religion and morality went hand in hand was not altogether without foundation. One historian of the period, reviewing the historical accomplishments of Victoria from the vantage point of 1888, looks with disdain at the laxity of public morals of an earlier period, but then goes on to say:

> during the past twenty-five years the earnestness displayed by the clergy of the old country has been communicated to the colonies. Hence we see a marked improvement in the religious attitude of the colonies (Leavitt, 1888: 45).

Similarly at the beginning of the twentieth century parsons blamed neglect of the church for a degeneracy in morals (Matthews, 1908: 11). Right up to the present day many clergymen have met the moral expectations of their various communities, sometimes at the expense of traditional theology. They have looked upon the reinforcement of an ethical code as an important, if not the most important contribution to Australian society. Henderson, (1923: 17) is an articulate representative of this view. He felt that the sharp reaction of many Australians to the Puritan code had not led 'to the building up of any recognised ethical standards except those of the easy virtues of good fellowship'. Christianity to him was what separated Australian society from moral anarchy.

The experiences of some chaplains during World War II do not essentially differ from their eighteenth and nineteenth century counterparts. As in the early convict settlements, the chaplains were regarded as 'God botherers' or 'Sin busters' (O'Reilly, 1947: 8-16). They were frustrated in whatever attempts they made 'to bring back careless souls' and hardly less so when they tried to do something about 'moral laxity'. Even so, society at large and the armed forces in particular found it very useful to have the 'God botherers' around, if only as a reassurance that moral standards were still 'physically' present in the guise of a living person whose separateness was as unavoidable as his social utility.

What about Australian society at present?

From whatever observations are available the churches are still primarily seen as sources of morality and civilisation, rather than as

Table 7.2 Percentage distribution of responses of types of believers and secularists to a variety of issues and statements (1966)

Percentage of respondents who	'orthodox believers' a	'private believers' b	'public believers' c	'believing secularists' d	'vacillating secularists' e	'consistent secularists' f
1 disapprove of the person who has a small job on the side and does not declare it for income tax purposes	56	49	40	32	22	21
2 disapprove of the person who takes too much change when the shop assistant has made a mistake	94	93	84	81	77	71
3 disapprove of the person who has sex relations before marriage	90	82	72	66	54	27
4 highly disapprove of the person who gambles heavily	83	75	60	63	58	53
5 admire the patriotic person	60	56	46	52	43	40
6 disapprove of the person against Asians emigrating to Australia	75	57	64	59	57	63
7 disapprove of the statement that it does not matter what one believes as long as one leads a moral life	54	24	30	18	11	6
8 agree that the most important thing for a child to learn is to obey rather than to think for himself	46	53	42	54	34	28
9 agree that it is more important to try to get ahead than to be satisfied with what one has	59	68	68	70	72	72
10 feel friendly and at ease with a Jew	74	58	66	60	57	55
11 feel friendly and at ease with a Japanese	58	42	55	43	41	44
12 are males	37	30	51	49	47	68
13 are over 40 years of age	61	70	40	56	43	49
14 are Anglicans	17	48	10	42	57	55
15 are Catholics	47	19	51	15	8	6
16 are Methodists/Presbyterians	20	22	29	34	26	20
17 had fathers who were regular church attenders when they grew up	65	36	66	33	24	23
18 had mothers who were regular church attenders when they grew up	81	50	72	46	36	32
19 had completed at least a secondary education	30	30	40	30	27	40
20 would like to see the Australian Labor Party win	12	28	23	25	36	33
21 would like to see the Liberal–Conservative Party win	51	39	47	44	43	44

repositories of supernatural truth. A union leader in Cessnock told an interviewer, 'I had a very strict Church upbringing, and it was all to the good, for it gave a sense of responsiblility and made me realise the difference between right and wrong' (Walker, 1945). A.J. and J.J. McIntyre, studying Victorian country towns, were told by one man, 'I don't suppose I back up the church as much as I should; it's just as well everyone isn't like me. Because if we had no church, we'd have no morals, would we?' The McIntyres report that they met this sentiment very often.

What are some of these areas where a reluctant population expects the churches to provide moral leadership?

The 1958 *Current Affairs Bulletin* on 'Church-going in Australia' has the following to say about such worldly pursuits as drinking, gambling and sports to which Australians are said to be abnormally devoted:

> Drinking and gambling have always been opposed vehemently by adherents to the Nonconformist tradition; and the leaders of Nonconformity in Australia remark from time to time on their inability to restrain these habits. The President-General of the Methodist Church, Dr. A.H. Wood, was reported last August thus: 'It was said that to belong to the Methodist Church a man should not drink or gamble, and these are the two greatest interests of many Australians.' Early this year Presbyterians joined with Methodists in Sydney to deplore what seemed to them a growing love of gambling. The record sales of tickets in the N.S.W. lottery, the popularity of the 'jackpot tote' at race meetings—on evidence of this sort, one minister said that N.S.W. was becoming a huge casino. The increase of Sunday sports disturbs many Protestants, who believe that the Sabbath should be set aside for worship.
>
> On the issues of this sort the Roman Catholic Church does not collide head-on with popular desires. The Roman Catholic Church has never been associated closely with the teetotal movement; it does not oppose gambling on principle; and it does not object to the pursuit of pleasure on Sunday, on the playing field or elsewhere, so long as the believer first attends religious worship. Is Roman Catholicism, then, on better terms with Australian society than any other form of Christianity? In some respects it is. But Roman Catholics do not always have the society on their side. Some crucial decisions in Australia go against them (*Current Affairs Bulletin*, 1958: 63–64).

It is with observations like this that the matter usually rests. The Religion in Australia Survey attempted to answer additional questions as to which dimension of religiousness (church going, prayer, or belief) had which effect on morals, and how much other factors such as age, sex or education supported or diminished this effect.

The first five items of Table 7.2 show an almost perfect trend of decreasing disapproval or admiration according to decreasing orthodoxy and decreasing religious involvement of the respondents. Those who have no doubts about God's existence, go to church and pray regularly, are more likely to disapprove than respondents who hold the same beliefs but attend church less regularly. The categories (e) and (f) perpetuate the trend of (a), (b), (c) and (d), complementing through differences in belief what in the other categories is associated with religious involvement as measured by church going and prayer. This tendency of the 'vacillating' and 'consistent secularists' to complement the pattern is evidence for the heterogeneity of the 53 per cent of the respondents of the sample who neither worship nor pray regularly. They can be differentiated on a variety of beliefs which in turn are associated with a slightly different set of norms.

Secondly, there is more variation between the extremes of 'orthodox believers' and 'consistent secularists' on some issues than on others. The percentage disapproving of sex relations before marriage varies as much as 63 per cent between 'orthodox believers' and 'consistent secularists'. The 'consistent secularists' can be separated in turn into three constituent groups: 159 deists who do not believe in a personal God but do believe in a higher power of some kind; 96 agnostics who do not know whether there is a God and do not think there is a way to find out; and 32 atheists who do not believe in God. Within this group there is a similar variation. Thirty-one per cent of the deists and 25 per cent of the agnostics, but only 9 per cent of the atheists disapprove of the person who has sex relations before marriage. This means that 9 out of 10 of the 'orthodox believers' disapprove, whereas only 1 out of 10 atheists objects. There is less difference on adultery. Ninety-three per cent of the 'orthodox believers' and 69 per cent of the atheists disapprove of the person who has sex relations after marriage with someone other than husband or wife.

There is in Australian society, or certainly was in 1966, sufficient consensus regarding the social importance of marriage to unite otherwise divergent sections of the population in disapproval of the person who has extramarital sexual liaisons. This also applies to items not in the table: of the 'orthodox believers' 94 per cent disapprove of the person who drives a car after a steady evening's drinking; of the 'consistent secularists' 84 per cent do.

There seems to be a fine distinction in the minds of the respondents between types of dishonesty. They are less inclined to disapprove cheating such an impersonal organisation as the Taxation Department than they are of taking advantage of a shop assistant's mistake.

Thirdly, another important distinction between 'orthodox believers' and 'consistent secularists' is that the latter are inclined to say that they 'are not worried' about a person who does these things. The differences are not that some are more likely to approve where others disapprove, but that some are more likely 'not to be worried' about the person whose conduct is judged. For instance, on tax evasion, few respondents approved, but 35 per cent of the 'orthodox believers' and 64 per cent of the 'consistent secularists' said that they were not worried compared with 50 per cent of the former and 21 per cent of the latter who disapproved.

The figures of Table 7.2 show that the popular identification of religiousness and stern moral standards contains a considerable amount of truth. The 'consistent secularists' seem to be more ready to leave the choice of conduct open, thereby minimising dissent and disapproval, and maximising the 'live and let live' philosophy. The 'orthodox believers' on the other hand appear more definite in their views of acceptable and unacceptable conduct, at least on the items which the survey investigated. To them society seems woven of one cloth, where fewer norms are optional.

Fourthly, regular prayer habits are more likely than regular church going habits to contribute to what may be called ethical conservatism or disapproval in items 1, 2, 3, and 4. On the other hand, regular church going habits, more than regular prayer habits seem to lead to greater tolerance of people and thought forms that are different (items 6, 8, 10, and 11). At any rate, this is what is suggested by a comparison of the 'private believers' who pray daily but do not attend public worship regularly, with the 'public believers' who attend public worship regularly, but pray occasionally, if at all. Why is this so? Is there something in private acts of worship which makes people more inclined to disapprove of the person who cheats on his income tax, takes advantage of the shop assistant's mistake, or who gambles heavily? It could be that daily prayer, either out of habit or out of need means communication with the source which is perceived to judge these types of conduct unfavourably. If this is so, daily prayer would reinforce disapproval of the person whose actions would be under scrutiny. Conversely, the person who prays irregularly, if at all, would not have these judgements reinforced, particularly when the groups in which he or she moves are more permissive. On the other hand the 'public believer' may be more effectively plugged into the 'communications network' of the churches which preach tolerance and understanding.

This may lead us to be dubious about those sociologists and thinkers who maintain that there is no actual difference between Christian and secular humanism (Schreuder, 1964: 39), and that both thoroughly respect and safeguard the worth of the individual. Provided that we are justified in thinking that the former is located more within the goups of columns (a), (b) and (c) and the latter in columns (e) and (f), Christian humanism appears to see the individual more in the context of the collectivity of the values for which he has responsibility, whereas secular humanism sees individual freedom more in terms of a 'live and let live' philosophy.

Fifthly, an interesting category of respondents are the 'believing secularists' who have no doubt about God's existence, but are anything but regular worshippers. They represent the average Australian who has a dislike for both those who do not believe in God and those who are very religious. They are effectively modal in that there is no significant difference between them and the total sample, on the issues, of Table 7.2. The category also accurately represents the sample on age (56 per cent being over 40) and sex (49 per cent being males). The 'consistent secularists' and the 'orthodox believers' were, of course, far from typical.

Categories of belief in God are independently correlated with a variety of ethical issues. Both the 'consistent secularists' and the 'believing secularists' who 'knew that God existed without doubt', hardly ever attended church or prayed regularly. And still they differ significantly on ethical permissiveness. This reinforces the theoretical justification of Glock and Stark's (1965: 19) treatment of religious belief as a separate dimension of religiosity.

Although David Moberg (1969: 106) investigated theological positions (fundamentalism, evangelism, liberalism, etc.) rather than beliefs in God, his finding that theological conservatism was associated with ascetic morality, and theological liberalism with non-asceticism appears rather similar. Moberg's research led him to deny that ascetic moral viewpoints were relics of a past age which would die with the departure of the older generation. The Religion in Australia research, too, suggests that age is less important than is sometimes thought.

Finally, Table 7.2 showed that some denominations were over-represented in specific categories of believers and underrepresented in others. There were almost twice as many Catholics in the column of 'orthodox believers' (47 per cent) as there were in the population at large (26 per cent at the 1966 census). The opposite was true for Anglicans. Only 17 per cent of the 'orthodox believers' were Anglicans, compared with 34 per cent of the population in the 1966 census. Anglicans were overrepresented also at the secular end of the continuum, justifying the complaint of the Church of England in Australia that they were burdened with large numbers of nominal adherents whose religious involvement is minimal. However, in the same way as the Catholics have more than their share (51 per cent) of 'public believers' who go to church regularly, but do not pray daily, so the Anglicans have more than their share (48 per cent) of 'private believers' who pray daily, but do not attend church regularly. The Methodists and Presbyterians are better spread over all categories, but have a higher proportion of 'believing secularists' and 'public believers'.

So far the Religion in Australia Survey, (Hogan, 1979: 399ff.) confirms that the data on the secular respondents of the 1977 Australian Social Barometer fit with the 1966 findings. The respondents who claimed not to have a religion usually skew in the opposite direction from that of the Christian respondents, he said. They reject authoritarianism in favour of permissiveness and tend 'to have a low regard for family and home-making values. They tend to be independently minded, fairly impulsive and rather self-assertive.'

The 1983 Australian Values Study similarly investigated beliefs and values. It asked approximately 1200 Australians, aged fourteen years and over, whether or not they believed that each of the ten commandments applied to them. Although 79 per cent professed to believe in God, a considerably smaller number (54 per cent) said that the first ('I am the Lord thy God, thou shalt not have other gods before me') applied to them. It would be interesting to find out whether or not the drop is caused by those for whom God is primarily innocuous rather than jealous. An even smaller percentage (47 and 28) was happy with the second (not using God's name in vain) and the third (keeping the sabbath holy). The respondents had much less trouble with the other seven. As many as 82 per cent and 91 per cent felt fully constrained by the fourth, 'honour thy parents' and the fifth, 'thou shalt not kill'. Not stealing (the seventh with 88 per cent), not bearing false witness (the eighth with 82 per cent), and not coveting thy neighbour's goods (the tenth with 79 per cent), also received wide support. Yet, strangely, the ninth commandment, (not coveting thy neighbour's wife) with 80 per cent, received stronger compliance than avoiding what must surely be the more grievous sin (committing adultery, the topic of the sixth commandment) with 75 per cent.

What does all this mean for the relation between belief and morality? There may be good reason to think that the moral function of religion, like so many of its other functions, such as education and philanthropy, is diminishing. There is conviction in some quarters that 'morals are private matters' (Wilson, 1966: 63) or that 'they are self-chosen' (Wilson et al., 1968: 370). In modern society the moral and religious demands of the community have undoubtedly been relaxed. Yet, in Australia, those who are involved in their religion have different moral expectations from those who are not. Religion makes a difference. It is premature to announce the demise of religion. An English study (Television and Religion, 1964: 41) found that the majority of its respondents, especially the young, wanted the churches to express their opinions on moral and social matters. In this study there were also ten times as many people who wanted religion to have more influence than people who wanted it to have less. The days of self chosen morals certainly have not arrived. In Australia, as in Britain, a majority of the people are still seeking moral guidance from somewhere. Yet in contrast to earlier periods in Australian history, the churches are now less universally regarded as the sole reinforcer of morality. They may, for many, even be the moral conscience of the nation, but the days when they were the sole voice and only conscience, are gone.

Lately there have been writers in Australia who have the well-being of both church and nation at heart and who want religion to have more of a voice in the nation. I am thinking about David Millikan's work (1981, 1982). Before elaborating and criticising his views, I must say that my own vision for Christianity in Australia, used to be rather similar. I said at the time:

> Some unique and basic Australian values were never, as far as I know, consistently reinforced and implicitly sanctioned by the churches. I am thinking here about what Max Harris (1962, 64–5) calls 'the ingrained disbelief in the "myth of progress" . . . the dry intelligence, good sense, a good humoured resistance to all pretensions and over-valuations . . . the ready acceptance of human beings'.
>
> Australian Protestantism seems on the whole to have been more inclined to sanction the Western middle-class values of ambition, aspiration and individualism (Mol, 1969: 6).

From here I go on to describe the Anzac myth with its mordant, macabre humour sublimating the predicament of the Gallipoli disaster, and blaming the churches for never having the courage 'to call the bluff of middle-class pretences. And yet . . . both the Anzac spirit and the Australian ethos provide in embryo a highly sophisticated and healthy response to the culturally induced neuroses of Western civilization (ibid.: 7).

Millikan (1872: 33), writing thirteen years later, has detected a quest for 'indigenisation' of Australian culture in the churches and the beginnings of an Australian apologetic, but then he laments:

> . . . the 'ocker' advertisements presented by Bill Lyle, who portrayed a blue singleted street cleaner speaking about Jesus, proved too colloquial for Sydney churchgoers.

He continues to point to the 'many conventions which alienate [the churches] from the egalitarian Australian spirit', and continues: 'When dealing with a society of knockers sensitive to the hollowness of pretension, we have got to recommend ourselves as good blokes before we have a hope of being heard'. He calls it unfortunate that 'many Christians took ... wowserism (a puritanical concern with mortification and ascetism) as an essential part of their witness to Australian society'. He wants to dispel this image, because there 'is something very healthy in the Australian grasp of life and the immediacy with which Australians pursue pleasure'.

From the vantage point of someone who has to be regrettably absent from Australia for six years out of every seven, I am convinced that its culture seems to become increasingly heterogeneous with every sabbatical interval. So much so that it is more and more hazardous to ferret out anything unique. Certainly the Anzac myth, mateship and 'knocking', the central features of an allegedly Australian identity, seem to be hidden in pockets of the older generations. If there is anything unique, apart from accent, it is bloody-minded toughness. Christian ethics will have no trouble wholeheartedly endorsing the honest and direct aspect of this character trait. Yet it can hardly condone the simplication and the discouragement of nuance which is also part of this set of attitudes. What strikes outsiders in 1984 is that Australia has in no way escaped the media hyperbole, the sensual titillations and neurotic trendiness pervading so much of Western culture.

If then Australia has inevitably become pluralistic like the rest of the developed West (and I am convinced it has) the search for a coherent set of values appears to be an impossible ideal. And that is why, if I had to write *Christianity in Chains* all over again, I would put even less stress on cultural relevance than I did at the time, and more on the relevance of an age-old Christian tradition. In a pluralistic culture it simply does not pay to hold together artificially what is intrinsically fragmented. The mainline denominations have tried to reach this increasingly unattainable goal. By contrast the sects assume pluralism and have always thrived under conditions of secular dysjunction.

Wowserism is 'out' in Australia at the present and pleasure is 'in'. And yet behind the God-bothering is a sense of responsibility for basic social institutions which is certainly missing in unrestrained pleasure-seeking. Maybe that's why our Victorian ancestors were so afraid of it! All cultures have insisted on a certain amount of repression to preserve families and communities. And vice versa, expression has always been good for the individual soul, but not necessarily for the common good. If I interpret the Australian data on value polarisation properly (and more will be said about this in the section on sexuality) religion has of necessity been on the side of repression rather than expression of self. Subduing the inevitable conflict this causes, compromising its stance for the sake of peace with the pleasure industry, surrendering to what are essentially competing (and I may add equally legitimate and valuable) ways of whole-making, such as art and play, would make the antidotal function of religion in Australia obsolete. Or to say this more clearly in terms of our six-fold continuum from 'orthodox believers' to 'consistent secularist': to give up one's polar stance and join the 'real' Australians in the middle is to condone what the modal group stands for—no church going, no praying, but believing in God. Yet this quixotic stance was not so long ago defended by major theologians when they defended the 'secular city' as intrinsically Christian. Of course for such a compromise to work our 'consistent secularists' would have to move towards the middle as well, and they would be much too pragmatic for such a thing. Polarisation of major values and beliefs may undermine the viability of a culture, but this is what pluralism is all about, and in Australia as elsewhere Christianity has no other choice but to defend its corner of the ring and do as well as it can while the audience is cheering the other side, and yet, paradoxically, also respecting the Christian.

Sexuality

The point about the polarity of self denial and self assertion, asceticism and pleasure, and repression and expression is well illustrated by the Australian data on sexuality. From the beginning of the settlement the religious authorities were battling against the debauchery of convicts, soldiers and officers. The felons, their guards and the sailors as well as scores of officers, the Judge Advocate, the Surveyor General, Surgeons and the Lieutenant Governor sired illegitimate children. A 'survey of 1806 showed that in New South Wales there were 395 wives and 1035 *de facto* wives; 807 legitimate children and 1025 illegitimate children' (Grocott, 1980: 72). The chaplains thundered against the moral decadence to no avail.

Through the entire 200 year history of Australia the population expected both Catholic and Protestant churches to have pronounced views on sex relations. Press reports on the sex revolution generally identify a conservative sex ethic with a Christian ethic. In late 1967 the Students Representative Council of the University of Sydney conducted a small opinion survey in which questions on church going, attitudes towards premarital sex and actual sexual experience were asked. A secondary analysis of the 117 single students from all faculties who answered the relevant questions showed that 73 per cent of the 56 who attended church were virgins as opposed to 46 per cent of the 61 who did not attend church. There were similar differences on whether or not the the students thought that premarital sex was wrong; of those who attended church, 95 per cent thought so, of those who did not 39 per cent.

This suggests that there is also a relationship between church attendance and attitude on the one hand and actual behaviour on the other. However, the association in weak. Of the 53 students who attended church and thought that premarital sex was morally wrong, 72 per cent were virgins. Of the 37 students who did not attend church and did not think that premarital sex was morally wrong 46 per cent were virgins. This difference of 26 per cent is smaller than one would expect. Presumably those who are not virgins in the first category think about their premarital experiences as regrettable lapses, whereas those who are in the second category must think in terms of a regrettable lack of opportunities.

Australian data on religion and sexuality seem to be generally confined to the student world. In an article, 'The Sex Revolution in Print' Rohan Rivett (1967: 2) summarises a Melbourne controversy raging around statements made by the head of the executive of the Students Representative Council of Melbourne University about the need and the availability of the contraceptive pill to unmarried girls. The clergy mentioned in the article were pitted against the permissive academics, 'advocating pre-marital chastity as a basis for post-marital happiness' and lamenting the lack of responsibility of a woman in charge of an educational centre. Still, in all writing of this kind there is no real evidence for the assumed association between religious beliefs and sex norms of the population at large.

The 1966 Religion in Australia Survey attempted to throw some more light on the situation. Of the 1825 respondents 7 per cent approved, 63 per cent disapproved and 28 per cent were not worried about people who had sex relations before marriage (2 per cent did not answer). However, 1 per cent approved, 86 per cent disapproved and 11 per cent were not worried about people who had sex relations after marriage with someone other than husband or wife.

The percentage disapproving of people who had sex relations before marriage varied considerably according to sex, age and belief. Table 7.3 shows this clearly. Using percentages as scores, the average difference between the sexes when age and beliefs are held constant is seventeen. Similarly when sex and beliefs are held constant, the average difference between those under and over 40 is also seventeen. However when age and sex are held constant, the average difference between those who believe that God really exists and those who hold deistic, agnostic or atheistic beliefs is as much as 39.

When in a similar table church going is substituted for beliefs, the average difference between those who go to church regularly, once a month or more, and those who go hardly ever, if at all, becomes 30, age and sex being held constant. It could be countered that the age categories were not very discriminating. Still, when the 20–24 year old respondents who have a high religious involvement, believe in God without doubt and pray daily (n = 41) are compared with similar respondents who are 60 and over (n = 124), the percentage disapproving of people who have sex relations before marriage is very high in both instances: 83 per cent and 93 per cent respectively.

Table 7.3   The effect of age, sex and beliefs on attitudes to sexual relations before marriage (1966)

Age	Respondents who	Percentage of respondents disapproving of people who have sex relations before marriage	
		Females	Males
Over 40	believe that God really exists and have no doubts about it (n = 322 females, n = 204 males)	87	78
	believe in God although they have doubts or although they do so only some of the time (n = 113 females, n = 116 males)	73	50
	don't believe in a personal God, but in a higher power of some kind, or who are agnostics or atheists (n = 77 females, n = 116 males)	69	37
20–40	believe that God really exists and have no doubts about it (n = 205 females, n = 164 males)	77	63
	believe in God although they have doubts or although they do so only some of the time (n = 151 females, n = 113 males)	60	48
	don't believe in a personal God, but in a higher power of some kind, or who are agnostics or atheists (n = 54 females, n = 108 males)	28	14
	Total sample (n = 922 females, n = 821 males)	74	53

Source: Religion in Australia Survey, 1966

Similarly when the deists, agnostics and atheists are analysed separately, the percentage disapproving decreases from 31 per cent (deists, n = 159) to 25 per cent (agnostics, n = 96) to 9 per cent (atheists, n = 32).

In the case of adultery the differences are much smaller, as Table 7.4

shows. The only significant differences (at the 5 per cent level of significance) are amongst males with 'consistent secularist' beliefs. They differ from all other categories by being less inclined to disapprove of the adulterous person.

Table 7.4   The effect of age, sex and beliefs on attitudes to the person who has sex relations after marriage with someone other than husband or wife (1966)

Age	Respondents who	Percentage of respondents disapproving of people who commit adultery	
		Females	Males
	believe that God really exists and have no doubts about it (n = 318 females, n = 201 males)	95	92
Over 40	believe in God although they have doubts or although they do so only some of the time (n = 113 females, n = 110 males)	94	86
	don't believe in a personal God but in a higher power of some kind, or who are agnostics or atheists (n = 77 females, n = 115 males)	90	74
	believe that God really exists and have no doubts about it (n = 203 females, n = 163 males)	90	88
20–40	believe in God although they have doubts or although they do so only some of the time (n = 150 females, n = 113 males)	92	86
	don't believe in a personal God but in a higher power of some kind, or who are agnostics or atheists (n = 53 females, n = 107 males)	89	66
	Total sample (n = 914 females, n = 814 males)	92	84

Source: Religion in Australia Survey, 1966

Fifteen years later when the sexual revolution began to show signs of abating, surveys still proved that respondents who were regular church attenders differed significantly from those who were irregular. The *Age* poll of August 1981 asked: 'Do you agree or disagree with the following statement: "Women should not have sex before they are married"'. Of the regular attenders 62 per cent (n = 343) agreed, of the irregular ones only 29 per cent (n = 1261) did. These figures are difficult to compare with the 1966 data, but it is fairly clear that the percentage agreeing with statements of this kind has dropped considerably in the 1970s while the large difference between regulars and irregulars has remained. The August 1981 poll also showed that the differences were not generally between denominations, but between the regulars and the irregulars in each of them. The smallest differences were amongst those who said they were Anglicans, with 51 per cent of the regulars agreeing (n = 49) and only 30 per cent of the irregulars (n = 30). The largest difference was amongst Catholics, with 60 per cent of regulars agreeing (n = 177) compared with 24 per cent of irregulars (n = 295).

The other interesting difference between the 1966 data and the August 1981 *Age* poll is that the sex differences seem to have disappeared (the difference between men and women when age and church attendance are held constant is negligible), but that age (the difference between those under 35 and those above 35 years of age is on average 26 per cent when sex and church going are held constant) and church going (the difference between those who say that they are regular and those who say they are irregular is on average also 26 per cent when sex and age are held constant) are now equally important indicators of attitudes towards premarital sex. For those interested in the data on the basis of which these comparisons were made: 38 per cent of regular church going males under 35 (n = 32), 65 per cent over 35 (n = 101), 19 per cent of irregular church going males under 35 (n = 241), 35 per cent over 35 (n = 384), 38 per cent of regular church going females under 35 (n = 50), 71 per cent over 35 (n = 160), 13 per cent of irregular church going females under 35 (n = 265) and 40 per cent over 35 (n = 371) agreed with the statement that women should not have sex before they are married.

In the same survey the same question was asked about men (Do you agree or disagree with the following statement: 'Men should not have sex before they are married?'). Again the major difference was between the regulars (56 per cent of whom agreed with the statement (n = 344)) and the irregulars (26 per cent of whom did so, [n = 1258]). It is interesting that there was little evidence of a double standard (one for men and one for women): the regulars gave the men only 6 per cent more leeway, the irregulars 3 per cent.

As with the previous question, the differences between males and females were negligible when age and church going were held constant. The difference between those under 35 and those over 35 years of age is on average 23.5 per cent when sex and church going are held constant. The differences between regular and irregular church goers is on average also 23.5 per cent when sex and age are held constant. The data for the comparison are as follows: 32 per cent of regular church going males under 35 (n = 34), 57 per cent over 35 (n = 103), 16 per cent of irregular church going males under 35 (n = 242), 33 per cent over 35 (n = 386), 38 per cent of regular church going females under 35 (n = 51), 66 per cent over 35 (n = 156), 13 per cent of irregular church going females under 35 (n = 267) and 34 per cent over 35 (n = 363) agreed that men should not have sex before they are married.

A few months later (in November 1981) the Melbourne *Age* poll asked another question about sexual mores. This time the question was: Do you agree or disagree with the following statement: 'It is wrong for a married person to have sex outside of marriage'? Predictably there was far less difference between regulars and irregulars on this issue: 77 per cent of the regulars (n = 456) agreed versus 70 per cent (n = 1250) of the irregulars. In this instance the big difference was between those who mentioned a denomination and those who said they did not have a religion: of the latter only 44 per cent (n = 185) agreed.

The answers to this question were as follows: 81 per cent of regular church going males under 35 years of age (n = 36), 76 per cent over 35 (n = 148), 62 per cent of irregular church going males under 35 (n = 264), 70 per cent over 35 (n = 383), 73 per cent of regular church going females under 35 (n = 83), 79 per cent over 35 (n = 189), 69 per cent of irregular church going females under 35 (n = 239) and 76 per cent over 35 (n = 364) agreed that it is wrong for a married person to have sex outside marriage.

How do these findings compare with overseas studies? In 1964 an English survey by Social Surveys (Gallup poll) Ltd. on behalf of ABC Television Ltd, asked identical questions on sex conduct. In that survey the average difference was 20 per cent for age when sex and church going were held constant; when age and church going were held constant the average difference was 21 per cent for sex; when age and sex were held constant the difference was 19 per cent for church going. In the sample of the Religion in Australia Survey, similar calculations showed that church going (30 per cent difference) had more effect than sex (19 per cent difference) and sex in turn had slightly more effect than age (16 per cent). It appeared that in Australia at the time church going had a stronger association with the premarital sex norm than in England, but that in both countries church going was at least as important as age and sex differences.

The importance of church going for sex conduct is brought out in another survey conducted by Britain's Central Council for Health Education and described by its research director, Michael Schofield, and others (1965: 148–49). They found that teenagers who did go to church were less likely to be sexually experienced, by which the authors meant having premarital intercourse. It did not matter whether these teenagers were Anglican, Catholic or Nonconformist or even whether parents attended church or not. What was relevant was their own church going.

In the USA the mutual effect of religion and sexual behaviour has been quantitatively measured by Kinsey, Pomeroy and Martin (1948: 465). They concluded that in all religious denominations the most devout respondents were also sexually the least active and that the religiously devout group had the least premarital and marital sexual intercourse. Also in the USA, Burgess and Wallin (1953: 339) found that the couples who attended church more frequently had premarital coitus less often than those who attended church less frequently.

Winston Ehrmann (1959: 93) reports that in his sample of over one thousand college students 'the number of virgins among the males who went to church regularly is almost four times as large as among the males who went to church irregularly, 63 as compared to 17 per cent'. For females too he found that irregularity of church attendance was associated with a higher incidence in stages of advanced sexual activity.

How can we interpret these findings?

Kinsey and his associates (1948: 468) presumed that the lesser sexual activity of their devout respondents was a direct result of social pressures which 'are primarily religious in their origin'. However, they gave no evidence for this 'one-way street' argument and their data could equally support the opposite presupposition that less frequent sexual activity results in greater religious devoutness.

Abram Kardiner (1954: 18) also presumed that in the context of sexuality, religion was only used as a superior order of authority and that it only reinforced a custom of proven expediency. According to Kardiner the real basis for sexual customs is the home or at any rate the observation of what other people do. This interpretation of the function of religion would be acceptable (and many sociologists have actually accepted it) if it were not for the fact that in both the British and Australian survey actual premarital sex relations, or disapproval of them, correlates with respondents' church going and beliefs, and not with parental church attendance. This finding should make us sceptical of identifying religion too closely and exclusively with its undoubted preservative function in the home or society. Although parental church going is not a sufficient indicator of the sexual morality of the home, it would be very difficult to deny the effect of church going indirectly through the parents and the home environment, and affirm it directly through the religious involvement of the respondent, without severely qualifying the Kinsey and Kardiner assumption that religion has no effect apart from reinforcing the mores of one's society and home environment. This independent effect of respondents' rather than parental religious involvement seems to suggest that we have to look in a psychological rather than a sociological direction.

If we treat all three empirical phenomena, the stricter premarital sex norm, the lesser premarital and marital sexual activity of the religiously involved respondent as a single pattern, it could be logically deduced that the lesser sex activity is associated with more religious involvement.

Is there something in religious activity as such which competes with sex activity? If we can answer this question satisfactorily we might avoid the pitfall of narrow assumptions regarding the function of religion, into which Kardiner and Kinsey appear to have fallen. There is evidence from church history that a whole line of theologians from St. Paul to Augustine, the early Pietists, Puritans and Jansenists thought of sex as a substitute God or as an alternative form of commitment. They felt that hedonism in general and sexual indulgence in particular implied an interpretation of life which contrasted sharply with a singleminded and simplehearted dedication to divine authority. Asceticism, a capacity to postpone gratification, be it sexual or a general control over any appetite, was seen as proof that the meaning bestowing order in one's life did not reside in what man could control, but in a God who controlled man. The ultimate criterion was the interpretation of one's existence, and any physically based appetite could easily deny what St. Paul called 'pneuma' or spirit, the only aspect of that existence which raised man above the animals and was man's only contact with the divine. The charismatic, personal, meaning-bestowing function of religion stressed by Max Weber, assists our understanding of the competitive aspects of religion and sex better than the social, preservative, integrative function of religion as stressed by Emile Durkheim. Both approaches deal essentially with the integrative function of religion, although in our instance the personality-integrative rather than the society-integrative aspect seems to be more useful. If faith is the focus of man's commitment 'the role of sexual gratification in the total motivational economy of the personality will be relatively minor' (Hardy, 1964: 15).

It appears then that religion can function as a world view which filters the penetration of cues from one's environment. The sex-stimulating content of some of these cues may affect the non-believer more than the believer, precisely because the religiously involved person has acquired a degree of immunity through his personality encompassing commitment. However, the sex drive is sufficiently forceful to be interpreted as a serious alternative commitment, and in Christianity this interpretation has resulted in an articulated set of norms stressing denial rather than indulgence.

This interpretation of the relation between sexuality and religion as competitive has the advantage of fitting in with a number of otherwise rather disparate sources. Kanter (1968: 505) uses celibacy or sexual abstinence as an indicator of the means by which a utopian community secured commitment. She has good evidence that sacrifices of this kind make commitment to the cause much stronger.

Wright and Cox (1967: 135–44) survey the studies in which the severity of moral judgment is associated with religious belief and practice. In their own sample of 2276 sixth form pupils of 96 Grammar Schools in England they found that the more ascetic the moral issue, the greater the difference between the responses of religious and non-religious subjects. This confirms the findings of an American study which they quote, where significant relationships were found between indices of religiosity and the condemnation of anti-ascetic behaviour (Middleton and Putney, 1962: 141–52). As in both studies the degree of sexual activity is an important indicator of asceticism the suggestion that sexuality and religion are competitive forms of commitment would fit their data.

Connell was puzzled by the Irish coincidence of little and late marriage and extramarital chastity, and wonders:

> What compensations have been found? What barriers built around sexual indulgence? Drink and dogs, cards, horses and gambling, religion, even the bombing and burning of Border posts, have been seen as the Irishman's way out (Connell, 1968: 120).

Connell's speculations imply that 'religion' is only one of many possible foci of man's commitment. This, I think, is more correct than Argyle's (1958: 128) theoretical fit of decrease of sexuality according to greater religious involvement. He suggests that 'religion is a product of conflict between superego and the instincts'. It may be more accurate to say that not just religion or sexuality, but also heavy gambling or militant politics can mitigate the conflict between superego and the instincts. At least from the Religion in Australia Survey it appeared that heavy gambling or militant politics as well as sexual indulgence are competitive forms of commitment, equally condemned by Catholic as well as Methodist respondents who have a high religious involvement. More basic is the suggestion that the important mechanism is not the resolution of the conflict in either the superego direction (religion) or the instinct direction (sexuality), but the level of commitment which alone unifies the person's meaning-bestowing order, and in this way contributes to his security.

How does our interpretation tie in with some of Maslow's observations? Maslow (1964) sees 'peak-experiences', whether religious, aesthetic or ideological, as meaning-bestowing and contributing to the integration of the personality. Maslow thinks of peak-experience in sex as providing a sense of the numinous as well as a religious experience. Apart from the fact that the concept of 'commitment' as an explanatory device has the advantages of constancy (how can a peak-experience integrate the personality unless it perpetually recurs?) and of comprehensiveness (as commitment to gambling is hardly a 'peak-experience'), both concepts have obviously much in common. Yet, the competitive aspect should be stressed more. Using Maslow's frame of reference, one could postulate that the inevitable institutionalisation of the processes of these 'peak-experiences', in order to guarantee their survival and pleasure, will sharpen the boundaries of the various areas in which these 'peak-experiences' occur. The perceived competition between these boundary-maintaining areas may explain why Puritans and Pietists highlighted the religious, and simultaneously played down sexual and artistic experiences. On a lower level of generality, where we are concerned with the concrete social structuring of these experiences, the actual institutional foci tend to be mutually exclusive.

However the argument should be qualified. It is possible that there are instances where either religion or sex do not serve at all as commitment requiring, unifying foci. There may be cultures, or sub cultures where sex is casual and not the intimate self giving act of fulfilling both ego and partner as the western world tends to emphasise.

This may be the case for instance in Negro culture in the United States, where premarital sexual permissiveness is only slightly less amongst church goers than amongst non-church goers. (Reiss, 1964: 693). More research is necessary to delineate commitment operationally and to discover whether religion and sexuality are competitive once the level of commitment to each has been established in particular instances. The modest intention of this section has only been to suggest unexplored explanatory directions.

Prejudices

In the mid-1960s the major Australian churches were at the vanguard of causes containing elements of humanitarianism and social justice. The White Australia issue was a case in point.

> The Australian Council of the World Council of Churches has consistently advocated a quota system or bilateral arrangements because it would "affirm our conviction of racial equality and remove suspicion that we are governed by colour prejudice". The Society of Friends has said that the White Australia Policy is "basically wrong" since it is a "denial of Christian love, of the fatherhood of God and the brotherhood of Man". The General Assembly of the Presbyterian Church has resolved that "the strict exclusion of non-European peoples from permanent residence in

Australia is detrimental to good relationships with non-white races and incompatible with Christian principles of human brotherhood ..."

The Australian Catholic Bishops have condemned the "false assumption of racial superiority which too often underlies the White Australian policy" and have declared that "absolute exclusion can hardly be justified". (*Current Affairs Bulletin*, 34, 4, 6 July 1964: 57).

This did not mean that the churches were able to affect the opinions of their following. Overseas sources suggest that there is a complex relationship between religious involvement and prejudice towards minorities. Particularly in Protestantism the active church goer is anything but inclined to have his opinions and attitudes determined by his religious organisations.

The Religion in Australia Survey of 1966 attempted to discover more about the religious involvement and the prejudices of its respondents. One of the questions was: 'Would you put yourself in the situation of just having met a person and the only thing you know about him is that he is an Englishman. Knowing only this one thing about him, what would your immediate reaction tend to be? Could you mark the box which comes closest to your reaction also for the following other characteristics?' The responses of the 1825 persons in the sample are in Table 7.5.

Table 7.5   Percentage distribution of the first reaction of the survey respondents to members of minority groups (1966 Religion in Australia Survey) (1966)

	Friendly and at ease	Friendly but somewhat uneasy	Uneasy and somewhat unfriendly	Quite unfriendly	Nothing either way
	%	%	%	%	%
An Englishman	70	8	1	1	17
A communist	17	21	18	22	18
An alcoholic	22	33	14	12	16
A Roman Catholic	69	9	1	1	17
A Dutchman	67	9	1	1	18
A Jew	60	12	3	2	18
An atheist	40	17	6	7	24
A teetotaller	69	8	1	1	17
An Italian	58	16	4	2	17
A Japanese	46	20	6	5	19

Note: The row percentages do not add up to 100 because the small number of respondents who did not answer the question were eliminated from the table, but not from the percentage calculations. To avoid response contagion the categories were scrambled, but in subsequent tables the categories were classified according to whether the minorities were ethnic, religious, political or 'social', such as alcoholics and teetotallers.
Source: Religion in Australia Survey, 1966

It contains some interesting facets. It shows how the percentage of respondents having negative feelings towards out-groups rises from 10 per cent for Englishmen to 11 per cent for Dutchmen, 22 per cent for Italians and 31 per cent for Japanese. It also shows that the first reactions to a communist and an alcoholic are very negative. Atheists are also unpopular.

What happens when we look separately at the most religious and the least religious section of the sample? For the sake of cross tabulations with religion, the small responses of columns 2, 3 and 4 were combined to form a new category of 'negative responses'. Columns 1 and 5 were subsequently named 'positive' and 'neutral' responses. Table 7.6 shows that in all instances the 'consistent secularists' are more inclined to select the neutral category of 'no feelings either way', whereas the 'orthodox believers' are more inclined to say that they feel 'friendly and at ease' with the various types of individuals. The percentage differences are not great, but it is unlikely that they are accidental. The 'consistent secularists' are more aloof and less involved. They seem to represent more than the 'orthodox believers' the neutral anonymity of a secular urban society. Yet they hardly differ from 'orthodox believers' on negative feelings. Like the 'orthodox believers' they are more inclined to feel uneasy with Japanese than Italians and more uneasy with Italians than with Dutchmen and Englishmen. They dislike the company of teetotallers slightly more, but they share equally the considerable unease felt with alcoholics. The few atheists and communists of the survey would be in the secularist column, and, as was to be expected, the only people for whom the secularists have less negative feelings are the communists and the atheists. Compared with the many negative reactions of the sample as a whole to communists, alcoholics and atheists, the degree of unease or unfriendliness felt in the company of Jews and Catholics is slight indeed. This may show that in Australia religious minorities and to a lesser extent ethnic minorities encounter comparatively little hostility, granted that we are justified in equating feelings of unease and/or unfriendliness with hostility. Whatever uneasy or unfriendly feelings Australians have towards out-groups, they seem to be channelled against general political and social deviants, such as communists and alcoholics rather than more specific groups such as Jews, Catholics, Italians and Dutchmen. The question remains whether they recognise the communist, the alcoholic and the atheist when they see them. The odds are that they do not, and that they are just as much at ease with them as anyone else. Still, in the popular mind, communists, alcoholics and atheists, as a class, seemed to break the existing political, social and religious order, and this may be the main significance of their poor showing.

The Religion in Australia Survey asked another question dealing with foreigners. It ran as follows:

There has always been a good deal of discussion as to how people ought to act in their daily lives. It is not always clear what characteristics ought to be admired and which ones we should disapprove of. Below you will find a series of descriptions of ways in which people act. For each would you decide how much you would admire or disapprove of a person who acted in this way?

If a person is against any Asians migrating to Australia, I would:

a Admire him for it
b Think it was all right
c Be mildly disapproving of him
d Be highly disapproving of him

Nine per cent of the 1825 respondents admired the person, 24 per cent thought it was all right, 35 per cent mildly disapproved, 27 per cent highly disapproved and 5 per cent gave no answer.

Irregular church goers (n = 1218) were more likely to admire the person (11 per cent) or to think it was all right (28 per cent) than regular church goers (n = 604) for whom the corresponding percentages were 7 and 18 per cent. And the other way round: irregular church goers were less likely to either mildly (33 per cent) or highly disapprove (25 per cent) of the person than regular church goers (38 per cent and 31 per cent).

The differences were particularly great between Methodist irregular church goers (53 per cent disapproving, n = 111) and regular church goers (75 per cent disapproving, n = 61). Similarly between Presbyterian irregular church goers (55 per cent disapproving, n = 189) and regular church goers (73 per cent disapproving, n = 91). For Anglicans (59 per cent of irregulars disapproving, n = 632; 66 per cent of regulars, n = 101) and Catholics (63 per cent of irregulars disapproving, n = 137; 69 per cent of regulars, n = 270) the differences were less.

Fifteen years after the Religion in Australia Survey similar differences between regular and irregular church goers still exist. The November 1981 Melbourne *Age* Poll asked two questions dealing with migration. Thirty one per cent of the regular attenders (n = 480), 18 per cent of the irregular ones (n = 1313), and 30 per cent of those who said they did not have a religion (n = 223) agreed that Australia should accept refugees. By contrast 26 per cent of the regulars, 35 per cent of the irregulars and 30 per cent of those without a religion agreed that Australia should not accept any migrants at the present time.

The same survey had another statement about migrants being encouraged to fit into the Australian community as soon as possible. Sixty per cent of the regulars, 67 per cent of the irregulars and 58 per cent of those without a religion agreed with that statement. The

Table 7.6 **Percentage distribution of responses of orthodox believers and consistent secularists according to their reaction to certain categories of people (Religion in Australia Survey, 1966)**

Percentage of respondents reporting positive, negative, and neutral feelings towards	Orthodox believers (n = 311)			Consistent secularists (n = 287)		
	Positive feelings	Negative feelings	Neutral feelings	Positive feelings	Negative feelings	Neutral feelings
An Englishman	80	9	9	62	11	26
A Dutchman	77	11	10	59	13	27
An Italian	69	19	10	50	22	27
A Japanese	58	28	12	44	29	27
A Roman Catholic	80	11	7	61	12	26
A Jew	74	13	10	55	17	25
An atheist	40	43	14	52	15	31
A communist	18	67	14	25	50	24
An alcoholic	31	57	10	20	57	22
A teetotaller	80	7	11	60	15	23

Note: When the percentages do not add up to 100, the reason is that the percentage of 'no answers' was left out. 'Orthodox believers' was the term given to respondents who went to church regularly, prayed daily and knew without doubt that God existed. 'Consistent secularists' was the name given to respondents who did not go to church (or at the most irregularly), did not pray daily and who either did not believe in God or did not know whether there was a God or did not believe in a personal God, but in a higher power of some kind.
Source: Religion in Australia Survey, 1966

opposite statement that 'migrants should be assisted by government funds (for instance funds for ethnic radio and language teaching) to maintain their own cultural traditions' was approved by only 20 per cent of the regulars, 15 per cent of the irregulars and 23 per cent of those without a religion.

The differences in the 1981 survey are not very great. Yet generally the regular church goers were bedfellows of those without any religion as over against the irregular church goers. Obviously the committed Christians feel more responsible for the disadvantaged, and those with no religion (similarly on the fringe of society) favour many enlightened causes. Both groups stand over against the large bulk of Australians who don't go to church, but display conservative attitudes.

Of course on other issues the committed Christians and the enlightened liberals are poles apart. In the same November 1981 survey as many as 68 per cent of those without a religion (n = 223) agreed that it was morally acceptable to be single and to have and bring up children, but only 25 per cent of the church goers (n = 480) did so.

There were also large differences between these groups on whether it was a good idea for husbands and wives sometimes to take separate holidays (60 per cent of those without religion and 39 per cent of regular attenders agreeing). Similarly those without a religion (n = 223) much less readily agreed (41 per cent) that a woman should put her husband and children ahead of her own career than the Christians (of the 480 regular respondents in this survey as many as 77 per cent agreed). On all these issues the large modal group of irregular Australians (n = 1313) took a position in between: 45 per cent agreeing on the single parent, 43 per cent on the holiday and 68 per cent on the career issue.

Looking at all three major variables (age, church attendance and sex) simultaneously for the single parent issue, sex again made on average little difference. However, age (being under and over 35) made a difference of 23.5 per cent when church attendance and sex were held constant and similarly church attendance made a difference of 23.5 per cent when age and sex were held constant. The data are as follows: 28 per cent of regular church going males under 35 (n = 40), 24 per cent over 35 (n = 150), 66 per cent of irregular church going males under 35 (n = 273), 34 per cent over 35 (n = 395), 39 per cent of regular church going females under 35 (n = 88), 13 per cent over 35 (n = 295), 65 per cent of irregular church going females under 35 (n = 242) and 33 per cent over 35 (n = 368) agreed with the statement that it was morally acceptable to be single and to have and bring up children. What do these figures mean?

There is no Australian evidence supporting the overseas research showing that church goers are more prejudiced; if anything it supports research which shows that they are less so. Argyle (1958: 83) attempts to explain why. The finding that devout people, compared with conventional church members, are less prejudiced, he says, is because they are less authoritarian. Their religiosity has less to do with God as a projection of the superego (the authoritarian way) but with other psychological mechanisms (for instance, reduction of guilt feelings).

This is doubtful to say the least. Religion, in any country, walks the tightrope between the countervailing integrities of person, family, society and world community. In Australia the Christians who through church going, are regularly exposed to information disseminated by religious bodies, feel responsible for those suffering from injustice and persecution in other countries. One can therefore expect them to favour the intake of refugees more than others. The international awareness of the 'no religion' intelligentsia and their proclivity for worthwhile (sometimes even 'trendy') causes leads in the same direction. By contrast the non-church going, modal Australians tend to look less beyond their shores and more to what is of immediate advantage to them personally.

By contrast the large differences between the regular church goers and those without a religion goes back to a strong sense of protection of family cohesion of the former (separate holidays, single parenting and career priorities undermine that, they fear) and an equally strong emphasis on self fulfilment (if necessary at the expense of the family) by the latter. Argyle's tendency to provide exclusively psychological explanations for data which fit much better with assumptions of 'countervailing integrities' points to the necessity for inter-disciplinary theorising rather than separate sociological, psychological or anthropological explanations when religious phenomena are under scrutiny.

Gambling and patriotism

Do religious people love their nation more and the gambler less? If the references in Australian history are any guide, the answer is a resounding yes. For long periods the Church of England and the other mainline Protestant churches stood for heart warming but dignified allegiance to throne, empire and nation. The prayers for king, queen and the national rulers were taken as a matter of course. Catholics did not necessarily share Protestant patriotism. Their equivalent allegiances had more to do with Ireland and its struggle for home rule.

With regard to gambling, the first Council of Churches was established in New South Wales in 1889, 'principally to defend the Christian Sunday and to combat gambling' (Phillips, 1981: xiv). It was in that era that Christians felt it to be their God-given task to balance the nation's excessive love for the vices of alcohol and gambling with an equally excessive denunciation of it all. Right up to the present, Europeans coming to Australia for the first time are astonished at the importance attributed by many church going Australians to refraining from betting, gambling and drinking.

The 1966 Religion in Australia Survey had a question dealing with both patriotism and gambling. It ran as follows:

There has always been a good deal of discussion as to how people ought to act in their daily lives. It is not always clear what characteristics ought to be admired and which ones we should disapprove of. Below you will find a series of descriptions of ways in which people act. For each would you decide how much you would admire or disapprove of a person who acted in this way?

There were four categories of reply, 'Admire him for it', 'Think it was all right', 'Be mildly disapproving of him', 'Be highly disapproving of him'. The two statements were, 'If a person is very patriotic, I would ...' and 'If a person gambles heavily, I would ...'.

Of the 1218 respondents who never or irregularly went to church, 46 per cent admired the very patriotic person, 42 per cent thought it was all right, 8 per cent disapproved and 4 per cent gave no answer at all. Of the 604 regular church goers the corresponding percentages were 53, 37, 6 and 4 per cent.

The differences in degree of admiration for the patriotic person were greater for Anglican church goers (60 per cent, n = 101) than Anglicans who attend church irregularly (51 per cent, n = 632), and noticeably more for Catholic church goers (54 per cent, n = 270) than Catholic non-attenders (29 per cent, n = 137).

Yet the larger difference was between the percentage of 'orthodox believers' (60 per cent, n = 311) and 'consistent secularists' (40 per cent, n = 287) admiring the patriotic person. The other categories fit into the continuum: of the 'private believers' (n = 146) 56 per cent admires the very patriotic person, of the 'vacillation secularists' (n = 364) only 43 per cent do. The less involved and the less orthodox one is, the less one is inclined to admire the very patriotic person.

Yet when age is introduced the differences between the younger age groups seems to disappear: of those in the age bracket of 20–24, 42 per cent of the orthodox and private believers (n = 41) and 41 per cent of the vacillating and consistent secularists (n = 106) admired the very patriotic person. By contrast the corresponding percentages for those 60 years and over were 74 per cent (n = 117) and 50 per cent (n = 78). This finding throws doubt on the assumption that reactions to the statement say something about the link between religion and national sentiment. It suggests that there are important differences between the generations as well. The younger ones who have not experienced war and its effects on patriotic feelings, are less inclined to admire the very patriotic person, irrespective of religious beliefs and practices. The older ones, on the other hand, are more divided according to their beliefs: those who hold orthodox beliefs and pray daily are more inclined to admire than those who are at the secular end of the continuum. However, even the latter are more likely to either admire or disapprove than the youngsters who prefer to think 'it is all right'.

No comparable data have become available since the Religion in Australia Survey. Yet differences between regular and irregular church goers and between Protestants and Catholics on related issues can be distilled from a reanalysis of the *Age* Poll of April 1980. Here the question was asked:

Which of these statements comes closest to your own opinion?
I would prefer Australia to remain a member of the Commonwealth with a
Governor-General as the Queen's representative in Australia
or
I would prefer Australia to become an independent republic with its own
elected president.

As many as 84 per cent of the regular Protestants (n = 202) favoured
the first option as compared with 68 per cent of the irregular ones
(n = 950). By contrast only 58 per cent of the Catholics who attended
church regularly (n = 202) and 51 per cent of those who went irregularly if at all (n = 279) preferred Australia to stay in the commonwealth.
Most revealing was the relatively small percentage (35 per cent) of
those without a religion (n = 210) who favoured a commonwealth over
a republic. These figures show that support for the commonwealth
rests for a great deal with the Protestant church goers. On this issue
denomination seems to be more important than church attendance: if
church attendance is held constant, on average 22 per cent more
Protestants favour the existing arrangements; if denomination is held
constant on average 12 per cent more regular church goers prefer
commonwealth and monarchy compared with irregular ones. All this
fits with the historical sources.

The above figures should not be interpreted to mean that Protestant
church goers are less nationalistic. When a year later in the May 1981
Age Poll individuals were asked whether they would prefer Prince
Charles or an Australian appointed to the position of Governor
General, only 29 per cent of regular church going Protestants (n = 164)
favoured the former. The corresponding percentages for irregular
church going Protestants (n = 890) was 27 per cent, regular church
going Catholics (n = 186) 24 per cent, irregular church going Catholics
(n = 265) 16 per cent and those without a religion (n = 264) 18 per cent.
The rank order is approximately the same as in the commonwealth
versus republic question, but church going makes on average only
5 per cent difference and denomination 8 per cent.

'Being very patriotic' seems to have as positive a connotation to the
people in the sample of the 1966 Religion in Australia Survey as 'being
a heavy gambler' has negative. Of irregular church goers only 14 per
cent think that it is all right, a further 22 per cent 'mildly' disapprove,
but as many as 60 per cent disapprove 'highly'. The regular church
goers are most outspoken: 5 per cent think it all right, 18 per cent
'mildly' disapprove and 75 per cent 'highly' disapprove. Again the
differences are accentuated when the extremes of the religious involvement continuum are compared: 'orthodox believers' 83 per cent,
'private believers' 75 per cent, 'public believers' 60 per cent, 'believing
secularists' 63 per cent, 'vacillating secularists' 58 per cent, and

'consistent secularists' 53 per cent, disapprove highly.

There are interesting denominational differences also: of church going Catholics 69 per cent highly disapprove, of church going Anglicans 73 per cent, Presbyterians 80 per cent and Methodists 90 per cent. This suggests that if we look at denomination in conjunction with type of believer we may get even greater differences, for example, between Nonconformist 'orthodox believers' on the one hand and Catholic 'Consistent secularists' on the other.

However, Table 7.7 shows that this does not happen. When categorised in this way, the differences between denominations are not as great, for the significant differences are between the 'orthodox believers' and the 'believing secularists' in each denomination. Catholics tend not to disapprove as strongly of the heavy gambler, but in no instance are the differences significant.

Table 7.7   **Percentage of respondents who highly disapprove of the person who gambles heavily, by denomination and beliefs (1966)**

Denomination	Orthodox believers	Believing secularists	Consistent secularists
Anglican	86	68	50
	(n = 50)	(n = 71)	(n = 154)
Catholic	81	55	53
	(n = 147)	(n = 38)	(n = 17)
Methodist/Presbyterian	90	61	53
	(n = 62)	(n = 84)	(n = 55)

Source: Religion in Australia Survey, 1966

What does this mean? One factor is probably that the orthodox believers feel that indulging in heavy gambling denies them a different source of fulfilment which is important (for instance Christian salvation). More significant from a sociological point of view is another factor running as a thread through all of Australian history: dedicated Christians always felt it to be their God given duty to protect and reinforce major units of social organisation. Excessive drinking, adultery and heavy gambling were never failing sources of disruption for orderly family and communal life. Children growing up in homes with alcoholic, unfaithful and gambling parents were as often as not a social liability, a burden for the law-enforcing agencies, a drain on welfare facilities and poor prospects for responsible citizenship. Even the unpleasant opprobrium of being called wowsers and kill-joys did not weigh against their distaste for chaotic behaviour, breakdown of decency and uncertainty of expectation.

8   Class and residence

Occupation and income

Historical sources agree that in the past Catholics and Methodists were overrepresented among the lower classes. Russel Ward (1965: 80) refers to 'a grossly disproportionate number' of Irishmen among the unskilled, wage earning section of the community. As Ireland was the main source of Catholic migrants to Australia in the nineteenth century, the statement by implication applies to Catholics. Ward makes the interesting point that they were the people who, more than anyone else, would embrace an Australian national sentiment, for 'Britishness' was anathema to them. Like working people generally they were less able to keep up cultural connections overseas and therefore took on the colour of their surroundings more rapidly.

The overrepresentation of Catholics in the lower occupational categories has been recorded by other observers. Roger Therry, the first Catholic to be given an administrative position in the colony of New South Wales, complained, 'In 1829 every office of importance was filled by members of other religious denominations and there were not half a dozen Catholic families belonging to the gentry' (Barcan, 1962: 48).

Henderson, (1911: 222) speaking of the last half of the nineteenth century in Victoria says, 'Irish Roman Catholics seldom rise above the lower levels, and never as a class represent the mercantile, banking and squatting interests'. The situation was similar in Western Australia, where Catholics were reported to occupy 'the humblest positions in society' (Reilly, 1903, 31), and South Australia where their poverty was stressed (Pike, 1957: 492). Bishop Dunne of Brisbane observed in a letter to Cardinal Moran in 1884 that Catholics in Queensland formed only a small proportion of the skilled labour force and that too many of them were to be found in the morally, socially and physically undesirable occupations, such as publicans, policemen, cab drivers, wharf labourers and pick-and-shovel men (Phillips, 1981: 17). Overrepresentation in the lower occupational categories was balanced by an underrepresentation in the upper. More recently, the proportion of Catholics among business executives has been reported as being particularly small (Spann, 1961: 123). They are better represented in the public service, but not in the higher echelons (Davies and Encel, 1965: 103). At universities too, Catholics are severely underrepresented, as shown by Tien's (1965: 65) sample of the academic staffs of Sydney and Melbourne Universities of which only 8 per cent was Catholic and 21 per cent atheist or no religion. The corresponding figures for the Australian population as a whole were 26 per cent Catholic and 1 per cent 'no religion' at the time (1966 census).

What about Methodism? In the last century Methodism was splintered into many denominations; Primitive Methodists, United Methodist Free Churches, Bible Christians, Free Connection and the bigger Wesleyan Methodist Church. Often, Methodists appear to have been associated with the lower, skilled occupations. Speaking about Brisbane, Lilley quotes someone as saying:

> The Free Methodists are workaday people, sturdy mechanics, small employers, thriving backmen and thrifty shop-keepers; they don't drive in gorgeous carriages behind liveried coachmen, but any one of them is worth two of the snobocracy when there is singing going on (Lilley, 1913: 56).

This was also true in Victoria. Renate Howe (1966: 22–3) identifies the Wesleyans as typically farmers, shop keepers and skilled tradesmen.

In South Australia, in Broken Hill and in Newcastle, Methodism was associated with mining (Pike, 1957: 493). This is understandable when we realise that the mining areas of Wales and Cornwall from where many of the miners came, were strongly Methodist.

What about Anglicans and Presbyterians? Historical sources again agree that generally these denominations were overrepresented in the upper occupational categories. The Church of England, being the largest Australian denomination, has always been fairly well represented in all categories. Twopenny (1883: 116–17) asserts that it was least strong in 'the middle class which governs Australia', and that Anglicanism was primarily the religion of the upper class. Whether or not we can accept his generalisation that the Church of England had its 'main sphere almost entirely among upper and lower classes', as was partly true in England, it is safe to say that no denomination could be regarded as homogeneously upper, middle or lower class. Presbyterianism is a good example. It found its supporters among both the working classes and the rich and influential, as in Bathurst (Walker, 1962: 49).

What is the statistical evidence for these various opinions in the historical sources?

Table 8.1 Percentage of male breadwinners in selected major occupational categories in NSW according to the major denominations

Occupation	Anglican	Catholic	Methodist	Presbyterian
Ministering to general or local government (n = 1894)	52.1	17.1	7.4	10.6
Ministering to law and order (n = 5404)	51.7	22.8	6.0	12.9
Ministering to religion (n = 1623)	28.1	24.3	14.3	13.1
Ministering to health (n = 3851)	50.0	14.7	7.9	11.4
Ministering to civil & mechanical engineering, architecture & surveying (n = 2382)	55.3	12.6	4.8	13.8
Ministering to education (n = 3806)	39.1	22.0	13.3	16.7
Ministering to amusements (n = 1797)	48.1	33.0	4.1	6.0
Engaged in supply of board & lodging (n = 8258)	46.6	32.8	3.2	7.5
Engaged in domestic service (n = 11 870)	46.9	26.2	5.5	8.0
Engaged in banking and finance (n = 3553)	60.0	8.2	5.5	13.8
Engaged in railway traffic (n = 9493)	46.8	25.8	11.5	9.7
Engaged in road traffic (n = 13 050)	48.6	30.9	7.1	7.0
Engaged in postal service (n = 2664)	46.3	29.5	7.2	11.0
Working in engines, machines, tools and implements (n = 5432)	47.4	13.5	10.4	15.2
Working in carriages and vehicles (n = 3364)	46.2	22.1	12.1	8.9
Working in ships, boats & their equipment (n = 1663)	47.6	17.2	8.5	16.1
Working in houses and building (n = 23 253)	48.5	16.3	11.1	11.7
Working in roads, railways, earthworks etc. (n = 13 645)	41.2	40.8	5.9	7.2
Engaged in agricultural pursuits (n = 75 884)	43.1	27.1	9.8	10.1
Engaged in pastoral pursuits (n = 47 162)	45.8	27.4	7.4	12.8
Engaged in mines & quarries (n = 38 378)	39.6	22.0	17.0	9.4
Under legal detention (n = 2330)	42.4	43.0	5.4	4.7
All male breadwinners (n = 451 403)	45.1	24.3	9.3	10.0

Source: Census, 1901

Table 8.1 shows that for New South Wales in 1901 the impressions are generally correct: in the occupational categories where high technical skill is required, such as engineering, or which are central to the business world such as banking and finance, Anglicans and Presbyterians are overrepresented, Catholics and Methodists under-represented. On the other hand, Methodists are overrepresented in mining, whereas Catholics are overrepresented among those who work in roads, railways, earthworks, provide amusements, or supply board and lodging. It is interesting that the Methodists and Presbyterians have more than their share of people 'ministering to religion', whereas Anglicans are strongly underrepresented in this category. Presbyterians are also overrepresented among those working in engines, machines, tools or ships and their equipment.

Approximately 50 years later (1947) the census table (8.2) shows that although the categories are not strictly comparable, denominational divergences do not appear to be as great. In 1901 Anglican occupational representation moved from a low in religious occupations (28.1 per cent) to a high of 60 per cent in banking and finance. In 1947 the low was in professional and semi-professional occupations (35.1 per cent) and the high (41.3 per cent) in administrative occupations.

In 1901 Catholic occupational representation moved from a low in banking and finance (8.2 per cent) to a high of 40.8 per cent (disregarding the 43.0 per cent under legal detention) amongst those working in roads, railways, earthworks, etc. In 1947 the low was in administrative occupations (15.1 per cent) and the high was among labourers (25 per cent).

In 1901 Methodist occupational representation moved from a low amongst those who supplied board and lodging (3.2 per cent) to a high of 17 per cent amongst those who were engaged in mines and quarries. In 1947 the low was amongst labourers (8.7 per cent) and the high in rural, fishing and hunting occupations (13.5 per cent).

In 1901 Presbyterian occupational representation moved from a low of 6 per cent amongst those supplying amusements (disregarding the 4.7 per cent amongst the legally detained) to a high of 16.7 per cent amongst those engaged in education. In 1947 the low was amongst labourers (6.5 per cent) and the high amongst the professional and semi-professional occupations (12.8 per cent).

Although the more specific categories of the 1901 census were submerged in the more general ones of the 1947 tabulations, it is remarkable that the 'highs' and the 'lows' for both 1901 and 1947 are so often in similar categories for the various denominations.

Three surveys in the 1960s showed that there were still rather similar over and underrepresentations in the major denominations. The

Table 8.2 Percentage of male breadwinners in the various occupational orders by denomination

Occupation	Anglican	Catholic	Presbyterians	Methodists	Total population
Rural, fishing and hunting	36.6	19.2	12.1	13.5	444 176
Professional and semi-professional	35.1	19.8	12.8	11.0	82 429
Administrative	41.3	15.1	11.6	10.4	139 201
Commercial and clerical	39.9	19.9	11.2	11.6	409 423
Domestic and protective	40.6	23.4	8.6	9.1	151 432
Craftsmen	41.0	17.0	9.9	11.6	497 602
Operatives	40.8	21.0	7.7	10.5	514 065
Labourers	30.2	25.0	6.5	8.7	159 505
Indefinite	39.5	23.3	7.6	9.0	81 436

Source: Australian Census, 1947

Religion in Australia Survey (1966) found that Anglicans (44 per cent) and Presbyterians (16 per cent) were slightly overrepresented amongst the professionals, managers, graziers and lower professionals (n = 340). In the population at large their percentages were 40 and 14 per cent respectively.

The Broom, Jones and Zubrzycki Stratification Survey of 1965, published in 1976, had more semi-skilled and unskilled workers, such as operatives, sales assistants, labourers, amongst Catholics (n = 429) than amongst non-Catholics (n = 1448): 36 per cent compared with 30 per cent. This was also the case in the Australian National University Survey Project (Political Science) in 1967: of Catholics 42 per cent were in the lower occupations, of non-Catholics, 33 per cent.

More detail is available from the 1971 and 1981 censuses. Particularly the Jews (18 per cent in 1971; 29 per cent in 1981) and those with 'no religion' (17 per cent in 1971; 25 per cent in 1981) have a much larger proportion of professionals in their membership than the population (10 per cent in 1971; 15 per cent in 1981). By professionals I mean not only doctors, engineers, lecturers, clergymen, pilots etc. but also nurses, teachers, artists, computer programmers and librarians who are usually categorised as 'lower' professionals. In the 1981 census, also the Uniting Church with 22 per cent, had more than its share of professionals. Baptists came third with 15 per cent in 1971 and fourth with 19 per cent in 1981.

Catholics (9 per cent in 1971; 12 per cent in 1981) and Anglicans

(10 per cent in 1971; 13 per cent in 1981) were in the middle of the spectrum, as one can expect from the two largest denominations. Far below the average for the population was the percentage of professionals amongst those who were Orthodox (3.2 per cent in 1971; 5 per cent in 1981), Jehovah's Witnesses (5 per cent in 1981) and Muslims (6 per cent in 1981). That too was more or less expected. The most recent immigrants usually start at the lowest rung of the occupational ladder and most of the sects appeal particularly to those who are marginal to the status ranking of a society.

Some denominations are better represented in the rural section of the Australian population than others. Adding together graziers, wheat, sheep and other farmers with farm and rural workers from the 1971 census (as tabulated by Harris, [1982a: 274] and from the 1 per cent sample of the 1981 census) we find that both in 1971 and in 1981, 7 per cent of the employed in Australia fell into this combined category. Yet almost 2.5 times as many Lutherans (17 per cent in both 1971 and 1981) could be classified this way, trailed in 1971 by the Presbyterians (12 per cent) and Methodists (11 per cent). In 1981 the Lutherans were closely followed by those belonging to the Uniting Church (16 per cent) with the Presbyterians this time in third place with 10 per cent. By contrast some denominations were hardly represented in rural occupations: there was only a single Jew who fell into the rural category (out of 297). Strongly underrepresented were also the Orthodox with 2 per cent and the Muslims with 3 per cent in the same census. They were followed by the Pentecostals, Jehovah's Witnesses and those belonging to the Salvation Army, all of whom had 5 per cent of their membership classified as rural. Again more in the middle were Anglicans (7 per cent in 1971 and 1981) and Catholics, slightly below them with 6 per cent in both years.

It is natural that when one occupational group is underrepresented another group in the same denomination is overrepresented. The Muslims and the Orthodox are a good example. In the Australian population according to the 1 per cent of the 1981 census, 7 per cent could be classified as labourers. Yet Muslims have 4.5 times that percentage (32 per cent) and the Orthodox almost 3.5 times (24 per cent). The sects too are overrepresented here: the Jehovah's Witnesses have 21 per cent, the Pentecostals 16 per cent and the Salvation Army 13 per cent. By contrast, the Jews are underrepresented with 2 per cent and the Uniting Church with 5 per cent. Anglicans (9 per cent) and Catholics (11 per cent) are again in the middle, but slightly over represented.

Dempsey (1983: 28) looked at the class divisions and religion in Smalltown (a rural community of 2800 people in Western Victoria). He writes that the 'middle and upper strata form the bulk of the active membership of the Anglican Church and the Presbyterian component of the Uniting Church'. The Methodist section of this church is much more disproportionately middle class, whereas the 'Church of Christ is a mixture of working and middle strata and the Salvation Army draws its support exclusively from the working stratum. Only in the Roman Catholic Church are all three strata proportionately represented'.

The Australian census has also asked individuals questions about their employment status. Tables 8.3 and 8.4 are based on calculations from selected censuses for which these data were available. The first shows that since 1921 the 'no religion' employer/employee ratio has been consistently below the national average. This was also true for Catholicism until 1981 when, like the Anglican Church, it achieved the national ratio. On the other hand, Methodists and notably Presbyterians have had consistently more employers per 1000 employees than the national average. The table indicates that while the ratio decreases over time, the denominational differences since 1947 have remained at approximately the same level. From 1921 to 1947 there was little decrease, with the exception of the Methodist and Presbyterian ratio. The depression year of 1933 severely affected all denominations: the steep increase of the ratio shows that unemployment hit employees more severely than employers, although bankruptcies must have thinned the ranks of the latter as well.

Table 8.3   Number of male employers per 1000 employees of each denomination

Census	Anglican	Catholic	Methodist	Presbyterian	No religion	Total (including rest)
1981	73	72	77	96	61	72
1961	94	74	108	126	78	92
1954	101	75	120	138	87	100
1947	103	85	122	137	112	108
1933	145	139	206	209	127	158
1921	101	85	144	157	99	113

Source: Selected Australian Censuses from 1921

The 1981 figures also show that large differences between the denominations are now a thing of the past. Particularly the ratio of Methodists and Presbyterians has dropped more than the others. However, if we now calculate the ratio for the Uniting Church for the one per cent sample of the population in 1981, we arrive at the very high figure of 121 employers per 1000 employees. This seems to suggest that the employers amongst the Uniting denominations have taken a more active part in the changeover, or at any rate, have tended to think more of themselves as 'Uniting' at census time.

Table 8.4   Number of unemployed per 1000 males in the workforce, by denomination

Census	Anglican	Catholic	Methodist	Presbyterian	No religion	Total (including rest)
1981	62	68	77	53	94	68
1961	37	54	26	28	62	42
1954	14	17	10	11	23	15
1947	28	32	21	22	47	28
1933	237	279	170	171	395	234
1921	85	115	61	69	156	86

Note: Unemployed (or 'not at work') was defined by the Census as: 'those who stated that they were usually engaged in work, but were not actively seeking a job at the time of the Census, by reason of sickness, accident, etc. or because they were on strike, changing jobs, or temporarily laid off, etc. It includes also, persons able and willing to work but unable to secure employment, as well as casual and seasonal workers not actually in a job at the time of the Census
Source: Selected Australian Censuses from 1921

Table 8.4 similarly shows the severity of unemployment in 1933, with some denominations suffering more than others. More than one-fourth of Catholics was unemployed, compared to one-sixth of Methodists and Presbyterians, while Anglicans because of their size, remained very close to the national average. Catholic overrepresentation in the unskilled labourer class comes to mind as a ready explanation, as the unskilled suffer most in times of economic recession. Whatever the cause, in 1981 Catholic unemployment was not any worse than unemployment in the nation at large. By contrast the 'no religion' category seems to have in all censuses the largest percentage of unemployed. The number of unemployed who say they belong to the Uniting Church (not in the table and separately calculated) is an incredibly low 19 per 1000. If we follow our previous reasoning, it appears that the unemployed or maybe the unemployable take a very scant interest in the new church. The most recent immigrants, who, as we have seen are overrepresented in the labourers' category, also suffer most from unemployment. The Orthodox ratio is 91 per 1000 and for the even more recent Muslims it is as high as 162.

It was because of the depression that the 1933 census included a question on income. As Table 8.5 shows, the differences were most obvious in the percentages of adherents in the lowest and highest income group. Of all Catholic breadwinners 41.4 per cent had earned less than £52 in the preceding year. The percentages for the others were lower: Anglicans 36.2 per cent, Methodist 32.4 per cent and Presbyterians 31.4 per cent. Some of the smaller denominations such as Congregationalists (27.5 per cent) and Jews (25 per cent) had an even lower percentage of adherents in this category. The reverse proves to be true when we look at the percentages of bread winners in each denomination who earned £260 or more. Here the Jews (28.9 per cent), Congregationalists (22.2 per cent) and Presbyterians (18.7 per cent) far surpassed Catholics (10.7 per cent), who are only ahead of the Salvation Army (5.3 per cent).

Questions about income were also asked in the most recent censuses. In 1976, 15 per cent of the population lived in homes where the family income was over $15 000. As in 1933, this income category was highly overrepresented amongst Jews (37 per cent). Presbyterians and those having 'no religion' (both with 18 per cent), followed at a distance. Anglicans (16 per cent) were slightly above, and Catholics (14 per cent) slightly below the average for the population. Again far below the average were the Muslims (7 per cent), the Orthodox (8 per cent), the Jehovah's Witnesses (4 per cent), The Salvation Army and the Pentecostals, both having 9 per cent of their membership in the above $15 000 family income category.

The pattern repeats itself for 1981 with a new and interesting twist for the Uniting Church. Twenty per cent of the population at the time lived in homes where the family income was over $22 000. Again the Jews (39 per cent) are way above this average, but this time the second place is occupied by those who designate themselves as 'Uniting' (27 per cent). The Presbyterians (21 per cent) have now fallen to slightly above the average, whereas the Methodists who in 1976 were still on average, have now dropped to 16 per cent which seems to suggest that the Uniting Church in 1977 creamed off the church going, well educated, high status, high income Methodists and Presbyterians leaving the others with the somewhat less endowed remnant.

As was also the case in 1976, Anglicans (21 per cent) have slightly more than the average share of families in the population with an income over $22 000, but Catholics have now caught up (20 per cent). Still much below the average for the population are the Muslims (8 per cent), the Orthodox (13 per cent), the Jehovah's Witnesses (11 per cent), the Salvation Army (12 per cent) and the Pentecostals (14 per cent).

Religious practices and occupation

Is it true that the lower classes or the lower occupational categories are less 'religious', that they go to church less, pray less and hold less

Table 8.5 Income distribution of male breadwinners for the major Australian religious denominations

Denomination	No income	Under £52	£52 to £103	£104 to £155	£156 to £207	£208 to £259	£260 and over	Total
Anglican (n = 914 034)	12.0	24.2	16.6	11.8	11.6	9.8	13.9	100
Catholic (n = 435 955)	15.1	26.3	16.3	11.4	11.3	8.9	10.7	100
Methodist (n = 228 604)	10.0	22.4	16.6	12.4	12.3	10.7	15.6	100
Presbyterian (n = 255 550)	10.1	21.3	15.7	11.8	11.7	10.7	18.7	100
Baptist (n = 34 883)	10.5	23.1	16.5	11.6	12.6	11.1	14.5	100
Congregational (n = 22 208)	8.4	19.1	15.5	11.7	11.1	11.8	22.2	100
Lutheran (n = 23 244)	12.6	24.6	19.5	12.7	9.1	6.3	15.1	100
Salvation Army (n = 9251)	11.2	33.5	18.6	11.9	10.8	8.6	5.3	100
Hebrew (n = 9230)	10.4	14.6	13.9	12.4	10.2	9.6	28.9	100
No Religion (n = 7645)	16.1	26.5	14.3	9.2	10.2	9.1	14.6	100
Total (per cent)	12.5	24.7	16.7	11.8	11.4	9.6	13.3	100
Total	296 206	585 422	394 450	279 227	270 866	226 935	314 674	2 367 780

Note: Income = income earned during the preceding year
Source: The Census, 1933

orthodox beliefs? What are the attitudes of the professional classes?

Since the establishment of the Australian colonies the lower classes are indeed said to have been less 'religious', and though they may never have expressed it verbally, their '"practical unbelief" led to a great deal of lying about on Sundays and to very little church attendance' (Barrett, 1966: 169). The middle rather than the upper classes were said to form the bulk of the church's support, both in terms of attendance and finance (ibid.: 66). They were the people for whom piety was 'a royal road to respectability' (Pike, 1957: 513). The upper classes were less evident (Henderson, 1953: 135), although the clergy could not be blamed for at least trying to get them involved.

Samuel Marsden, the second Anglican chaplain to the colony of New South Wales, was excessively obsequious to the powerful, and condescending of those of lesser rank:

> In his sermons he was capable of saying that throne and altar fell together, or that religion was the great and essential comfort of the poor, the old and the sick, that in the sanctuary of God men learned the significance of those gradations of rank and wealth which in His infinite wisdom God had thought fit to establish in this transitory life as stimulants to the industry and energy of men (Clark, 1962: 205).

Marsden's sanctification of the class structure was a short step to the justification of his personal 'multitudinous temporal affairs' (Clark, 1963: 63), a concern which he had in common with some of his English contemporaries, such as the Archbishop of Canterbury, Dr. Manners Sutton (1808–1828) who 'distributed sixteen livings and other cathedral appointments among seven members of his family' (Pike, 1957: 12–13). What was true of Marsden was also true of many of the later clergy of the Church of England who because of birth, education and upbringing identified themselves with the upper classes (Roe, 1965: 12–13), inevitably alienating themselves from the working class.

The situation was different among Catholics, for the working classes were never lost to the church. In Ireland priests had been deeply aligned with the peasants: frequently they had been brought up in a peasant home and sympathised with the people's aspirations. In Australia 'this association between the priests and the lower classes was perpetuated because both bond and free tended to remain on the bottom rungs of the social ladders' (Clark, 1962: 105–10).

In the Broom, Jones and Zubrzycki Social Stratification Survey carried out in 1965, 76 per cent of adult Catholic respondents in the upper occupational bracket (n = 120) had been to church in the preceding month, 57 per cent in middle (n = 154) and 63 per cent in the lower (n = 155) bracket. For non-Catholics the corresponding percentages were 36 per cent upper (n = 498), 25 per cent middle (n = 513) and 23 per cent lower (n = 437).

In the Australian Survey Project carried out in 1967, 72 per cent of Catholic heads of households in the upper occupational bracket (n = 67) went to church once a month or more, 48 per cent in middle (n = 79) and 47 per cent in the lower (n = 107) brackets. For non-Catholics the corresponding percentages were 27 per cent upper (n = 261), 21 per cent middle (n = 229) and 16 per cent lower (n = 245).

Table 8.6 has the percentage of regular church goers by occupation and denomination for the 1966 Religion in Australia survey. It shows that manual workers are least regular, closely followed by the upper professionals and managers. The strength of the churches seems to lie with the rural occupations and the lower-professionals and clerical workers.

The more recent data from the November 1979 *Age* poll show that compared with 1966 (33 per cent) only 20 per cent (n = 1314) of those in the work-force thought of themselves as regular church goers. Actually if those in the work force who put themselves in the 'No Religion' (n = 125) are added, the percentage decreases even further to 18 per cent. Two years later (November 1981) another *Age* poll saw the percentage of regular church goers in the workforce increase to 23 per cent (n = 1001) or to 20 per cent if the 151 'No Religion' respondents are added.

In both surveys the respondents with skilled occupations (plumbers, hairdressers etc.) who belonged to a denomination were least regular (11 and 16 per cent respectively). The unskilled (labourers, domestics) and semi-skilled (process-workers, apprentices etc.) had corresponding percentages of 25 (1979) and 21 (1981), lower-professionals and clerical workers 26 and 29, professionals managers 20 and 31 per cent. The pattern of the skilled being the least regular maintains itself for all denominations in those two polls.

The Age polls also asked to which class respondents felt they belonged. As over one third chose 'working class' and almost one half 'middle class' it may be interesting to compare their church attendance by denomination. In 1979, 20 per cent of the working class (n = 710) regarded itself as regular compared with 28 per cent of the middle class (n = 994). The denominations followed the same pattern: the percentage of Anglican regulars in the working class (n = 253) was 7 per cent and 14 per cent in the middle class (n = 359). Corresponding percentages for Catholics were 39 (n = 224) and 43 (n = 276), and for members of the Uniting/Presbyterian/Methodist section 10 (n = 138) and 23 (n = 214).

For the 1981 poll the percentages were 22 per cent regulars in the

Table 8.6 Percentage of regular church goers by occupation and denomination (1966)

Denomination	Graziers & farmers	Professionals (doctors, architects, etc.) and managers	Lower professionals (teachers, etc.) & clerical workers	Manual workers, police force, armed services & shop-owners	Total of those in work-force
Anglicans	26	12	26	11	15
	n = 54	n = 138	n = 143	n = 449	n = 784
Catholics	83	78	77	58	66
	n = 42	n = 58	n = 98	n = 302	n = 500
Methodists	43	22	46	25	30
	n = 21	n = 23	n = 33	n = 126	n = 203
Presbyterians	38	36	35	19	28
	n = 43	n = 44	n = 66	n = 155	n = 310
Others	59	23	46	29	33
	n = 27	n = 44	n = 39	n = 185	n = 295
TOTAL	48	30	45	28	33
	n = 189	n = 307	n = 379	n = 1217	n = 2092

Note: Occupation includes the wives or respondents in the workforce; wives were assigned the husband's occupational status
Source: Religion in Australia Survey, 1966

working class (n = 649) and 29 per cent for the middle class (n = 807). The denominational distribution was as follows: Anglican working class 10 per cent (n = 229), middle class 15 per cent (n = 285), Catholics 37 per cent (n = 201) and 48 per cent (n = 215), Uniting/Presbyterian/ Methodist 16 per cent (n = 120) and 25 (n = 215).

The main conclusion one can draw is that in Australia the differences between denominations are more striking than the differences between classes and occupational groups. A comparison of the extremes in the marginals of Table 8.6 shows that the difference between Catholics (66 per cent) and Anglicans (15 per cent) in regular church going is greater than those between the rural occupations (48 per cent) and the manual workers (28 per cent). In the 1980s the differences between the major denominations has narrowed. Yet they are still greater than between classes or occupational groups. It is certainly incorrect to speak of the religious alienation of any one class of the Australian population. What the data seem to show is that the boundaries around some of the major denominations (e.g. Catholic) are still stronger than around others, in spite of the increasing fluidity of these boundaries and the ensuing reduction of loyalty as expressed in church attendance since the mid-1960s. Yet the boundaries between classes and occupational groups seems to be even more fluid, certainly exerting little pressure on separating life style, accents, behaviour patterns and religious observances.

Occupational mobility

Are Australians more inclined to be 'religious' when they have climbed steeply the social ladder?

Sometimes in private conversations one overhears remarks that highly mobile individuals change denominations in order to belong to a fashionable Anglican church. These remarks come from free thinkers who have read this kind of thing in books, but who have not observed the Australian religious scene close at hand.

The books often come from the USA, where there is evidence that individuals 'play musical church to a status-striving tune' (Demerath, 1965: 22). Allingham's (1965: 277) study of occupational mobility in Australia concluded that there was no consistent relationship between religious affiliation and mobility patterns among the various classes in his sample and that religion was 'the least useful of the variables considered in contributing toward an understanding of factors affecting mobility'. As Table 8.7 shows, the 1966 Religion in Australia Survey confirms his finding. It is true that Anglicans are overrepresented among the high upwardly mobile group, and underrepresented among the high downwardly mobil respondents, and that among the latter, Catholics and Presbyterians are overrepresented. However, comparing the small numbers in categories 1 and 7 with the sample as a whole, the underrepresentation of 12 per cent of Anglicans in column 7 is significant. Columns 1 and 2 give no evidence that Catholics are less mobile than Protestants, as has been reported in some studies of American Catholics (Kane, 1955: 7). Their share of both categories of mobile respondents is equal to their share of the total sample. Our findings seem to support other American studies, which found that Catholics are as achievement oriented as Protestants, and that the Protestant ethic

> appears now to have become effectively disconnected with its point of origin. Catholics appear to be as manifestly imbued with Puritan values, in relation to work and achievements as are Protestants in the modern world (Wilson, 1966: 123).

In church going too the differences between the various categories are small. Eleven per cent more of the respondents in the high downwardly mobile category were regular church goers, compared with the total sample. The sample size is small, but there is a suggestion that the overseas findings (Lenski, 1961: 103) of a correlation between greater religiosity and status deprivation may also be true for Australia.

More significant is the overrepresentation of respondents in row 6 (denominational school attendance) and column 3 (no mobility—both father and respondent or husband of respondent having 'upper' occupations): 52 per cent of this group had been to a denominational school compared with 27 per cent of the total sample. It is interesting that there is no overrepresentation among respondents with high upward mobility. This may indicate that denominational school attendance has generally no effect on upward mobility in Australia. Greeley and Rossi (1966: 225–26) say that Catholic schools in the USA accelerate upward mobility of Catholics. This is not true for Australia. When Catholics who have gone to denominational schools (n = 416) are compared with Catholics who have not (n = 200), the percentage of highly upwardly mobile respondents (5 per cent) and medium upwardly mobile respondents (16 per cent) is the same in both instances. Row 7 of Table 8.7 gives a negative answer to our original question: do highly mobile respondents change to other denominations? There is no significant difference between the percentages of any of the categories, although there is a tendency for upwardly mobile respondents to have changed more. However, further inspection of the data shows that the direction and reasons for the change are fairly random. A good reason why there should be so little difference lies in the fact that the four major denominations are big enough to encompass a whole variety of churches. One does not have to step outside one's denomination if one wants to 'play musical church to a status-striving tune'. All one has to do if one is Protestant is to join a more fashionable church within the same denomination, although there is no evidence of this happening. No questions were asked to investigate this possibility, but it is doubtful whether the percentage that use the church to manipulate social connections is sufficiently large to warrant further research. Average Australians would hotly deny that their own church going has anything to do with status striving, even when they may be suspicious about their neighbour, but to verbalise these suspicions would be almost as heinous as the act itself.

The percentages in rows 8 and 9 are unexpected, for the more upwardly mobile respondents are, the less they reported regular church going and vice versa: the more downwardly mobile, the more they reported regular parental church going. The percentages of columns 3, 4 and 5 (rows 8 and 9) conform to those in row 5, showing that there is a tendency for respondents who are not mobile and in lower occupation groups, to attend church less than mobile individuals from the same class origins. In all non-mobile groups the respondents' church going

Table 8.7 Mobility of respondents by selected characteristics (1966)

Percentage of respondents who	High upward mobility (n=117)	Medium upward mobility (n=409)	No mobility upper occupational categories (n=177)	No mobility middle occupational categories (n=487)	No mobility lower occupational categories (n=287)	Medium downward mobility (n=342)	High downward mobility (n=72)	Total sample (n=2601)
	1	2	3	4	5	6	7	8
1 were Anglican	46	36	43	35	40	34	28	40
2 were Catholic	23	24	19	24	22	24	31	24
3 were Methodist	9	11	6	8	15	10	7	9
4 were Presbyterian	14	15	21	15	13	15	21	14
5 were regular church goers (once a month or more)	33	33	38	37	24	33	44	33
6 had attended a denominational school	27	27	52	26	19	26	29	27
7 never had any other religious affiliation	82	86	87	89	89	92	90	88
8 had fathers who were regular church goers when they grew up	26	36	47	48	30	46	57	41
9 had mothers who were regular church goers when they grew up	40	53	57	56	46	58	62	53
10 were born in non-English speaking countries	7	7	11	14	10	20	18	12
11 had lived in the suburb or area of interview less than 5 years	36	32	36	27	28	31	29	28

12 had completed a secondary education	55	30	67	30	15	24	38	29
13 never attend non-church meetings or activities	49	61	41	58	67	66	61	62

Notes: Mobility has been measured by respondents' present occupation in comparison with father's occupation when he (or she) was of high school age. For the purpose of this Table wives were assigned their husband's occupation which was then compared with her father's occupation. Of the 2601 respondents in the first section of the survey 709 could not be classified either because they were not in the work force or because their father was not. Although these 709 were excluded from further analysis they were included in the percentages of column 8 (total sample).

1 High upward mobility was operationally defined as: all respondents (or wives of respondents) who belonged to the professional, managerial or graziers categories and whose fathers had semi- or unskilled occupations (shop assistants, process workers, drivers, service workers, and labourers). Added to this category were those respondents who were in the upper professional brackets and whose fathers had a clerical, craftsman or foreman occupation.

2 Medium upward mobility: all respondents (or wives of respondents) who had skilled occupations and whose fathers had semi- or unskilled occupations. This category also included the respondents (or wives of respondents) who were in the professional/managerial/grazier bracket and whose fathers were in the skilled categories.

3 No mobility (upper group) consisted of all respondents (or wives of respondents) who like their fathers had professional/managerial/grazier occupations.

4 No mobility (middle group) consisted of all respondents (or wives of respondents) who like their fathers had clerical or skilled occupations (included were also 'other farmers' and members of armed services and police force).

5 No mobility (lower group) consisted of all respondents (or wives of respondents) who like their fathers had unskilled occupations.

6 Medium downward mobility is the reverse of category 2.

7 High downward mobility is the reverse of category 1.

Source: Religion in Australia Survey, 1966

is approximately 10 per cent less than the father's, and 20 per cent less regular than the mother's. The high upwardly mobile respondents differ less from their parents than any other category, and are slightly more regular than their fathers and slightly less regular than their mothers in church attendance.

It is difficult to say what this means. Have respondents from secular homes been more ambitious or more able to grasp opportunities? And once these opportunities have been realised have fewer of them turned from religion?

A more likely explanation is that manual worker parents are less active church goers (columns 1 and 5) than professional parents (columns 3 and 7); the differences within these pairs of columns are not significant. As a result fewer of the upwardly mobile respondents come from church going homes and more of the downwardly mobile respondents do. However small the differences, it is interesting that the more mobile respondents adjust to the church going patterns of their new status, whereas the downwardly mobile continue the patterns of their parental status.

The differences in row 10 are not significant, but suggest that recent European migrants are likely to be downwardly rather than upwardly mobile.

Row 12 on the other hand contains the greatest differences of all data related to mobility, showing that there is a strong correlation between education and mobility. Although the fathers of the respondents in column 1 and 5 are generally in the same lower occupational categories, respondents who had secondary education or more moved into the upper class occupations.

Row 13 shows that those in upper occupations are more likely to attend outside organisations such as Rotary, Parents and Citizens, and that upwardly and downwardly mobile people adjust themselves to the greater or lesser activities of their respective categories. However, the differences are slight.

Other data on mobility and religion can be found in an earlier study (Mol, 1971: 100). They have a bearing on the international discussion about mobility and values. For instance, Gerhard Lenski (1967: 225) said that the reason Catholics are less mobile than Protestants is that the former are more inclined to rate obedience ahead of intellectual independence. He suggests that because the more responsible positions go together with a capacity to think for oneself, Catholics are less successful. However, the Religion in Australia Survey data showed that the differences were not between those who had been either upwardly or downwardly mobile, but between those who occupied upper, middle and lower positions. In other words, this attitude does not generate upward mobility, but results from different socialisation processes in the various occupational groupings, processes in which parental ambition and levels of education may be crucial.

If these speculations have any ground, the 1966 Religion in Australia Survey data should show that, contrary to Lenski's data, mobile Catholics continue to differ from mobile Protestants. This is indeed the case. Of the upwardly mobile Catholics (n = 85), 41 per cent agree that the most important thing for a child is to obey rather than to think for himself. Of the upwardly mobile non-Catholics (n = 299) 33 per cent agree with the statement. Of downwardly mobile Catholics (n = 66) 65 per cent agree, while of corresponding non-Catholics (n = 213) 42 per cent do.

Some of the Religion in Australia Survey data seemed to suggest (Mol, 1971: 100) that upwardly mobile respondents are more achievement oriented while downwardly mobile respondents are more ascription oriented, presumably because each group derives some ego strength from either occupational achievement or family origin according to one's status gratification or frustration. Yet there were few differences on such achievement values as getting ahead or on admiration of the very ambitious person. If anything, the differences were within the immobile, rather than between the upwardly and downwardly mobile groups. Those who occupy high status occupations appear to play down ambition and 'getting ahead' more than those who are on the lower rungs of the social ladder. Are they more blasé or do they perceive the relativity of these values since they have 'arrived'? Do they suffer from status envy in reverse, opposing those values which may threaten their position at the top of the pyramid? Whatever is the answer, it is clear that in Australia the working classes do not represent a separate ethos denigrating ambition and success. Maybe one should not expect this in a country where the opportunity structure is more open than in those European countries where Marxism originally took root. If this is so, one may have to take a second look at the so-called Australian habit of 'lopping off the tall poppies', or what Russel Ward (1965: 16) calls 'the unusually widespread delight that Australians feel in taking down the mighty from their seats—a pastime known in the vernacular as "knocking"'. Many observers of Australian society have remarked on this phenomenon. Blainey (1966: 171) says: 'Ambition and the desire to raise oneself beyond one's station were considered to be vices by a majority or an influential minority of Australian men.'

It may be that Australian egalitarianism manifests itself in an emphasis on equal opportunities more than on a relativisation of ambition. Although preoccupation with occupational or financial success appears much stronger in the USA (Williams, 1956: 39), a common western culture rewarding ambition and career aggressiveness could not have failed to make its impact here, for there is a certain amount of striving, even if it is not as desperate or neurotic as in many other western countries.

McGregor (1966: 366) similarly wonders whether Australia is not changing in more ambitious directions. On the one hand he says that Australians do not let ambition interfere with the good life, 'they are quite content to work hard for what they consider the necessities of life—a home, a car, a TV set—and then leave the coronaries to some other silly bastard'. However, on the same page he warns that it is foolish 'to think that this [egalitarian] ethic is not crumbling slowly before the pressures which have been generated in the new society. In the last few years Australia has become rapidly more success-riddled, its society more status-conscious and pettily stratified.'

Since the Religion in Australia Survey little work has been done on religion and mobility. An exception is De Vaus who investigated geographical (rather than occupational) mobility and its effect on adolescent religious behaviour of 375 students in 12 Victorian high schools. He found that it led to a decline in church attendance but not of beliefs and private religious practices because moving did not entail change in reference groups (De Vaus, 1982: 401).

What conclusions can we draw from the Australian research on religion and mobility? The major finding is that occupational mobility or lack of it does not correlate strongly with any item in the 1966 Religion in Australia Survey. The differences in Table 8.7 are generally between the immobile upper and lower occupational groups rather than between the upwardly and downwardly mobile individuals. There seems to be nothing in mobility as such which is worthy of attention. The clue to the mobility of respondents seems to be located in whatever differences there are between the occupational groupings, but this observation should be seen in the light of the relative inadequacy of the survey to investigate these matters in depth.

It is obvious that mobility or lack of it does not tie in with denomination, church going, praying, beliefs regarding God and the Church, and the various religious experiences.

A possible explanation is that Australians do not have a heavy emotional involvement in their social status. Consequently their self-image or identity is not seriously affected by occupational success, and even if religion is relevant for the integration of the self, it is irrelevant for changes in social status. Therefore religion is neither widely used to provide an anchorage for those whose status has changed, nor exploited as a vehicle for upward mobility.

The point could also be taken the other way: that religion has not been perceived as a potential vehicle for upward mobility nor as a convenient comfort for those trampled under in the status rush. Religion may not be sufficiently tied in with the Australian ethos and the way an individual sees himself, to serve any purpose in this respect. However this answer presumes too much, that climbing the occupational status ladder is important to Australians. It may be that both status climbing and religion are irrelevant to the Australian ethos and so irrelevant for one another. However, this view is an over simplification, for although religious dimensions do not differ from one mobility category to another, the strongly upwardly mobile go to church as regularly as their parents, whereas respondents in the other categories go much less. While those who have been strongly downwardly mobile are going to church less regularly than their parents, they still go to church more than the respondents in any other category. They also are more likely to have had an experience of being punished by God for something they had done than the respondents who had similar high status fathers but managed to remain where their fathers were. In other words, although the evidence is faint, one of the many theories regarding the function of religion (that it provides compensation for the frustrated) is likely to be of some relevance here.

One interesting final point of speculation and comparison is whether the weak mobility–religion pattern in Australia resembles the one in Britain. The American hypotheses in this field do not hold true for Australia, and the occupation–religion pattern was rather similar to the British one. Bryan Wilson (1966: 118) has speculated about the American–British difference on this point. His thesis is that in the USA churches are status-confirming agencies whereas in England they are not. In the USA the normalcy of social mobility enhanced the status of whole religious movements, and individuals who rose more rapidly than their fellows switched to higher status churches (ibid.: 104, 107). This occurred because of the demand for congruence of statuses. The adjustment of the American churches to the mobility of their membership runs parallel to their general capacity and willingness to be assimilated to the wider society and all its values (ibid.: 111). They put greater stress on values such as competition, love, joy and personal security. On the other hand, the English churches have not adjusted in this way. Mobility was not so strong, status was more ascriptive and consequently social control functions were more prominent. All this had a different effect on secularisation, so that in England religion continues as a compartmentalised marginal item, while in America it is institutionally more central, but ideationally much more bankrupt (ibid.: 114).

There are a few fallacies and omissions in Wilson's argument. First-ly, in a country such as Australia, mobility patterns resemble those in America, but the whole religious scene is reminiscent of England.

Therefore to link differential mobility with absence or presence of status-conferring functions is manifestly wrong, for in Australia religious affiliation or behaviour does not appear to have much to do with occupational status or mobility.

Secondly, differences between the English emphasis on social control functions versus the American stress on personal security is an interesting, but rather dubious hypothesis. However, it could be verified by an historical content analysis of sermons. In all countries, including Australia, both emphases seem to have occurred. On the whole, the social control function is probably even more strongly stressed in evangelical–fundamentalist circles which in the USA are not any less influential or more numerous than in Britain. A more interesting hypothesis would be that in countries where mobility, change and success are a way of life, the saliency of the objectification function of religion increases. By this I mean that the provision of a moral anchorage outside the immediate contingencies, or the projection of the source of meaning in an objective datum, such as the revealed will of God, may be associated with mobility. The proliferation of sects in the USA precisely in areas of large scale migration (the West Coast) rather than in long established areas (the East Coast) seems to point to the possible fruitfulness of such a hypothesis. Unfortunately the function of religion for objectification, and consequent strengthening of norms and systems of meaning, is an underdeveloped area of investigation in the sociology of religion.

Thirdly, the thesis that American secularisation can be satisfactorily understood in terms of the churches' adjustment to mobility patterns seems far fetched. It leads to Wilson's underestimation of the historical theological content of much American religiosity. I think that the peculiar, peaceful symbiosis of aggressive secularisation and religiosity in American society has its origin much further back in the pre-industrial, but culture-creating era of American history. The Great Awakening in the eighteenth century and the fervent religion of earlier periods made for the Americanisation and therefore vitalisation of European religious forms. It also led to the inevitable profanation or secularisation of American society once the charismatic phase had become irrelevant for the now self propelling cultural forces (Mol, 1968: 71).

At any rate the similarities between the religious scene in England and Australia and the dissimilarities between Australia and the USA make sense only in terms of some such historical argument. After all, unlike the USA, Australia has never had anything like this religious fervency dissolving it from the old world heritage.

Fourthly, Wilson underestimates (actually does not mention), the importance of size of religious denominations. The possibility that certain denominations become catalysts for social status categories exists only when there are sufficient religious organisations available for this division of labour. It is for this reason that in the USA the Episcopal Church could become the bastion of old English aristocracy, whereas in Britain and Australia the same Church of England could only represent the whole spectrum of the population.

Residence

Are Anglicans more numerous in the 'better' suburbs, and Roman Catholics overrepresented in the industrial areas of town?

From various censuses in the nineteenth century, and all censuses of the twentieth century, one can calculate the percentage of denominational adherents for specific districts. They show that some denominations have been over or underrepresented in the 'desirable' areas of towns and cities. Yet these over or underrepresentations have been slight and give no hint of a 'denominational monopoly' in any district. Australia has always been 'pluralistic' in the religious sense. Still, this should not prevent us from looking at denominational imbalance.

Some nineteenth century observers have referred particularly to underrepresentation of Catholics in well-to-do areas. Cardinal Moran (Inglis, 1961: 8) found that his fellow Catholics occupied the poorest section of the community. Burns makes a similar observation for Melbourne in the twentieth century.

> In both 1931 and 1933 ... the proportion of Catholics to non-Catholics was highest in the areas of low economic status ... the ranking of areas according to the proportion of Catholics went in inverse order to the ranking on socio-economic status (Brennan, 1965: 307).

James Jupp, speaking about Melbourne, also mentions that even 'after generations of settling down, there are far more Catholics in the industrial suburbs than in the higher class residential districts' (Inglis, 1961: 8). Additional evidence is given by Jones (1967: 98) in his analysis of the 1961 census data. He says, 'The pattern of factor coefficients indicates that in Melbourne in 1961 areas of low socio-economic status tended also to have relatively high proportions of Catholics, southern Europeans and their nationals'. As Catholic migration to Australia since 1947 has been higher than Protestant migration it is well to bear in mind that recent migrants have settled in the inner city areas where cheaper rents may be a more salient factor than denomination as such.

The same pattern occurs in Sydney. Spann compared the 1901 with the 1954 census. He found that in 1901, 32 per cent of the population of seven 'inner' municipalities were Catholic, compared with only 15 per cent of the population in eighteen 'outer' suburbs and in the exclusive suburb of Woollahra. In 1954 Catholics again formed 32 per cent of the population of seven 'inner' municipalities, but only 20 per cent of the population living north of the harbour, in Woollahra and in Sutherland shire. Spann throws an interesting and perceptive sidelight on these findings when the writes:

> It is not implied by this that there is, among Sydney Catholics, much conscious sense of there being 'Catholic' areas of the city. No matter where they go, there is a Catholic church within a mile or so, and a local Catholic school. As a Catholic friend has written: 'What is important is a fairly strong sense of the need for congenial neighbours, and quite a strong feeling that in some areas they may feel unwelcome, either because the local society is rather strongly "Masonic" (typically such places as Epping, Longueville and parts of the Manly district) or stand-offish. An Australian Catholic wants to live in an atmosphere where nobody but a few cranks will regard him as in any way unusual, and where most people will accept him as the ordinary decent bloke he is'. This is, among other things, a striking testimony to the Australianism of Australian Catholics; this sort of demand, and the reserves and fears that go along with it, is characteristic of the whole society, only reinforced in this case by the character of the sub-group (Spann, 1961: 128).

What is true of Catholicism in Melbourne and Sydney also applies to the federal capital. Jones (1965: 98), investigating the 1961 census results for collectors' districts in Canberra, found that in two adjacent areas in Narrabundah, consisting predominantly of timber prefabricated cottages built to house workmen engaged on the post-1948 construction programme, the percentage of Catholic residents was forty-six. On the other hand, at the opposite end of the scale were two adjacent collectors' districts in Deakin and Forrest, where 70 per cent of the male workforce was composed of men engaged in public authourity or in business and professional services and where less than 20 per cent was Catholic. Again, the factor of recent immigrants seeking cheap housing is more likely to explain this finding than Catholicism as such.

What about other denominations and other cities? Peter Scott (1965: 471) from the University of Tasmania subjected the 1961 census figures to a detailed analysis and found a significant relationship between high per capita income and Anglican affiliation, particularly in such areas as northern Sydney, Walkerville in north-eastern Adelaide and south-western Perth, and to a lesser extent in east-central Melbourne, and the small inland tracts of St. Lucia and Ascot in Brisbane.

Methodism tends 'to be overrepresented in districts of predominantly middle, particularly lower-middle income'. On the other hand, both Methodists and Presbyterians are underrepresented in the inner metropolitan areas. The latter 'become conspicuous in districts enjoying a high social status [and] . . . therefore reduce the margin of Anglican supremacy in northern Sydney, in areas east of central Melbourne, and at Kenmore and St. Lucia in south-western Brisbane' (ibid.: 472).

Are the people living in higher socio-economic sections of town also more regular church goers? There is little available evidence in historical records that they are. The only evidence comes from the Report on the Decline in Church-going carried out in Newcastle in 1951, where it was found that only 17.5 per cent of 348 Anglican respondents living in D type (poorest) housing were regular church goers, whereas the corresponding percentage for those living in better housing was 30.2.

The 1966 Religion in Australia Survey ranked the Sydney respondents in accordance with Congalton's status-ranking of suburbs. This 7 point scale is based on the amount of prestige assigned to the 348 suburbs by 143 Sydney residents. Suburbs with the highest prestige were accorded 1, those with the lowest seven. Melbourne respondents were ranked in accordance with a socio-economic and ethnic status scale based on such data as proportion of male work force in finance and property, in employer status etc., and developed by Jones (1967: 95). The Melbourne suburbs were ranked in 8 groups according to their socio-economic status scores. Although Congalton's reputational and Jones' objective method are not strictly comparable the data show that in both cities religious behaviour, beliefs and experiences do not differ much from one type of suburb to another.

Yet historians have enlivened many conversations with their remark about Sydney's godless pragmatism and Melbourne's godfearing reserve. Speaking towards the middle of the nineteenth century Turner (1904: 325) referred to Melbourne as 'noticeably a church-going town, partly from force of habit, and partly perhaps from the lack of facilities for getting away from it'. However in the 1880s it was a city where vigorous and militant atheism flowered and, where more than in any other Australian capital, the influence of Darwin, Spencer, Huxley and the English materialists 'struck healthy roots' (Smith: 1963).

This apparently did not affect the churches, because round about the same time Francis Adams (1892: 45) observed cynically: 'Melbourne is still genuinely Sabbatarian, keeping its public galleries closed on Sundays and trying to be unctuously thankful for at least one day's intolerable dullness out of the seven.'

Dale (1889: 231) noted that in Victoria, (with most of the population living in Melbourne) 35 per cent of the people attended the principal church services compared with 24 per cent in New South

Wales. He also noted that the churches could accommodate 58 per cent of the population in Victoria and only 38 per cent in New South Wales. In Victoria the number of Sunday School scholars equalled 71 per cent of children between six and fifteen, compared with 56 per cent of children between seven and fifteen in New South Wales. Dale wondered how these interesting differences came about. As the proportion of the population living in cities, towns and villages in each colony appears to be about the same, he does not think that urban/rural differences can explain the greater concern with religion in Victoria.

However, he believes that the fact that New South Wales was settled earlier had an effect. Considerable numbers of persons had left England and settled in New South Wales before the great period of church building had started. In Victoria, he says, the immense development had only just begun when the disclosures of inadequate religious accommodation in the large towns contained in the Report on the Religious Census (England and Wales) of, 1851 had created something like a religious panic. He continues:

> The passion for church building, which the Report had created at home, revealed its power in the young colony; large numbers of the settlers carried with them the sacred fire (ibid.: 232).

Another reason Dale advances for the religious differences between the colonies was that New South Wales trained the people to rely on the government for the provision and maintenance of the religious institutions, whereas Victoria abolished the system of concurrent endowment in 1875. He felt that Victorian self reliance made the people more conscious of the need for active financial participation.

More recently Clark (1962a: 84) has characterised some of the differences between Melbourne and Sydney in terms of two schools of faiths dividing the unbelievers. The Melbourne one, he says, believes in enlightenment and happiness for all. It wants to change things. It supports all left wing causes, all peace movements, all attempts to ban the bomb. The Sydney one, on the other hand, is indifferent to the fate of the uneducated masses; it would not have things any different if it had the power to change them. It believes in self improvement and seeks the power of a higher good in the self. There is (or was?) an interesting bit of truth in this spoof which appeals particularly to academics who know both Melbourne and Sydney universities.

Did the Religion in Australia Survey detect any variation between the two cities? There were few differences between respondents in Sydney and Melbourne. Of all men, women and children in Sydney (n = 1179) 32 per cent had been to church on the Sunday preceding the interview compared with 31 per cent (n = 1253) in Melbourne.

Of the Sydney adults who answered the questionnaire containing the items of personal beliefs and values (n = 518) 33 per cent claimed that they prayed daily. In Melbourne (n = 648) the corresponding figure was 32 per cent.

In Sydney 47 per cent believed in the existence of God without doubt, in Melbourne 51 per cent did. In Sydney 2 per cent did not believe in God, in Melbourne 1 per cent did not. In both Sydney and Melbourne, 7 per cent did not know whether there was a God and did not think there was any way of finding out.

However there was a difference between the two cities, in that 22 per cent of the Sydney respondents fell in the category of 'consistent secularists' (n = 510), while in Melbourne this per cent was only 14 (n = 638). The comparable figures for the non-metropolitan areas of New South Wales and Victoria were 16 per cent and 11 per cent. Although the differences were small, they pointed to an element of truth in the stereotype of Melbourne as a less 'secular' city than Sydney. Again there are no significant differences between the percentages of 'orthodox believers' in the Sydney and Melbourne sample (17 per cent and 18 per cent). However Melbourne has more of what were called 'public believers', people who believe in God without doubt and go to church regularly but do not pray daily. These constitute 11 per cent for Melbourne, but 7 per cent for Sydney, and 9 per cent for non-metropolitan Victoria, but 3 per cent for non-metropolitan New South Wales.

There were even fewer differences on the 'religious experience' items. In Sydney the percentage of respondents who claimed to have had an experience of God's presence since they grew up was 45 per cent. In Melbourne this percentage was forty-eight. In Sydney 34 per cent claimed to have had a sense of being saved in Christ, in Melbourne thirty.

More interesting differences have to do with recollection of past church attendance frequency. In Sydney 13 per cent of the 793 adult respondents said that five years ago they attended church more often. In Melbourne 19 per cent of 770 said so. In Sydney 37 per cent of the same respondents claimed that their fathers were regular church goers when they grew up; in Melbourne 45 per cent. In Sydney 47 per cent claimed that their mothers were regular worshippers; in Melbourne 58 per cent. These figures suggest that although there was little difference between Melbourne and Sydney on church going in 1966, there may have been some ground for thinking that Melbournites attended church more regularly in the past.

The largest difference between the Sydney and Melbourne respondents was on the statement: 'A person whose family has had a high social standing for many generations is therefore entitled to more respect'. In Melbourne only 48 per cent of the respondents disagreed with the statement, in Sydney as many as 66 per cent did. To a lesser extent this was true for another statement condoning unequal treatment: in Melbourne 42 per cent disapproved of the person who treated people differently according to status; in Sydney the corresponding percentage was 52.

In the entire survey there was a slight association between acceptance of inegalitarianism and negative feelings towards out-groups and so one could expect the Melbourne respondents to be somewhat less positive towards outsiders. This proved to be so: in Melbourne 21 per cent of the respondents were against any merger of their denomination with others: in Sydney the percentage was only 13. In Melbourne the percentage of respondents with negative feelings towards atheists was 33, in Sydney twenty-five. It becomes smaller when one looks at negative feelings towards Jews (Melbourne 20, Sydney 14) or Italians (Melbourne 22, Sydney 17) or Japanese (Melbourne 31, Sydney 27). Actually the percentage difference on negative feelings towards communists becomes almost non existent in the two cities (60 per cent in Sydney, 62 per cent in Melbourne), and disappears in the disapproval rate of the person who is against any Asian migration to Australia (63 per cent in both cities).

Urban rural differences

In the first half of the nineteenth century facilities for religious worship became progressively worse as one moved away from established centres. Barrett (1966: 169) says that even the itinerant chaplains did not realise how completely bushworkers were estranged from the church. He relates a story about Reverend J.D. Mereweather who described a service held in a woolshed in the Riverina for some attentive shearers and rouseabouts. Barrett discovered from other sources that the station owner, after realising that all twenty-odd men had some excuse for not attending, had bribed the men into coming by promising them a glass of rum. Carruthers observed the same lack of religious interest in a later period:

> A common saying was that there was 'no God beyond the Range'. Sunday certainly was very much the same as any other day, except that the bush pubs did more business usually on it than during the rest of the week. 'Sunday is a day for putting on a clean shirt' was the sole distinction a prominent station manager was willing to accord to it (Carruthers, 1922: 54).

There were proportionately more freethinkers and agnostics in the outback than anywhere else. According to the 1891 census, in the plains east of the Darling, 1 in 187 of the population was a freethinker or agnostic; in Trans Darling 1 in 200; in the metropolis 1 in 324; in country municipalities 1 in 514 (Walker, 1962: 49). The inhabitants of the outback blamed the absence of religious facilities for excessive drinking and crime. Towards the end of the nineteenth century things began to change. Phillips (1969: 52) mentioned that in 1880 church attendance in country areas of New South Wales (29 per cent of the population) was slightly below that of Sydney (31 per cent), but by 1890 the situation had reversed: 28 per cent of the rural population attended church regularly, but only 25 per cent in Sydney and suburbs.

In the diocese of Newcastle, the 1949 Report on the Decline of Church-going (p.47) found that 33 per cent of Anglicans in country towns went to church regularly compared with 20 per cent in Newcastle itself. The report also found that regular church goers in the country were less satisfied with church and clergy than city Anglicans (ibid.: 49). Thirty two per cent of country town dwellers (n = 103) compared with 19 per cent of Newcastle inhabitants (n = 101) thought that the average Anglican minister was not in touch with practical everyday affairs. More of the same country town dwellers opposed the minister preaching sermons dealing with personal, family and moral problems than their Newcastle counterparts (39 per cent compared with 32 per cent). A larger percentage of the former (81 per cent compared with 68 per cent) answered 'No' to the question: 'Would you like to have more sermons dealing with political issues such as communism, immigration, housing and so on? (ibid.: 60).

A 1946 Gallup poll found that the proportion of church goers was generally greater in the country than in cities. The 1976 and 1980 polls detected only a slight difference: 20.5 and 19.6 per cent regular attendance in country areas as compared with 19.9 and 18.3 per cent in metropolitan ones. The Religion in Australia Survey analysed the urban/rural differences in Victoria, but found that the differences were not very great.

Table 8.8 shows that with regard to respondents' church going, parental attendance, daily prayer, experience of God's presence, and beliefs regarding God and the church, the differences between metropolitan, urban and rural areas in Victoria were either small or nonexistent. Differences are greater on some items. More rural respondents listened to or watched religious services regularly on radio or television: more of them opposed the merging of their denomination with others. The ecumenical conservatism of non-metropolitan Victoria does not come as a surprise. Even in the 1920s the rural Presbyterians were primarily responsible for the breakdown of merger negotiations with the Methodist and Congregational churches.

Table 8.8 **Percentage of respondents in metropolitan, urban and rural areas of Victoria by church attendance and other items**

Percentage of respondents who	Victoria metropolitan	Victoria other urban towns with more than 1000 inhabitants, but not Melbourne	Victoria rural (all other)
1 attended church regularly had been to church on the previous Sunday	40 / 31	43 / 33	41 / 26
2 usually listened to or watched religious services on radio or television	14	21	29
3 reported that their fathers attended regularly when they grew up	45	43	46
4 reported that their mothers attended regularly when they grew up	58	53	61
5 prayed daily	32	31	30
6 reported to have had an experience of God's presence since childhood	48	50	44
7 reported to have had an experience of being afraid of God	24	16	11
8 were of the opinion that the Church was appointed by God	31	37	31
9 believed without doubt that God existed	52	55	50
10 were opposed to the merging of their denomination with any other	21	35	37
11 had a majority of their five best friends belonging to the local church	27	39	46
12 had finished at least a secondary education	29	22	17
13 attend non-church meetings at least once a month	23	34	41
14 agree that the most important thing for a child to learn is to obey rather than think for himself	39	66	48
15 agree that a person whose family has had a high social standing for many generations is therefore entitled to some respect	43	39	32
16 admire the person who is very ambitious	55	39	42
Total sample (items 1 and 2)	1250	369	401
Total sample (items 3, 4, 5, 13 and 14)	770	219	219
Total sample (all other items)	648	186	158

It is difficult to understand why more of the Melbourne respondents reported having had an experience of being afraid of God. The fact that in the smaller communities more respondents attend non-church meetings, could be attributed to the greater pressure and desire for community involvement in these areas. It is also understandable that so many respondents in rural areas have the majority of their five best friends in the local congregation; there are fewer sources for finding friends.

Comparing the survey results for Victoria with overseas findings, it is surprising that city and country differ so little on the major religious items. In most countries of the world there are substantial differences, the rural areas showing more activity than the urban (see entry under rural/urban difference in Mol et al., 1972). One factor that may explain why differences in Australia are not as large is the early history of irreligion in the outback. In the older countries religion has always been strongly interwoven with rural existence. In Australia on the other hand the outback was originally so sparsely populated that the traditions of rural Britain could not be readily transferred. Moreover the early settlers, both emancipated and free, often arrived with indifferent feelings about religion. Australian cities, on the other hand, have always consisted of suburban communities where mainline religion could flourish more than in the abject slums of European towns and cities.

Comparison and conclusion

How do the Australian data compare with those of other countries?

In a sample survey of 998 inhabitants of Christchurch, New Zealand, in 1962, 22 per cent of Presbyterians (n = 241), 19 per cent of Anglicans (n = 403), 16 per cent of Methodists (n = 105), and 6 per cent of Catholics (n = 143) belonged to a professional category comprising managers, graziers, teachers, or lived in homes where the husband or father had an occupation of this kind (Mol, 1962: 11). The relative preponderance of professionals in the denominations follows the Australian rank order.

Other New Zealand surveys found that the occupational profiles of the major denominations hardly differed (Blaikie: 1969). Regarding church attendance of the various categories, here too there was not much difference: 21 per cent of professional (n = 43), and 18 per cent of the non-professional men (n = 209), had been to church on the preceding Sunday (Mol, 1962: 10–11). This compared with 26 per cent professional (n = 340) and 23 per cent non-professional men (n = 919) of the Religion in Australia Survey. Again, the slightly better attendance of the professionals is similar in both countries. The slightly lower attendance of both New Zealand categories is probably caused by the smaller percentage of Catholics in the Christchurch survey, 15 per cent as compared with 27 per cent in Australia.

There are also many similarities with Great Britain. Historical sources in both countries speak almost uniformly about the alienation of the working classes from the churches. In England the Catholic Church (Inglis, 1963: 16) and some of the sectarian groups are exceptions, but the Church of England and the larger Nonconformist bodies lost their hold on the workers in the nineteenth century. 'As with every census available from 1851, the point is made for every section of London that the poor and the working classes are substantially estranged from the churches ...' (Wickham, 1957, 173). Wickham makes the same point for other areas in England, such as Sheffield and York. Charles Booth (1902–1903: 327) noticed the great differences between the religious behaviour of the middle class compared with the working class. The twentieth century saw a change. 'Since 1900 ... the differences of religious behaviour between classes, though still discernible, are less striking than they were in Charles Booth's day', says Inglis (1963: 322). 'It is the middle class which is losing its religion', wrote Masterman (1960: 14) in 1909. Looking back over the last two generations from the vantage point of the mid-1950s in the twentieth century, Wickham (1957: 218) observes the same phenomenon: '... the losses from the churches ... were substantially from the middling classes of society—the industrial and professional middle classes, the inhabitants of suburbia, shopkeepers, black-coated workers, superior craftsmen, foremen and such like. Losses from the working classes have also occurred, but relatively less, since fewer of this class, as adults, were within the churches'. This may be why, both in the Religion in Australia Survey and the 1964 English Gallup poll the differences between occupational groups or classes are not as great as historical literature leads us to expect. In the 1964 English TV study, 23 per cent of the lower class (mainly manual workers, shop assistants, unskilled labourers) went to church 'most Sundays' or about once a month. Of the upper class, (professionals, managers, teachers, supervisors, and farmers) 32 per cent went with similar regularity.

In the Religion in Australia Survey 24 per cent of the unskilled or semi-skilled workers were regular church goers (at least once a month) compared with 35 per cent of the middle and 34 per cent of the upper categories. In the November 1981 *Age* poll, 22 per cent of the working and 29 per cent of the middle class were regular church goers.

Similarly with prayer. Of the upper class in the English TV study, 49 per cent prayed regularly compared with 42 per cent of the lower class. In the Australian study 29 per cent of the professional respondents claimed to pray daily compared with 25 per cent of skilled and 26 per cent of unskilled. The difference between the two countries may be the result of the differences between 'daily' and 'regular'. In the Australian survey, apart from the 26 per cent who claimed to pray daily and the 34 per cent who said they never did, there was a large percentage (39) who said that they prayed occasionally. It is likely that at least some of these would have put themselves in a 'regular' category if that had been the choice. But the main point, that the class differences on prayer habits in either country are small, is seen clearly from the data.

Another similarity between English and Australian data shows in the comparison of classes and denominations. There are few differences between the four major denominations in both Australia and England. The TV study showed the upper class to consist of 68 per cent Anglican, 13 per cent Nonconformist, 8 per cent Catholic and the lower class to consist of 67 per cent Anglican, 14 per cent Nonconformist and 10 per cent Catholic.

The differences with the USA are much greater. Episcopalians or Anglicans have twice as many members (63 per cent) in the non-manual groups (professions, managers and clerical) as the population at large (31 per cent). Presbyterians (47 per cent), and particularly Jews (67 per cent), have a strong overrepresentation of non-manual workers in their membership. On the other hand, Catholicism (29 per cent non-manual) and Methodism (32 per cent non-manual) do not differ substantially from the occupational profile of the nation as a whole, whereas white Baptists (26 per cent) and particularly negro Baptists (9 per cent) have less than average non-manual membership (Lazerwitz, 1964: 428).

On church going the differences with Australia are also substantial: 70 per cent of Protestant professionals in the USA went to church once a month or more, while percentages for owners, managers and officials were 63, for clerical and sales workers 65, skilled workers 56, semi-skilled 57, unskilled 62, and farmers 74. For Catholics the percentages were professions 92, owners, managers and officials 91, clerical and sales workers 92, skilled 83, semi-skilled 82, unskilled 83, farmers 76 per cent (ibid.: 431). Although the overall levels are much higher than in either Australia or England, in the USA too, Protestants are less regular church goers than Catholics, and manual workers less regular than the non-manual.

Yet the differences within the English speaking world are not as great as the differences within European countries.

In some of the large cities of France, such as Paris and Toulouse, the percentage of working class males that attend mass regularly is

2 per cent, whereas the percentage of business executives and professionals is much higher (Isambert, 1972: 180). This applies also to Protestants in some areas of France such as Strassbourg, where 5 per cent of the working, 30 per cent of the middle class and 40 per cent of the upper class proved to be regular church goers.

In almost all European countries there is a pronounced difference between urban and rural areas. The latter are more likely to maintain traditions of church going. But there are also vast regional and occupational differences cutting across the urban/rural divisions. In the Metaro district of Spain 81 per cent of the big industrialists attend mass, but only 5 per cent of the industrial labourers (Almerich, 1972: 470). In a survey in Lausanne, Switzerland, 69 per cent of executives had attended mass on a specific Sunday, but only 27 per cent of the skilled workers and 15 per cent of the manual labourers. However, in a Genevan survey only 2.5 per cent of Protestant workmen had attended church on the survey date and only 4 per cent of the upper middle class (Campiche, 1972: 520).

Recently Stoetzel (1983: 83) summarised the data from the European Value Systems Study on religion and occupation and concluded that farmers were the most religious group. They exceeded the average by 10 per cent. Employers, managers and professional workers represented the average. The unskilled manual, office and clerical workers were less religious, but least religious of all were the unemployed and skilled manual workers. Stoetzel (ibid.: 106) bases these observations on a variety of indicators of 'religiousness': worship, beliefs, prayer, importance of God, claims of being religious etc. The problem with this summary of European data is that it obscures large regional and local differences much more than a similar summary in Australia.

It is interesting to conjecture why Australian patterns resemble English rather than American patterns. It seems that the greater the contrast in life styles, income levels, and occupational milieux in the past, the less effectively churches have been able to integrate particular communities. In other words, although religion has contributed to the integration of a community, it has not been strong enough always to offset the inexorable forces of social differentiation. The world wide tendency of country dwellers to be more involved religiously can be explained partly by the existing homogeneity of rural communities and the visibility of occupational tasks and social behaviour. If, as in the USA, suburban interest in religion is high, it is the very invisibility of large segments of individual existence and the occupational atomisation which has increased the attraction of the relatively few integrative institutions.

Religion is sometimes seen as an antidote to the anxieties of a world which is moving too fast, but if a religious institution is to fulfil this function, it must have behind it a tradition of religious strength. In Europe the sharp divisions between occupational classes and life styles appear to have impaired the historical integrative function of the churches more than in the English speaking world. If in Europe specific population segments have become alienated from religion, it is because the religious institutions served to integrate other segments, generally those with which there were historic ties of power, life style and recruitment. Often this was the older bourgeoisie. To some extent this was true in nineteenth century England as well, for MacIntyre (1967: 15) relates the apostasy of the rural workers moving to the cities to the segmentation of their new environment. They came from a 'community in which it could be intelligibly and credibly claimed that the norms which govern social life had universal and cosmic significance, and were God-given'. However, in the industrial cities, 'the officially endorsed norms (were) so clearly of utility only to certain partial and partisan human interests that it [was] impossible to clothe them with universal and cosmic significance'. MacIntyre goes on to explain that the reason why working class people in England continued to believe in God and lacked the anticlericalism of their European counterparts, lies in the development of crucial relations of class cooperation from 1865 to 1875 (ibid.: 23) and the basic agreement on such values as pragmatism, cooperativeness, fair play, tolerance, a gift for compromise, and fairness (ibid.: 24). This ruled out any kind of metaphysical exclusivism and cosmic sanction for one class compared with another; 'hence, in part at least, the failure of the Labour Churches and of Marxism' (ibid.: 30). This also allowed for the survival of a 'strong vestigial Christianity, manifested whenever at times of birth, marriage and death questions about meaning, purpose, and survival became inescapable' (ibid.: 31).

A certain amount of levelling also appears to occur in Europe. The churches' alliance with the old bourgeoisie is less exclusive than it used to be. In expanding areas the newer middle classes form the fundamental support of religious institutions. In future the churches' alienation of population segments may decrease, if only because divisions in life styles and economic differences are now less noticeable. Still, the very forces of secularisation which have accompanied both social differentiation and the ethos of rationality are likely to provide a counter balance, resulting in stabilisation rather than increase of influence of religious institutions.

The level of stabilisation is also likely to differ from country to country or, in Europe, from region to region, according to the historic forces which pushed the churches on the periphery. In American culture, the foundations of which were laid in a climate conducive to religion, the lower classes were never estranged; firstly because of the favourable opportunity structures of a rural frontier, secondly because of the virility of the lower class religions, such as the Methodist and Baptist churches, and thirdly because an ever expanding frontier allowed the lower classes to participate equally in community building. None of these factors was present to the same extent in Australia.

MacIntyre in his attempt to explain the difference between American and English class-religiosity overlooks these factors, and focuses on the secularisation of the American churches. Still, the religious adjustment to man's more mundane values took place in all other countries. The discriminating variable is not the churches' capacity to accommodate values such as egalitarianism, but the accessibility of upper class symbols to the lower classes in the USA and the resulting lack of religious legitimation of particular classes.

In Australia, on the other hand, the frontier was generally more congenial to the man with capital who could afford large holdings. The worker was more inclined to seek urban areas than his American counterpart, and the fervent Protestant lower class denominations never had the impact on the worker that the Methodist and Baptist churches had in the United States.

Yet these workers were not alienated from Australian society and its religious institutions, partly because of the egalitarian tradition of all newly settled countries where labour of any kind is scarce, but mainly because the mother country itself managed to keep lower classes and religious institutions in some kind of accord, however strained. In Australia, as well as Britain, the worker attempts to justify and excuse himself for his general lack of interest in the churches, whereas in many parts of Europe his anticlericalism would preclude any such accord. The strands of ethical and Christian idealism in both the British and Australian labour parties contrast with the anti-church militancy of many European socialists and Marxists. However, on the other hand the favourable attitude to religion of all political parties seems to show that in the USA the religious involvement of the worker precludes even the lukewarm British/Australian variety of leftist convictions and neutral religious sentiments.

So far, the burden of the argument has been that the relative similarity of religious interest of the various occupational classes in Australia is the result of the absence of deep class cleavages, and the absence of a militant leftist movement which would have provided similar integrative functions for the working class as religious institutions provided for the bourgeoisie.

There are however other factors. There is evidence that in the homogeneously Catholic or Protestant countries of Europe, Catholicism was better able to keep a hold on the various classes than Protestantism. There is also evidence that in the religiously heterogeneous countries the churches are stronger than in homogeneous ones. Australia is not an exception to this general rule. Religious pluralism prevented any of the churches from resting on their laurels, or from being unconcerned about their lack of influence on any of the occupational classes. In Australia the capacity of the Catholic Church to keep all classes more effectively under its wing than the Protestant churches, appears to fit in with the general pattern. Yet, any national pattern has its own idiosyncracies. The Irish issue, Catholic schools, the dedication of celibate clergy and brothers, all had an effect on the maintenance of Catholic influence over all its members. In Australia and the newer countries one can often lean on global variables for one's explanation, whereas in some European countries specific regional and local differences have to enter into any analysis.

Two global conclusions stand out from our investigations of class and religion in Australia.

Firstly, items such as education and voting behaviour in Australia are more bound up with stratification or class than religion. Religious practices and many attitudinal variables do not relate strongly with items of class. This may caution us to take the sociological reality behind the 'myth' of egalitarianism and classlessness in Australia more seriously. There are many countries where these relations are much stronger. The following may be a good criterion of the classlessness of a society: over how wide a field are indicators of class significantly and strongly associated with other variables and values? If there are not many of the latter one may be justified in speaking of a relatively classless society. In research the really significant questions lie in this word 'relatively' and in the charting of those areas where 'class' has no effect.

Secondly, it is because of the comparative absence of strong correlations of the religious items with occupation, mobility, education, kind and length of residence, that the inter-denominational differences on these religious items are highlighted. The research points spontaneously to such questions as: why are the significant religious differences so often related to types of denomination or ethical issues, rather than to items of class?

9 Politics

I have assumed that society consists of jostling subsystems, co-operating but also contending, and that the amount of collaboration is determined by whatever contributes to the survival of either the system as a whole or its subordinate parts. In this chapter therefore I will look first at the initial close cooperation between church and state, making place for an increasing separation between the two. Because formal or informal alliances continued to persist I shall then look at the links between political parties and churches. The final section investigates whether or not religious practices have an effect on voting patterns.

Church and state

When Australia was colonised the political authorities did not depend, as they had in other countries in earlier eras, on religious legitimation. Certainly religion was regarded as a necessary force to promote good morals. However, the struggle of the first clergy for facilities, emoluments and recognition is a telling expression of the ambiguous place assigned to them by the state. Johnson, the first chaplain, had to conduct worship in the open and when after more than five years he completed a wattle and daub church, his expenditures were not refunded until four years later (Border, 1962: 18). There was, of course, the British state church precedent. Common sense of the rulers encouraged the official protection of the churches. A successful governor was one who could control friction and disorder in the new settlement. A semblance of moral unanimity, a self enforcement of norms and a taken for granted acceptance of his rule greatly advanced his personal success.

'Religion' to the early governors of New South Wales meant the Church of England. Two years after the establishment of the colony, instructions were issued to Governor Phillip 'to allot to each township, which should be marked out, 400 acres for the maintenance of the minister, and 200 acres for the maintenance of a schoolmaster'

(Burton, 1840: 19). 'The minister' was, 'the Church of England Minister' but opinions differ as to whether the Church of England actually was the established church. Gregory (1960: 6) says: 'One can cite legal opinion for and against; viewed historically, the answer seems to be that until about 1836, the Church of England was the most favoured church and that, in so far as the Home government thought about its legal position at all, it thought of it as an established church.'

It soon became necessary to clarify the situation. The Church of England could hardly claim a majority of the New South Wales population. Other denominations such as the Catholic (Clark, 1962: 350–351) and Presbyterian protested loudly against the favouritism shown to the Church of England. By 1825 Catholic and Presbyterian chaplains were also given allowances from colonial funds, although a disproportionate share still went to the Church of England. In 1836 a Church Act revised the unequal system by allocating colonial funds to supplement the voluntary contributions of the three denominations without discrimination. It provided that the government would subsidise pound for pound (up to a limit of £1000) the amount raised by individuals for building a church or parsonage after the initial £300 had been collected. It also agreed to pay £100 for the minister's stipend, if 100 adult residents indicated through their signatures that they wanted to attend the church in question. The amount was increased to £200 for 500 signatures. The system remained in spite of Anglican Bishop Broughton's angry protests that it was morally wrong and socially dangerous for the state to support true and false doctrines alike (Gregory, 1960: 22). This pattern of multiple establishment was followed by the other Australian colonies when they were founded. Grants to churches were substantial. In 1841 about 8 per cent of the total estimated expenditure of New South Wales went to the churches (ibid.: 19).

The result of the act was that between '1836 and 1850 church accommodation increased four and a half times while population grew only one and a half times; the number of clergymen in New South Wales increased from 35 to 150' (Bollen, 1973: 21).

One wonders why a system so favourable to the churches was abandoned later in the nineteenth century. Gregory rejects the view that agnosticism, voluntaryism (with its attacks by the believers on the debilitating influence of state support) and sectarian suspicion were the prime reasons.

> . . . at bottom the abolition of State aid to religion and the introduction of a secular system of public education were pieces of liberal reform not inspired by any doctrinaire rejection of the value of religion nor by any desire to persecute the Church, Protestant or Roman Catholic, but rather by a

determination to make the State, in action and in law, the symbol of a common citizenship (Gregory, 1960: 88).

Yet Gregory is suggesting a reason which does not differ essentially from the sectarianism he has just rejected. When the society-integrating role of religion has been weakened by contention between religious institutions, the state may take over that role and become the carrier of a unifying symbolism. This is more likely to take place in times of incipient nationhood and strong nationalism. In countries with one religion, specific churches are 'established' even now and derive at least some of their finances from the state.

More pertinent to the argument and equally applicable to all western countries in the nineteenth century is the increasing differentiation of religious and political functions. The abandonment of state aid is the Australian expression of this process. The more stable, autonomously legitimate and representative the political order, the less it was obliged to lean on other social institutions.

Yet this did not mean that at the time of federation in 1901 religion was absent from documents and ceremonies. The preamble to the Constitution Act included (at the instigation of various churchmen) the words 'humbly relying on the blessing of Almighty God' (Black, 1983a: 7), and the actual ceremony was opened with the singing of the old One Hundreth Psalm. Prayers were offered and up to the present both Houses of Parliament still open their sittings with an act of worship. Phillips (1981: 3) mentions that this practice of daily prayer followed also in the states, although before federation the habit had been rejected in New South Wales.

As in the USA, the separation of church and state in Australia is stated in the constitution. Section 116 of the Federal Constitution provides that:

> The Commonwealth shall not make any law for establishing any religion, or for imposing any religious observance, or for prohibiting the free exercise of any religion, and no religious test shall be required for any office or public trust under the Commonwealth.

Contrary to the First Amendment to the USA Constitution, however, section 116 is rarely litigated (Webb, 1960: 113). In Australia at present financial aid is given by the federal and state governments to denominational schools, religious instruction is provided in government schools, and religious programmes, both on national and commercial radio and television, are given preferential treatment. (ibid.: 116). This does not perturb the population at large. Various Gallup polls show a decreasing objection to financial aid for denominational schools.

Yet the population objects to advice from the pulpit as to how it should vote. In a 1956 Gallup poll 87 per cent were opposed to church leaders advising members how to vote. In a 1960 poll, 88 per cent was of the opinion that church leaders had no right to tell their members whom to select. Although the Catholic percentages were lower (80 per cent in the 1956 poll, 71 per cent in the 1960 poll), there seems to be a fairly well established unanimity on the issue by all denominations. At least some Catholic leaders are content for the Catholic layman to make up his own mind. On 8 March 1969 the Catholic Archbishop Knox of Melbourne said on television, in reply to a question regarding political choices, that it was in this area that 'we leave the laity to do their own jobs, and I think it is their responsibility' (Grant, 1969). This 'hands off' consensus is counterbalanced by a similar agreement to protect church leaders against abuse, including such a mild and common invective as 'bloody' in their presence. Blasphemy is punished, but is carefully defined by the law. The Tasmanian Criminal Code declares that it is not blasphemy 'to express in good faith and in decent language, or to attempt to establish by arguments used in good faith and conveyed in decent language, any opinion whatever upon any religious subject' (Campbell and Whitmore, 1966: 207). All of which goes to show that in Australia law and popular opinion go hand in hand to protect and separate the religious sector.

Yet this does not mean that there is no interaction between religion and politics. Several abortive attempts have been made in the past to establish denominational parties. Catholics in New South Wales launched the Democratic Party after World War 1 (Spann, 1961: 130). It had one candidate elected in 1922, but soon disappeared from the scene. The Protestant Labor Party ran nineteen candidates at the 1925 New South Wales state elections, but won only one seat. A Protestant Labor Party in Queensland similarly won only one seat in 1938. The reason these parties were not successful, when their counterparts in Europe could establish themselves, lies in the Australian electoral system. Regional representation, as in other English speaking countries, makes it almost impossible for a minority party to survive, unless like the Australian Country Party (nowadays the National Party) it can obtain a majority in at least some regions. The electoral system also made existence difficult for the Democratic Labor Party. This party emerged from the 1955 split in the Australian Labor Party over Catholic versus communist influence. Although the Democratic Labor Party has taken great pains not to become Catholic, in actual fact it is 'mainly organised by, and largely voted for by Catholics acting consciously as such' (ibid.: 132).

Interaction between the religious and the political scene can and does take other forms. Religious institutions can be effective pressure groups. Some examples are the many attempts by the Catholic Church to obtain state aid for denominational education. At the beginning of the twentieth century the Catholic press urged their readers to join a branch of the Labor Party (Clark, 1963: 182). During World War 1 Archbishop Mannix successfully opposed conscription. He declared himself 'totally opposed to the War and to enlistment' (Scott, 1943: 431).

Catholic pressure from 1947–1955 resulted in changes in obscenity/ blasphemy laws in several states. In the latter half of the 1960s a group of prominent Protestant Australian clergymen vociferously opposed the war in Vietnam in a widely publicised letter to the Prime Minister. During the New South Wales election of 1978 church leaders spoke out on many issues such as uranium mining, *de facto* and homosexual relations, and the morals of the politicians up for election (Millikan, 1982: 42).

Religious denominations in Australia have not been equally represented amongst the various party members: Catholics have been over-represented in the leadership of the Australian Labor Party, Protestants in the Liberal and Country Parties. This is clearly shown in the percentages of Catholic Federal Labor Members since Federation: 1901–1910, 14 per cent; 1910–1917, 21 per cent; 1917–1929, 45 per cent; 1929–1931, 45 per cent; 1931–1940, 49 per cent and 1940–1949, 50 per cent (Crisp and Bennett, 1954). Spann sums up the various investigations regarding the denominational allegiance of members of Parliament and cabinet ministers as follows:

> Overall, about two-fifths of Labor ministers, Federal and State, have been Catholics . . . The contrast with non-Labor parties is startling. There are said to be only four Catholics among non-Labor Federal Members, and only two Catholic Liberals in all the State Parliaments put together (Spann, 1961: 121).

Since Spann wrote there has been a notable decline in Catholic representation in the Australian Labor Party leadership.

More important, however, than over- and underrepresentations in the various political parties is the tendency of all nations (and sometimes even regions within nations) to sacralise their own identity. Wars have generally heightened the patriotic sentiments of Australians, and the Crown and monarchy have always solemnly objectified the sense of nationhood. The queen and her representatives legitimate hierarchical relations between federal and state governments and act as the conscience of the nation by defending the law, pardoning prisoners, rewarding performances and achievements. The National Anthem and the Australian flag reinforce commitment to the nation.

People may often fidget during its singing, but there are also occasions, when an important international sporting event (such as the America's Cup in sailing) is won, that the playing of the anthem and the sight of the flag tug at heartstrings. Unique to Australia and New Zealand is the Anzac myth unifying both nations. It celebrates the mateship of the fighting troops, yet also re-lives the tragic defeat at Gallipoli in 1915.

To call these sentiments 'religious' is not stretching the definition of religion. Religion in any of its forms, orders through transcendental-isation, anchors emotions, enacts sameness and dramatises through reconciling opposites. If through separation and organisational competition the churches are hindered in reinforcing the national identity, sacralisation seems to emerge from the social fabric and to express itself through pageants, anthems, parades, solemn flag raising and national myths. This has happened in Australia as much as anywhere else.

Parties and churches

There is little documented evidence of Protestant church leaders influencing the political allegiance of their flocks in the nineteenth century. This does not mean that they did not do so. They were usual-ly conservative in outlook and supported the opponents of Labor at a time when the Catholic hierarchy began to develop some sympathies towards that party (O'Farrell, 1968: 184).

In the twentieth century Protestant clergy were vocal about the con-scription issue on World War 1. During the depression several of them did not hide their political inclination. During the Victorian State elections of April 1932 the Anglican Archbishop of Melbourne pub-lished a letter in the *Church of England Messenger*,

... in which he told upright and Protestant Melbourne that they had an opportunity to save the rest of Australia from financial collapse if they as Christians and churchmen displayed their stand for honesty by voting for the United Australia Party (Clark, 1963: 212).

The Catholic hierarchy has been quite openly involved in Australian politics. In the 1890s, Cardinal Moran of Sydney expressed his sym-pathy for the Labor Party, not so much because it was led by Cath-olics as because it was a party of wage workers (Ford, 1966: 97). So did Archbishop Carr in Melbourne (O'Farrell, 1968: 188). Yet the relationship between Catholicism and Labor, both then and later re-mained tenuous, for in that same period Bishop Dunne of Brisbane was not well disposed towards it and neither were the two Sydney Catholic newspapers. O'Farrell (ibid.: 187ff.), again and again uses the word 'drift'. Catholics drifted, he says, into the Labor Party, partly because it was, in Catholic eyes, the only party not patently tainted by bigotry, partly because of the principles of Leo XIII's *Rerum Novarum*, but, more important, because it was more amenable to the social and economic circumstances of its membership. Still Catholics were uneasy about alignment with the militantly socialist sections of the Labor movement, even when they were led by apostles of their own church (Clark, 1955: 662). In the second decade of the twentieth century Archbishop Mannix of Melbourne illustrated the ambiguity of the Labor/Catholic relationship. He strongly denounced Labor's secular education plank as violating Catholic conscience (ibid.: 210). Yet he was also a friend of the men who controlled the Labor Party Machine in that state and was 'prominent in the fight against conscription when the Labor Movement opposed their Federal Leader, Prime Minister W.M. Hughes during World War 1' (Truman, 1960: 11). Until this controversy, Labor's leadership was in the hands of those of Scottish or English rather than those of Irish descent. 'Most of these leaders were Protestants who supported conscription and when they left the party, or were expelled, many of them were replaced by Catholics' (Overacker, 1968: 36-37).

Although the majority of the Catholic hierarchy was on the anti-conscription side, a small group of 'upper class' Catholics vociferously opposed them (O'Farrell, 1968: 227). This lack of Catholic unanimity was even more obvious in 1955, when Catholic and communist tensions within the Australian Labor Party came to a head and Archbishop Mannix of Melbourne supported what later became the new Democratic Labor Party. It was then that Cardinal Gilroy of Sydney 'disapproved of these activities and took the position that by withdrawing from the Australian Labor Party Catholics weakened their chances of influencing its policy and opened the way for extremist elements, including the communists' (Overacker, 1968: 146).

All this could not fail to have an effect on the Catholic vote. Catholics in the past have been consistently more inclined than Protestants to vote Labor. After the split in 1955, Catholics in Victoria were more inclined to vote Democratic Labor Party. (McCoy, 1965: 199). Evidence of overrepresentation of the Australian Labor Party vote amongst Catholics comes from Gallup poll data. In the September 1951 Gallup poll, 69 per cent of Catholics preferred the Australian Labor Party, but only 49 per cent of Anglicans, 51 per cent of Methodists and 40 per cent of Presbyterians. Even after the Australian Labor Party/Democratic Labor Party split, the majority of Catholics in five polls from 1955-1961 preferred the Australian Labor Party (percentages range from 52–58 with a median of 54). Similar percentages for Anglicans range from 42–53 (median 46), for Methodists 40–50 (median 48), and for Presbyterians 38–43 (median 42). Alford (1963: 202) shows convincingly that even within similar types of occupation Catholics are still more likely to prefer the Australian Labor Party, but that religious rather than class voting is usually more marked among persons in non-manual occupations. The Democratic Labor Party supporters came disproportionately from Catholic non-manual workers who go to church regularly. Similar differences between voting patterns of Catholics and Protestants have been found in other countries (Lipset, 1964: 60–89).

As in the Gallup polls, the 1966 Religion in Australia Survey found that Catholics were slightly underrepresented among those who favoured the Liberal and Country Parties and much overrepresented among those who favoured the Democratic Labor Party. Methodists and Presbyterian on the other hand were overrepresented among those favouring the Liberal and Country Parties.

Religious practices and voting

The contribution of the 1966 Religion in Australia Survey was not so much in confirming what was already known about voting and denomination but in the finding that church going and conservative voting went together. It showed that of those who preferred the Australian Labor Party to win if there were an election 21 per cent were regular church goers: corresponding percentages for the Liberal and Country Parties and the Democratic Labor Party were 37 per cent and 69 per cent. Those who preferred the Australian Labor Party were also less likely to pray daily (24 per cent) than those who preferred the Liberal/Country Parties (34 per cent) and particularly those who preferred the Democratic Labor Party (66 per cent).

These differences were unexpected to Australians in general and to Labor members in particular. Yet at least one foreign observer writing about the Australian worker in 1901 expressed astonishment that the differences were not any greater. After saying that the Australian worker had become a 'gentleman' and that except during working hours the external difference between the worker and the *bourgeois* was diminishing, he goes on to say:

> Religion and religious forms are the object of even greater veneration, if that is possible. Many of the supporters of the "Labor Policy" say grace before every meal, go to church on Sundays and strictly observe the Sabbath as a day of rest. They would not tolerate the principles of Christianity to be questioned. (Métin, 1955: 676).

Returning to the Religion in Australia Survey: of those who preferred the Australian Labor Party, 41 per cent have had an experience of the presence of God; the percentage for those who prefer the Liberal/Country Parties is 51 per cent and the Democratic Labor Party 68 per cent.

Similarly with belief in God. Of those who would like to see the Australian Labor Party win, 39 per cent know that God really exists. The corresponding percentage for the Liberal/Country Parties is 50 per cent, for the Democratic Labor Party 77 per cent.

There is another difference between the Democratic Labor Party on the one hand and the Australian Labor Party, Liberal/Country Parties on the other. Fifty-two per cent of those who prefer the Democratic Labor Party have the majority of their closest friends in the local church. Corresponding percentages for the Australian Labor Party and Liberal/Country Parties are both 30.

There were also significant differences in attitudes and opinions among the respondents according to which party they would like to see win. For instance: percentages of those who agreed that it does not matter what one believes as long as one leads a moral life were: Australian Labor Party 84 per cent, Liberal/Country Parties 70 per cent, Democratic Labor Party 49 per cent. Percentages of those who thought that it was not necessary to go to church to be a Christian were: Australian Labor Party 80 per cent, Liberal/Country Parties 71 per cent, Democratic Labor Party 54 per cent. Percentages of those who admired the person who was very patriotic were: Australian Labor Party 41 per cent, Liberal/Country Parties 56 per cent, Democratic Labor Party 59 per cent. Percentages of those who disapproved of the person who had sex relations before marriage were: Australian Labor Party 50 per cent, Liberal/Country Parties 67 per cent, Democratic Labor Party 80 per cent. Percentages of those who disapproved of people who had a small job on the side and did not declare it for income tax purposes were: Australian Labor Party 26 per cent, Liberal/Country Parties 42 per cent, Democratic Labor Party 35 per cent.

On other issues, such as adultery, driving and drinking, being very ambitious, trying to get ahead, there were hardly any differences between the respondents.

What happens when we look at both denomination and church going together? Which variable is the stronger predictor? The 1966 Religion in Australia Survey found that church attendance was stronger than denomination. Other surveys at the time showed the same pattern. Is this still true in the 1980s, when, as we have seen in previous chapters church attendance has dropped considerably compared with the 1960s?

Four Melbourne *Age* surveys, analysed with this question in mind, show that church going is even now the stronger of the two variables. The November 1979 survey showed that 28 per cent of the regular Anglicans (n = 85) would vote ALP if a federal election was held, compared with 47 per cent of irregular ones (n = 664). For Catholics the comparable figures were 41 per cent (n = 248) and 57 per cent (n = 338). This means that if church going is held constant, denomination makes on average 11.5 per cent difference; if denomination is held constant church going makes on average 17.5 per cent difference.

The September 1980 survey showed that of the regular Anglicans (n = 70) 30 per cent would vote ALP if a federal election were held, compared with 54 per cent of irregular ones (n = 492). For Catholics the comparable figures were 42 per cent (n = 176) and 66 per cent (n = 280). This means that if church going is held constant, denomination makes on average 12 per cent difference; if denomination is held constant church going makes 24 per cent difference.

The only exception to the tendency of church going to be the stronger determinant is the October 1980 survey. It showed that 40 per cent of the regular Anglicans (n = 82) would vote ALP if a federal election were held, compared with 47 per cent of the irregular ones (n = 541). For Catholics the comparable figures were 49 per cent (n = 211) and 60 per cent (n = 284). This means that if church going is held constant, denomination makes on average 11 per cent difference; if denomination is held constant, church going makes on average 9 per cent difference.

The last of the four surveys (November 1981) showed that 40 per cent of the regular Anglicans (n = 82) would vote ALP if a federal election were held, compared with 48 per cent of irregular ones (n = 539). For Catholics the comparable figures were 38 per cent (n = 222) and 61 per cent (n = 288). This means that if church going is held constant, denomination makes on average 5.5 per cent difference; if denomination is held constant church going makes on average 15.5 per cent difference.

How can we explain these findings? One explanatory variable which comes to mind is class or occupation. It is on this factor that Australian political scientists have concentrated. The lower occupational categories (unskilled workers, for example) may both prefer the Australian Labor Party and rarely attend church. In other words 'church going' as a distinguishing or independent category may disappear when we look at each of the occupational categories in turn. Of all respondents of the 1966 Religion in Australia Survey who hoped to see the Australian Labor Party win at an election, and who were either in the workforce or were wives of respondents in the work force (n = 403), 49 per cent were in the lower occupational categories. Corresponding percentages for the Democratic Labor Party (n = 64) and Liberal/Country Parties (n = 628) were 16 per cent and 17 per cent.

Table 9.1 shows that occupation is an important factor: on average 22 per cent more of the lower occupations favour the Australian Labor Party than the upper ones, when denomination and church going are held constant. Yet on average 17 per cent more of the irregulars tend to vote Labor when occupation and denomination are held constant. By contrast on average only 5 per cent more Catholics favour the Australian Labor Party than non-Catholics. Does this mean that although we set out to find an intervening variable in occupation for the church going/party preference pattern, we end up by finding the relative independence of both church going and occupation, and that in actual fact whether one is Catholic or not is less relevant?

Table 9.1   Percentage of respondents hoping to see ALP (L/CP in brackets)
win, by denomination, church attendance and occupation (1966)

Occupation	Catholics		Non-Catholics	
	irregular	regular	irregular	regular
Upper	31 (46)	7 (42)	17 (64)	5 (77)
(professionals, managers,	n = 13	n = 60	n = 245	n = 82
lower professionals, graziers)				
Middle	39 (27)	15 (45)	28 (44)	14 (62)
(skilled and clerical workers)	n = 44	n = 103	n = 362	n = 129
Lower	46 (24)	33 (25)	47 (24)	32 (34)
(semi-skilled and unskilled)	n = 46	n = 60	n = 292	n = 65

Note: Only respondents in the work force and their wives, who were given their husbands' occupational designation, are considered
Source: Religion in Australia Survey, 1966

The percentage of DLP voters is only significant amongst Catholics who are regular church goers: upper occupations (27 per cent), middle occupations (20 per cent), lower occupations (13 per cent). As there were few differences amongst the Protestant denominations, they were all combined in the one category 'Non-Catholics'. This had the advantage of increasing our cells. Other data (see Alford, 1963: 205) from Australian Public Opinion polls 1951–1961 suggest that generally the differences between Anglicans, Methodists and Presbyterians are small, although Presbyterians have always a lower percentage of ALP voters than Anglicans or Methodists. This was also true for the Religion in Australia Survey which found that 32 per cent of Anglicans (n = 732), 23 per cent of Methodists (n = 172) and 18 per cent of Presbyterians (n = 276) favoured the ALP. The difference between these denominations was smaller when the regular church goers were compared.

It seems to be the case that being a Catholic is less relevant than being a church goer. Yet denomination may have been more important in the past as the Gallup poll differences between 1955–1961 and 1966–1968 suggest. Some authors think that the more Catholics become equally represented in all the occupational categories, the less inclined they will be to vote Australian Labor Party (Webb, 1960: 102). In other words, what appeared in the past to be denominational voting was actually class voting. On the other hand, scholars such as Davies (1958: 146) and Alford (1963: 192) reject this view by saying that there is still a significant Australian Labor Party bias amongst Catholics, although the 1947 census showed no significant divergence in any major denomination from the average occupational pattern of membership. For another, the irregular church attending Catholics of the middle and upper occupations are true to pattern. Thirdly, denomination is still a significant variable when Liberal/Country Party voting is considered, to which topic we may now turn.

When occupation and church going are held constant, 16 per cent more non-Catholics on the average favour the Liberal/Country Parties than Catholics. When occupation and denomination are held constant, 9 per cent more regular church goers favour the Liberal/Country Parties than do irregular church goers. On the other hand, when denomination and church going are held constant, the percentage increase of respondents favouring the Liberal/Country Parties is as high as 28 per cent when upper and lower occupations are compared.

Two other national surveys carried out at about the same time as the Religion in Australia Survey made it possible to compare results. Both the 1965 Social Stratification Survey and the 1967 Australian Survey Project (see for details and acknowledgements Mol, 1971: 295ff.) showed differences on voting Labor (of 15 and 17 per cent respectively) almost identical to the Religion in Australia Survey (17 per cent) when regular and irregular church goers were compared, holding both occupation and denomination constant.

More recently Clive Bean (1983: 23) using 1979 data confirmed the independence of the church attendance variable. Using the percentages of Labor Party voters as presented in his Table 5, the difference between non-manual and manual workers is on average 22 per cent, when denomination and church going are held constant; the difference between Anglican and Catholics is 15 per cent when occupation and church going are controlled; the difference between regular and irregular church goers is 13 per cent when occupation and denomination are held constant. Bean (ibid.: 16) compared these data with New Zealand and found that from 1963 to 1981 the power of the denominational and the church attendance variables in that country had increased over the occupational one.

Hyam Gold (1979) reanalysed the 1967 Australian National Political Attitudes Survey and found that the association between religious practice and anti-Labor partisanship disappeared if he controlled for what he called 'class-alienation' among the working class Protestants (for instance manual workers identifying themselves and their closest friends as middle class). As the association does not disappear for Catholics and middle class Protestants the relative independence of the church going variable is not in question. However Gold's article draws attention to a variable (class-alienation) which should be considered in future analysis of more recent surveys. Gold suggests that in Australia religious practice is associated both with decreased identification with the working class and increased affiliation with the middle class. Yet in our chapter on class we concluded that 'class' proved not to be so important when church attendance was analysed.

Another possible 'intervening' variable which might explain the religious behaviour of the different party adherents is education. In the Religion in Australia Survey only 22 per cent of those who hoped to see the Australian Labor Party win an election had finished a secondary education. Corresponding percentages for the Democratic Labor Party and Liberal/Country Parties were 38 per cent and 39 per cent. When denomination and church going were held constant, on an average 12 per cent more of the lesser educated favoured the Australian Labor Party. When denomination and education were held constant, on an average 16 per cent more of the irregular church goers favoured the Australian Labor Party. When church going and education were held constant, on an average only 5 per cent more Catholics favoured the Australian Labor Party.

What difference do age and sex make? In the Religion in Australia Survey more males (29 per cent) than females (24 per cent) favoured the Australian Labor Party. However when age and sex were held constant, church attendance still proved to play a much more important and independent part (Mol, 1971: 298).

A recent international survey, the European Value Systems, found similar correlations between voting and religiousness. Stoetzel (1983: 79) produced an index showing the importance of God for European respondents on a scale of 100 (no importance) to 1000 (of very great importance). On this index the extreme left has a score of 410, whereas the extreme right has one of 775 with the less strongly held political positions fitting in between.

If church going is a more significant factor of voting patterns in

Australia than denomination, why is it that church going and political conservatism seem to go together? Do politically conservative citizens go to church more? 'Conservative' here should be taken to mean 'being right of centre'. It is likely that religiosity predisposes towards political conservatism rather than the other way round. The forces of secularisation are very pervasive indeed and certainly in Australia there are no known instances of people who began to go to church more often because of political orientation. There are a number of possible reasons why church goers are more conservative.

Firstly, in the past the policy of the Liberal/Country Parties regarding state aid to denominational schools must have impressed particularly those Australian Catholics with high allegiance to their Church. However, this factor does not operate in other countries where church attendance and conservative voting are associated. Nor does this account for the differences between church going and non-church going Protestants. Nor is it valid for the 1980s.

Secondly, Lipset (1964: 81) argues that the more religious members of a group are more likely to follow the dominant tendency of the group. When the average socio-economic status of the members of a given denomination is low, the whole group will tend to prefer the more liberal or leftist parties which challenge the *status quo*. The marginal members, the irregular church goers, will tend to follow less the trend of the religious group as a whole. To apply this argument to the Australian situation: nominal Catholics who disproportionately prefer the Australian Labor Party do so because they are not properly plugged into the 'communications network' of the Catholic Church. They have not kept up with the changing trend of fellow church going Catholics, which is away from Labor sympathies. However this answer begs the question. Why have church going Catholics and Labor moved away from each other? Also it cannot be presumed that in amorphous Protestantism the local bodies of church goers have a similar effect on the voting patterns.

Thirdly, Lipset (ibid.: 87) has another answer. It may be, he says, that doctrinal emphases, such as Catholic sympathy for collective trade union objectives and community responsibility and Protestant stress on individual self reliance, can explain why in the USA Catholics are more prone to vote for the Democratic Party. In Australia, Crisp (1955: 293) has pointed to the congruence of Papal teachings and the Australian Labor Party understanding of 'socialisation'. However, this should have kept church going Catholics in the Democratic or Labor corner. Instead we see that Catholics who attend church regularly have a stronger preference for conservative parties than those who do not attend regularly.

Fourthly, maybe the answer lies in an area even more basic than institutional loyalties and allegiance. In Australian history the Labor Party was least liked by Catholics when it was at its most militant. This was true for the early beginnings as well as the 1950s when the aversion felt by Catholics for the methodical dedication of the extreme left wingers and communists was at a fever pitch. Maybe church going Catholics and non-Catholics alike will feel more inclined to compromise religious and political orientations, if the latter do not encroach on the former through an emotion laden, commitment requiring, unifying view of reality, but concern themselves solely with technical, even opportunistic service to a religiously pluralistic constituency. Whatever the merits of this answer, it at least makes sense in terms of the institutional division of labour in society: the more 'religious' a political orientation, the more it will appear to compete with the religious commitment of the church goer. Still, it is deficient in that it presumes that church goers have a high religious commitment. This is not necessarily so. Nevertheless the merit of the answer increases when we compare the percentage of regular church goers (n = 603) of the 1966 Religion in Australia Survey who hope to see the Australian Labor Party win (17 per cent) with the percentage of regular church goers who pray daily and believe in God without doubt (n = 311) and who hope to see the Australian Labor Party win (12 per cent). The value of the answer increases even more when we compare the 12 per cent who prefer the Australian Labor Party to win with the 23 per cent of Australian Labor Party voters in the category of 'public' believers (n = 177), who go to church regularly but do *not* pray daily.

Fifthly, parallel to the fourth reason is the suggestion that the integrative function of religion for both society and the individual predisposes the believer to accept meaning in terms of what is given by consolidation of the *status quo*, or to tie the divergent strands of existence together in terms of future salvation by transcending the incongenial *status quo*. In both instances salvation is not seen in terms of political and social change for which the political left aims.

Whatever the answer, there is evidence in Australia that it is risky to maintain that there is an independent Catholic pro-Australian Labor Party tradition. All one can say is that this independent Catholic tradition may be more typical for the non-church going Catholic than for the church going one.

Conclusion

Rather than summarise what might seem to be an avalanche of dispersed data I will suggest a frame of reference for the findings of this book. What do they mean in a coherent context? Elsewhere I have defined religion as 'the sacralisation of identity' (Mol, 1976: 1). By this I meant that religion in any shape or form tends to reinforce a large variety of units of social organisation (identities). Yet in any viable society these units (persons, families, communities, tribes, ethnic groups, nations etc.) are often at odds with one another; then religion attempts to reconcile them, sometimes through ethnic repression or sublimation of instincts (when they get in the way of family cohesion for instance), sometimes through promotion of justice (when individuals are unduly oppressed for instance), sometimes through providing the larger context for the conflict (stressing, e.g., that God loves the repentant sinner and expects individuals to treat their neighbour as they would like to be treated).

Both the historical survey data presented in this book and attendance at an Australian church on any Sunday illustrate the previous paragraph. In Chapter 1 the denominational distribution in Australia was shown to reflect the ethnic origin of the population: Anglicanism initially reinforced Englishness; Catholicism Irishness and after World War II also Polish, Italian and other national groups; Presbyterianism played a similar role in fostering Scottishness. Yet there is much more: any religious organisation is also in the business of whole-making on other than just ethnic levels. That is to say it attempts to heal what is broken and restore what is fragmented. Salvation is contrasted with sin. Nevertheless personal integrity is not defended without reservation: self denial for the sake of other forms of integrity is lauded and self affirmation at the expense of family or community is censured. Assertiveness may be good for the ego but it usually does not contribute to harmonious relations with others.

Both 'wowserism' (disapproval of gambling, drinking and other pleasures) and the survey findings that church goers are much more likely to disapprove of premarital sex and of single parenting, fit this picture. Active Christians stand on guard over normal family life and

217

therefore many insist that sexuality, being such a potent instinct, must be constrained to strengthen marital union rather than remain unconstrained for personal self-expression.

Pronouncements on social justice by the Australian mainline churches ultimately reflect the longstanding Christian and Judaic tradition of defending the good of the nation, rather than the good of one class or group in that nation. Nowadays the churches (for instance in their anti-nuclear and disarmament lobbies) often take worldwide rather than nationwide stances. The tendency of the church goer in Australia, rather than the non-church goer, to have positive feelings towards other races is a case in point: the unity of mankind rather than the unity of the predominating culture of a single country seems to have become, more than in a previous era, part of the vision.

In Australia, or more generally in the developed world, Catholicism has been more hesitant than Protestantism to favour a free rein over individual expression. Catholicism has always been more apprehensive of the damage posed by individualism to collectivities. Therefore for long periods of Australian history Catholics tended to be somewhat less prominent in both tertiary education and economic entrepreneurship where a high degree of independent thinking and private enterprise were required. Not in Australia (as far as I am aware), but in Latin countries such hesitancy has retarded the progress of lasting democratic forms of government. For the latter too a strange mixture of confident individualism and social conformity is necessary.

Yet from 1962–1965 Vatican II opened the Pandoras box and loosened its grip on its tightly controlled institutions. The effect in Australia, as in other Anglo-Celtic countries, was that in a short span of time Catholics began to differ less and less from Protestants. The percentage of individuals with tertiary degrees is now the same for both Anglicans and Catholics, if one compares those who were born in Australia of Australia born parents. Yet this loosening of grip also meant that Catholics began more and more to adopt the Protestant habit of regarding church attendance as optional: in 1966, 61 per cent of all Catholics had been to church on the preceding Sunday; in 1981 this percentage had dropped to thirty-seven. All of a sudden Catholics and Protestants found themselves united against those sections of the Australian population who took individualism (Protestants also, were tempered by allegiance to God in Whom many important collective values were summed up) to its extreme: in 1981, 68 per cent of the secularists who claimed to have 'no religion' (n = 223) found it morally acceptable to be single and to have and bring up children. Only 50 per cent agreed that it was wrong for a married person to have sex outside marriage, and only 41 per cent felt that a woman should put her husband and children ahead of her own career. These opinions stood in stark contrast to those of the church goers (Catholic and Protestant, n = 480) for whom the corresponding percentages were 25, 73 and 77.

So far we have looked primarily at 'person' and 'family' in their contending relation to one another: the church goers coming down on the family side, the secularists on the individual one. Yet it is quite clear that the cooperating relation is just as strong if not more so; individuals are shaped by their families and religion is heavily involved in the sacralisation of those values which preserve the integrity of both. Persons are also moulded by their work environment. In Australia as elsewhere women are consistently more religious than men on any of the criteria used. This may be because wives and mothers seem to be emotionally somewhat better equipped to unify through love and affection, and it this integrative and expressive role which fits well with the religious sphere. By contrast the workaday world of men appears to reward the aggressive doer; the instrumental and the expressive religious roles have much less in common. This suggestion has gained much credence recently through Stoetzel's (1983: 83) analysis of the data from the European Value System Survey. He found that women who worked full time had religious views close to those of men.

There are other units (identities) which contend and cooperate. We could have mentioned the divided allegiance between nation and ethnic group: Orthodoxy strengthens Greek ethnicity, while mainline Anglo-Celtic churches implicitly reinforce English speaking culture. There is also competition between religious organisations for the loyalty of the membership, in spite of the intrinsic unifying nature of the religious beliefs and practices of these organisations. The increasingly looser weave of modern Western societies ('pluralism' in the jargon) has put a premium on those religious organisations which have set themselves off against others. By far the fastest growing religious organisations in Australia, are the sects: Jehovah's Witnesses, Mormons, Pentecostals. In spite of the large differences between them, they all transmit a strong sense of purpose and belonging. They insist on their uniqueness, and the resulting boundaries provide a safe haven for the increasing number of individuals who feel that they are on the fringe of mainstream society, although the apparent cohesion of the latter is also something of an illusion.

Before Vatican II Catholicism in Australia had some of these same qualities associated with its purposive separation from society at large. Ever since the Catholic Church started a separate school system towards the end of last century, church attendance (which towards the middle of that century was not any higher than it is now) increased, maybe because the financial and personnel sacrifices required, paid off in terms of correspondingly greater allegiance. Thus it seems clear that although competition may clash with the intrinsic nature of religious beliefs, it has important advantages in a pluralistic world where the demand for strong guidelines balances the inevitable pragmatism and lack of concern for meaning in the secular environment.

If this is the case, the message for the mainline denominations in Australia is that in the future the accent may have to shift even more than it already has from a priestly, understanding and consoling concern for Australian culture and society, to a prophetic, critical and separatist stance. After all the secular culture may respect the churches and even hold them in high esteem, but is not likely to be persuaded by their call for self denial, self discipline and search for greater profundity. Not that true Christianity can in any way give up its priestly concern for any of man's structures! Yet for the sake of a more effective promotion of its tradition of good news and redemption, it may have to follow more closely the sectarian example of sharp boundaries.

So far I have not spelt out what I meant by 'sacralisation' and the positive way in which it reinforces the various units of social organisation. Elsewhere (Mol, 1976: 11 ff.; 1983: 112) I have said that it consists primarily of four components: transcendental ordering, emotional anchoring, sameness enacting and dialectic dramatisation. All these are involved in the reinforcing or reconciling of 'identities' as I have mentioned them so far. But something more can be said, if we take each of them separately.

1   Transcendental ordering (objectification or making order into an object) refers primarily to beliefs. It is the belief in God (however vaguely held by three-quarters of Australians) which legitimates major values and ways of acting and reacting. For most Australians it seems to be a potential refuge if the going gets rough or if confusion rears its ugly head. For a much smaller proportion God, or Jesus (His concretisation) is a source of strong belief, actually rather than potentially, guiding the interpretation of events that hurt, those that heal, those that subvert and those that build up.

Yet the majority of Australians seem to call on the consolations of belief and the churches primarily at major points of change in their lives, such as birth, death and marriage. But since Australia is affluent, the social security system encompassing and life's satisfactions plentiful, a pragmatic form of hedonism is usually sufficient. That being the case, the relativisations and the perspectives of Christianity on events and experiences are obscured by disuse. They will be dusted off once in a while, but the average non-church going Australian, who believes in God hopes secretly that there will be little necessity for getting Him out of the closet.

On the other hand the relativising aspect of belief has another connotation as well for the active laymen and church leaders: they have an articulate and detailed vision of what these beliefs entail. For them they contain criteria and blueprints for life and culture and, acting on this principle, such believers do not hesitate to decry injustices, corruptions and inequalities, wherever they find them. In other words the transcendental order in which they believe does not just conserve, it also contains prescriptions for change.

A much less Christian belief, underlying the patterns of thought and action of large numbers of successful academics may be called individual rationalism. It is the belief that the rational mind and individual scrutiny alone can interpret events and experiences. It is probably more strongly held in Australian universities than anywhere else in the non-communist world, partly because it is in Australia that theology or religious studies have such a comparatively minuscule place and effect in academia. Even if Christian intellectuals successfully argue that individual rationalism is essentially a tunnel vision because it undervalues the collective (for instance a taken for granted social order and paradigm) and the non-rational (for instance love and loyalty), their voices are not heard. Those with no religion or with atheistic beliefs are strongly overrepresented in Australian universities and assume as a matter of course that their horizons are the widest. They fail to appreciate that the Religion in Australia Survey in 1966 showed that the consistent secularists and the values they stand for are not any less a minority than the orthodox believers at the other end of the continuum.

2 Emotional anchoring (commitment) refers primarily to non-rational feelings unifying (or *not* unifying if they are absent) all the units of social organisations. Christians call it faith or trusting God, and stress it as an essential cornerstone for salvation (whole-making). Yet for the description of both boundary strengthening and reconciliation of these units of social organisation non-religious language is just as effective. Loyalty and allegiance can be measured by the sense of belonging. In the European Value System Survey (extended to Australia in 1983) 90 per cent of Australians said they were very proud of their nationality, compared with 96 per cent of Americans, 60 per cent of Dutchmen and 59 per cent of West Germans. So we have a measure of allegiance, even though we have to know a lot more in order to achieve a comprehensive analysis. Obviously in Australia Christians and non-Christians do not differ on their allegiance. Yet there are other differences; individuals who say they do not have a

religion are much more likely to favour a republic than Protestants for whom commonwealth ties are important, with Catholics somewhere in between.

The strong emphasis on love in all churches in Australia (I cannot remember ever having been to a service of a sect or denomination in which the word was not mentioned in either hymns, sermons, prayers or benedictions) is closely linked to the integrating effect it has on personality, family and group; in short on any 'identity'. It is a powerful boundary maintaining force and yet also transcends the boundary of self and family (where it is so essential for upbringing) when it includes larger groups and nations.

In the previous chapters commitment (in the form of church) attendance proved to be a rather important measurement of the strength of a religious organisation, the assumption being that the very act of going to church meant not only loyalty to God but also to the local church in which one worshipped. Like all measurements it has its inadequacies: many church goers have few links with others in the same worship service, and to assume that there is a 'community' is often assuming too much. Yet church attendance is at least one indicator of the effect a religious denomination has in Australian society. The changes in church attendance over the nearly 200 years of Australian history say something about both the receptivity of the culture to a particular Christian imprint and the waxing and waning of religious organisational strength. Taking the large view it is patently premature to think about Australia as inescapably sliding into complete secularisation. The 1970s witnessed a downfall in church attendance as compared with the 1960s, but the 22 per cent of the population who had attended church on an average Sunday in 1983 is, to all intents and purposes, the same as the 23 per cent which did the same in 1950. And both figures certainly look splendid if compared with the 40 individuals who attended the Christmas service in the newly built first church in the colony of New South Wales in 1793!

If commitment, faith, love and loyalty have conserving unifying consequences, this very unity can stand in the way of necessary change. Cooperation between denominations (I am leaving out sects because they derive their strength from boundary maintenance rather than cooperation) is more likely to occur when religious organisations also have mechanisms for de-commitment. Recently in Australia the formation of the Uniting Church showed that Congregationalism, Methodism and most of Presbyterianism could manage to de-commit. Yet this act of de-commitment proved to be facilitated by common allegiance to a source of tradition and theology which transcends organisational boundaries. And of course the uniting of the various factions of Methodism and Presbyterianism in nineteenth century

Australia is another instance of de-commitment and new commitment.

De-commitment however does not in any way apply only to the changing configurations of religious organisations. It plays a much more active part in the fragmentation of unfavoured habits and values or defunct identities about which those churches (such as Methodism and Salvation Army in the nineteenth century churches and many more sects and some denominations in the twentieth) had and have much to say. Conversion experience in all instances goes through phases of de-commitment of one pattern and commitment to another. The same applies on the more social level to charismatic leadership which spends as much time on de-committing followers from the evil past as on committing them to a glorious future. Similarly de-commitment is an essential part of all rites of passage, such as birth initiation, confirmation, marriage and burial rites. The churches contribute to orderly change by cleaning up the past before investing the future. And they can do this so effectively because of their basic commitment to a source of order, stability and continuity which resides in heaven where neither moth nor rust corrupts, rather than on earth.

3 Sameness enacting (ritual) refers to the universal tendency of religion to save the transcendental order and commitment to it from oblivion. It retraces the grooves of order. Again and again, every Sunday, in spite of the kaleidoscopic variety of articulation and expression, a church service reinforces in the participants the familiar loci of interpretation and sentiments. Most often church goers speak about being re-newed in worship, or being re-integrated after a week of onslaughts on the psyche. Yet in actual fact, but much more covertly, the non-personal sources of integrity are bolstered as well. This is illustrated by the prayer of confession which restores the sense of responsibility for others even though overtly it speaks about the sin of the individual.

In Australia as elsewhere (in Western Europe, according to Stoetzel [1983: 94], one third of those who never go to church, one quarter of those who have no religion and almost one fifth of all atheists spend some moments in prayer, meditation or contemplation) those who pray regularly and privately have stronger other-directed values and adhere less to a live-and-let-live philosophy than those who do not pray.

Under (2) I have already begun to discuss those rites (called rites of passage in the scholarly literature) which detach individuals and groups from the grooves of sameness and attach them to a new identity. The marriage ceremony (even a civil wedding) has a phase of emotional stripping from the old status or identity to the new one. The ritual guides the transition in order to contain the chaotic potential of change and to maximise sameness.

4 Dialectic dramatisation (myth, theology) refers to the represen-tation of major elements of existence, generally through contrasting basic elements or categories of that existence. Good examples are Yin (softness, receptivity, femininity) and Yang (hardness, aggressiveness, masculinity) in Chinese mythology. In Christianity heaven and hell, crucifixion and resurrection, sin and salvation, good and evil, God and satan are examples of dramatisations of beliefs. Although myth and theology are authentic repositories of the basic outlines of a culture, as such eminently 'true' and therefore legitimate objects of research in the social scientific study of religion, they have not figured much at all in this book. The main reason is the focus on historical and survey data. And yet for a comprehensive account of religion in Australia they should have a more important position. After all, these dramatisations are close to the essence of what confronts church goers Sunday after Sunday, in sermons, hymns and prayers. Their effects in terms of peace of mind or their contribution to the integration of the other units of social organisation can be examined. To date they have not attracted much attention, although anthropologists studying myths in Aboriginal society have considered them—see my own *The Firm and the Formless, Religion and Identity in Aboriginal Australia* (1982), there is certanly much scope for further research in this area in Australia. Apart from their effect, these dramatisations must also be compared with those in literature, films and TV programmes. Are the latter functional substitutes, thereby adding to the irrelevance of religion? Or does the titillating character of many of the media dramatisations leave room for the more reflective, depth centred nature of theological exposition? There are certainly no answers yet for these and other questions raised in this conclusion.

Bibliography

This list contains publishing details of books mentioned in the text

Abbott, Walter M.S.J. (ed.), *The Documents of Vatican II* London: Chapman, 1966

Acquaviva, Sabino S. *Der Untergang des Heiligen in der Industriellen Gesellschaft* Essen: Ludgerus Verlag, 1964

Adams, Francis W.L. *The Australians: A Social Sketch* London: Unwin, 1893

Albinski, Henry S. *The Australian Labor Party and the Aid to Parochial Schools Controversy* Pennsylvania State University Studies, No. 19, July 1966

Allan, J. Alexander *Men and Manners in Australia* Melbourne: Cheshire, 1945

Alford, Robert R. *Party and Society: The Anglo-American Democracies* Chicago: Rand McNally, 1963

—— 'Class Voting in the Anglo-American Political Systems' in *Party Systems and Voting Alignments: Cross-National Perspectives* Seymour M. Lipset and Stein Rokkan (eds.), New York: Free Press, 1967

Allingham, John D. 'Occupational Mobility in Australia' unpublished PhD Thesis Canberra: Australian National University, 1965

Allport, Gordon, *The Individual and his Religion: A Psychological Interpretation* New York: Macmillan, 1957

—— 'Behavioural Science, Religion and Mental Health' *Journal of Religion and Health*, 2 (3), 1963

—— 'The Religious Context of Prejudice' *Journal for the Scientific Study of Religion* 5 (3), Fall 1966

Almerich, Paulina 'Spain' in Mol et al. (eds.) *Western Religion* The Hague: Mouton, 1972

Anderson, Don. S., 'Do Catholic Schools Cause People to go to Church' *The Australian and New Zealand Journal of Sociology* 7, 1, 1971, pp. 65–67

Anderson, Kevin V., *Report of the Board of Inquiry into Scientology* Melbourne: Government Printer, 1965

Arendsberg, C.M. and Kimball, S.T. *Family and Community in Ireland* Cambridge, Mass: Harvard University Press, 1948

Argyle, Michael *Religious Behaviour* London: Routledge and Kegan Paul, 1958

225

Austin, A.G. *Australian Education 1788–1900* Melbourne: Pitman, 1961

Barcan, A. 'Education and Catholic Social Status' *Australian Quarterly* 34, 1962

Barrett, John *That Better Country (The Religious Aspect of Life in Eastern Australia, 1835–1850)* Melbourne: Melbourne University Press, 1966

Bean, Clive 'Some aspects of Social Structure and Party Support in Australia and New Zealand' unpublished paper given at the Australian National University on Monday 31 October 1983

Bennie, Christopher 'Personal Meaning in the Charismatic Renewal Movement: A Verstehen Approach' in Hayes, Victor, C. (ed.) *Religious Experience in World Religions* Bedford Park, S.A.: The Australian Association for the Study of Religion, 1980, pp. 60–77

Benson, C.I. *A Century of Victorian Methodism* Melbourne: Spectator Publishing Co., 1935

Berger, Peter L. and Luckmann, Thomas A., *The Social Construction of Reality* London: The Penguin Press, 1967

Berthelsen, Lionel D. 'Protestant Church Membership' in Harris, Dorothy; Hynd, Douglas; Millikan, David (eds). *The Shape of Belief* Homebush NSW: Lancer 1982, pp. 289–293

Bigge, J.T. *Report of the Commissioner of Inquiry into the State of the Colony of New South Wales* 3 Volumes, London: House of Commons, 1822, 1823

Binney, Thomas, *Lights and Shadows of Church-life in Australia* London: Jackson and Walford, 1860

Black, Alan W. and Glasner, Peter E. *Practice and Belief (Studies in the Sociology of Australian Religion)* Sydney: Allen and Unwin, 1983

Black, Alan W. 'Introduction' in Black, Alan W. and Glasner, Peter E. (eds.), *Practice and Belief* Sydney: Allen and Unwin 1983a, pp. 1–14

Black, Alan, W. 'The Sociology of Ecumenism: Initial Observations on the formation of the Uniting Church in Australia' in Black, Alan and Glasner, Peter (eds.), *Practice and Beliefs* Sydney: Allen and Unwin 1983b, pp. 86–107

Black, Alan, W. 'Organised Irreligion: The New South Wales Humanist Society' in Black, Alan, and Glasner, Peter (eds.), *Practice and Belief* Sydney: Allen and Unwin 1983c pp. 154–166

Black, Alan, W. 'Church Union in Canada and Australia: A Comparative Analysis' *Australian-Canadian Studies* vol. 1. 1983d pp. 44–56

Black, Alan, W. 'The Impact of Theological Orientation and of Breadth of Perspective on Church Members' Attitudes and Behaviours: Roof, Mol and Kaill Revisited' *Journal for the Scientific Study of Religion* forthcoming 1985

Blaikie, Norman W.H. 'Religion and Social Status *The Australian and New Zealand Journal of Sociology* vol. 5, no. 1, April 1963, pp. 14–41

Blaikie, N.W.H. 'Religious Groups and World Views' in Hunt, F.J. (ed.) *Socialization in Australia* Melbourne: Australian International Press, 1978, pp. 147–169

Blaikie, N.W.H. *The Plight of the Australian Clergy: To Convert, Care or Challenge* St. Lucia: University of Queensland Press, 1979

Blaikie, N.W.H. 'Styles of Ministry: Some Aspects of the Relationships between "The Church" and "the World"' in Black, Alan and Glasner, Peter (eds.), *Practice and Belief* Sydney: Allen and Unwin 1983, pp. 43–61

Blainey, Geoffrey *The Tyranny of Distance* Melbourne: Sun Books, 1966

Bodycomb, J. *The Naked Clergyman* Melbourne: Joint Board of Christian Education of Australia and New Zealand, 1979

Bollen, J.D. *Religion in Australian Society* Sydney: Leigh College Open Lectures, 1973

Bonwick, James *Australia's First Preacher: the Rev. Richard Johnson* London: Sampson Low, Marston & Co., 1898

Booth, Charles 'Life and Labour of the People in London', *Religious Influences* Third Series, 7, London: Macmillan, 1902–3

Border, J.T. Ross, *Church and State in Australia 1788–1872: A Constitutional Study of the Church of England in Australia* London: SPCK, 1962

Bos, Robert 'Fusing Aboriginal and Christian Tradition' in (eds.) Harris, Dorothy, Hynd, Douglas and Millikan, David (eds.), *The Shape of Belief* Homebush NSW: Lancer, 1982, pp. 132–139

Bossard, James H.S. and Boll, Eleanor Stoker *One Marriage Two Faiths* New York: The Ronald Press Co., 1957

Boulard, F., *An Introduction to Religious Sociology* London: Darton, Longman and Todd, 1960

Bouma, Gary, D. 'Australian Religiosity: Some Trends Since 1966' in Black, Alan and Glasner, Peter (eds.), *Practice and Belief* Sydney: Allen and Unwin, 1983, pp. 15–24

Brady, V. *A Crucible of Prophets: Australians and Question of God* Sydney: Theological Explorations, 1981

Brauer, A., *Under the Southern Cross: History of the Evangelical Lutheran Church of Australia* Adelaide: Lutheran Publishing House, 1956

Brennan, T. 'Urban Communities' in *Australian Society* (ed. A. Davies and S. Encel), Melbourne: Cheshire, 1965

Brooks, Hugh E. and Henry, Franklin J. 'An Empirical Study of the Relationship of Catholic Practice and Occupational Mobility to Fertility' *Millbank Memorial Fund Quarterly*, 36 (3), 1958

Broom, Leonard and Glenn, Norvall D. 'Religious Differences in Reported Attitudes and Behaviour' *Sociological Analysis*, 27 (4), Winter 1966

Broom, Leonard and Jones, F. Lancaster *Opportunity and Attainment in Australia* Canberra: Australian National University Press, 1976

Broome, Richard. *Treasure in Earthern Vessels (Protestant Christianity in New South Wales Society 1900–1914)*. St. Lucia: University of Queensland Press 1980

Brown, Morven S. 'Changing Functions of the Australian Family' in *Marriage and Family in Australia* (ed. A.P. Elkin), Sydney: Angus and Robertson, 1957

Burgess, Ernest W. and Wallin, Paul *Engagement and Marriage* Philadelphia: J.B. Lipincott, 1953

Burns, Creighton L. *Parties and People: A Survey Based on the La Trobe Electorate* Melbourne: Melbourne University Press, 1961

Burton, William Westbrooke *The State of Religion and Education in New South Wales* London: Cross, Simpkin and Marshall, 1840

Cameron, James *Centenary History of the Presbyterian Church in New South Wales* Sydney: Angus and Robertson, 1905

Campbell, A.J. *Fifty Years of Presbyterianism in Victoria: A Jubilee Sketch* Melbourne: Hutchinson, 1889

Campbell, Enid and Whitmore, Harry *Freedom in Australia* Sydney: Sydney University Press, 1966

Campiche, Roland. J. 'Switzerland' in Mol et al. (eds.) *Western Religion* The Hague: Mouton, 1972, pp. 511–528

Carpenter, S.R. *Church and People 1789–1889* London: SPCK, 1959

Carruthers, J.E. *Suburban Methodism* Sydney: Epworth Press, 1901

—— *Memories of an Australian Ministry 1868 to 1921* London: The Epworth Press, 1922

'Catholics Worse in First Year' *Canberra Times*, 19 December 1966

'The Catholic School in Australia', *Current Affairs Bulletin* 22 (9), 28 August 1958

Cavan, R.S., Burgess, E.W., Havighurst, R.J. and Goldhamer, H., *Personal Adjustment in Old Age* Chicago: Science Research Association, 1949

Chant, Barry 'The Promise of the Charismatic Movement' in Harris, Dorothy, Hynd, Douglas and Millikan, David (eds.) *The Shape of Belief* Homebush NSW: Lancer, 1982, pp. 109–122

Christensen, Harold T. and Barber, Kenneth E. 'Interfaith versus Intrafaith Marriage in Indiana' *Journal of Marriage and the Family* August 1967

Chryssavgis, Miltiades 'Orthodoxy in Australia' in Harris et al. (eds.) *The Shape of Belief* Homebush NSW: Lancer 1982, pp. 95–108

'Church-going in Australia', *Current Affairs Bulletin*, 22 (4), 16 June 1958

Clark, C.M.H. (Manning) *Select Documents in Australian History,* Vol. I, 1788–1850, Vol. II, 1851–1900 Sydney: Angus and Roberson, 1950 and 1955

—— *A History of Australia* vol. I, Cambridge: Cambridge University Press, Cambridge, 1962

—— 'Faith' in Peter Coleman (ed.), *Australian Civilisation* Melbourne: Cheshire, 1962a

—— *A Short History of Australia* Sydney: Tudor, 1963

Clark, C.M.H. *A Discovery of Australia* Sydney: Australian Broadcasting Commission Boyer Lectures, 1976

Cohen, David *Myths of the Space Age* New York: Dodd and Mead, 1967

Collins, D. *An Account of the English Colony in New South Wales* London: I. Caddell & W. Davies, 1798–1802

Colwell, J. *An Illustrated History of Methodism* Sydney: Brooks, 1904

Congalton, Athol A. 'Status Ranking of Sydney Suburbs', mimeographed, Sydney: School of Sociology, University of New South Wales, 1961

—— *Status and Prestige in Australia* Melbourne: F.W. Cheshire, 1969

'The Conjugal Condition of the People', *Statistician's Report*, Census of New South Wales, 1891

Connell, Kenneth 'Irish Peasant Marriages' in *Economic Historical Review*, second series, 14 (3), April 1962
—— *Irish Peasant Society* Oxford: Clarendon Press, 1968
Connell, W.F. *Growing up in an Australian City* Melbourne: ACER, 1957
—— *The Foundations of Secondary Education* Melbourne: ACER, 1961
Cox, Harvey G. *The Secular City* SCM Press, London: SEM Press, 1966
Crisp L.F. *The Australian Federal Labor Party, 1901–1951* London: Longmans Green, London, 1955
Crisp, L.F. and Bennet, S.P. 'Australian Labor Party Federal Personnel 1901–1954', unpublished monograph, Canberra: September 1954
Croog, Sydney H. and Teele, James E. 'Religious Identity and Church Attendance of Religious Intermarriage' *American Sociological Review* 32 (1), February 1967
Curtis, Richard F. 'Occupational Mobility and Church Participation' *Social Forces*, XXXVIII, 1960
Dale, R.W. *Impressions of Australia* London: Hodder and Stoughton, 1889
Davies, A.F. *Australian Damocracy* London: Longmans Green, 1958
Davies, A.F. and Encel, S. (eds.), *Australian Society* Melbourne: F.W. Cheshire, 1965
Davis, Gerald, Charles 'Australia's Religious Press' in Harris et al. (eds) *The Shape of Belief* Homebush NSW: Lancer, 1982, pp. 189–193
Davis, Kingsley *Human Society* New York: Macmillan, 1964
Day, Lincoln H. 'Family Size and Fertility' in Davies and Encel (eds), *Australian Society* Melbourne: F.W. Cheshire, 1965
—— 'Divorce' in *Australian Society* in Davies and Encel (eds), Melbourne: F.W. Cheshire, 1965
'The Declining Political Power of the Churches', *Sydney Morning Herald*, 4 May 1963
Demerath, N.J. III, *Social Class in American Protestantism* Chicago: McNally, 1965
Dempsey, Kenneth 'Country Town Religion' in Black and Glasner (eds), *Practice and Belief* Sydney: Allen and Unwin, 1983, pp. 25–42
De Vaus, David 'The Impact of Catholic Schools on the Religious Orientation of Boys and Girls' *Journal of Christian Education* July 1981, pp. 44–51
—— 'The Impact of Geographical Mobility on Adolescent Religious Orientation; An Australian Study' *Review of Religious Research* vol. 23 (4), 1982, pp. 391–405
Dicker, Gordon. 'The Search for Transcendence' in Harris et al. (eds.) *The Shape of Belief* Homebush NSW: Lancer, 1982, pp. 61–69
Dowdy, Edwin and Lupton, Gillian 'Some Aspects of Organisational Efficacy in Australian Churches' in Black and Glasner (eds.), *Practice and Belief* Sydney: Allen and Unwin, 1983, pp. 62–65
Duffy, Paul 'The Democratic Labor Party' in Henry Mayer (ed.), *Australian Politics: A Reader*, 1st edn, Melbourne: F. W. Cheshire, 1966
Ehrmann, Winston *Premarital Dating Behaviour* New York: Holt, 1959
Ely, R. 'Secularization and The Sacred in Australian History' *Historical Studies*, October 1981 pp. 553–566
Encel, S. 'The Old School Tie in Business' *Nation* 10 October 1959

Fairbanks, George 'Attitudes to Religion' *Australian Humanist* December 1968

Federal Catholic Education Office, *Information Bulletin* No. 7, March 1969

Feeney, Dianne 'The Changing Role of the Clergy' in Harris et al. (eds.) *The Shape of Belief*. Homebush, NSW: Lancer, 1982, pp. 123–131

Fichter, Joseph H., S.J. *Southern Parish* Chicago: University of Chicago Press, 1951

Fitzpatrick, J.M. *Belief in Australia: Some Figures on the State of Christian Belief in Australia* Maroubra: Catholic Enquiry Centre, 1979

Flynn, Marcellin *Some Catholic Schools in Action (A Sociological Study of Sixth Form Students in 21 Catholic Boys' High Schools)* Sydney: Catholic Education Office, 1975

Fogarty, Michael *Christian Democracy in Western Europes, 1820–1933* London: Routledge and Kegan Paul, 1957

Fogarty, Ronald *Catholic Education in Australia 1806–1950*, vol. III Melbourne University Press, Melbourne, 1959

Foote, A.E. 'Survey of the Methodist Combined Mission Area' Unpublished, Melbourne: 1958

Ford, Patrick *Cardinal Moran and the ALP* Melbourne: Melbourne University Press, 1966

Fowler, Stuart 'Christian Concern in the Parliamentary Lobbies' in Harris et al. (eds.) *The Shape of Belief* Homebush NSW: Lancer, 1982 pp. 147–158

Freedman, Ronald, Whelpton, Pascal, K. and Smit, John W. 'Socioeconomic Factors in Religious Differentials in Fertility', *American Sociological Review*, 26 (4), 1961

French, E.L. (ed.), *Melbourne Studies in Education, 1958–59* Melbourne: Melbourne University Press, 1960

—— *Melbourne Studies in Education, 1962–63* Melbourne: Melbourne University Press, 1964

—— review of T.L. Sutton's 'Hierarchy and Democracy in Australia 1780–1870' *Dialogue*, 1(1), Spring 1966; p. 44

Froude, J.A. *Oceana* London: Longmans, Green & Co., 1886

Gablentz, Otto Heinrich von der 'Secular Religions', mimeographed, New York: Goethe House Lecture, 17 November 1966

—— 'Religiöse Legitimation Politischer Macht' in Carl-Joachim Friedrich and Benno Reifenberg (eds.), *Sprache and Pditik* Heidelberg: Verlag Lambert Schneide, 1968

'Gallup on New Catholic Outlook' *Sun-Herald*, 2 April 1967

Garrison, Omar V. *The Hidden Secret of Scientology* London: Arlington Books, 1974

Geaney, Kieran 'The Catholic School in our Times', *Dialogue*, 2 (1), 1967

Giles, R.A. *The Constitutional History of the Australian Church* London: Skeffingdon, 1929

Glasner, Peter E. 'The Study of Australian Folk Religion: Some Theoretical and Practical Problems' in Black and Glasner (eds.) *Practice and Belief*, Sydney: Allen and Unwin, 1983, pp. 167–180

Glock, Charles Y. and Stark, Rodney *Religion and Society in Tension* Chicago: Rand McNally, 1965

—— *Christian Belief and Anti-Semitism* New York: Harper and Row, 1966

Glock, Charles Y., Ringer, Benjamin B. and Babbie, Earl R. *To Comfort and to Challenge* Berkeley: University of California Press, 1967

Gold, Hyam 'Religious Practice and Anti-Labor Partisanship: A Class-based Analysis' *Politics* no. 14, 1979, pp. 47–54

Goode, Eric 'Social Class and Church Participation' *American Journal of Sociology*, 72 (1), 1966

Gorer, Geoffrey *Exploring English Character* London: Cressett Press, 1955

Grant, Bruce 'Catholics and Politics' The *Age*, 26 April, 1969

Grassby, A. J. 'Religion in a Multicultural Society' *St. Mark's Review*, no. 107, pp. 50–58

Greeley, Andrew *Religion and Career* New York: Sheed and Ward, 1963

—— 'Some Results of Catholic Education in the United States', *Dialogue* 2 (1), 1967

Greeley, Andrew *Crisis in the Church* Chicago: Thomas More, 1979

Greeley, Andrew M. and Rossi, Peter H. *The Education of Catholic Americans* Chicago: Aldine Publishing Co., 1966

Gregory, J.S. 'Church and State and Education in Victoria to 1872' in E.L. French (ed.) *Melbourne Studies in Education, 1958–59* Melbourne: Melbourne University Press, 1960

Grocott, Allan M. *Convicts, Clergymen and Churches (Attitudes of Convicts and ex-Convicts towards the Churches and Clergy in New South Wales from 1788 to 1851)* Sydney: Sydney University Press, 1980

Habel, Norman C. 'Carols by Candlelight' in Hayes, Victor C. (ed.) *Religious Experience in World Religions*: Bedford Park, S.A.: The Australian Association for the Study of Religion, 1980, pp. 160–174

Hally, Cyril T. 'Growth Patterns in the Catholic Church' in Harris et al. (eds.) *The Shape of Belief* Homebush, NSW: Lancer, 1982, pp. 78–88

Hammond, S.B. 'Social Institutions and the Community' in Oeser and Hammond (eds.) *Social Structure and Personality in a City* London: Routledge and Kegan Paul, 1954

Hammond, S.B. 'Problems of Assimilation: Attitudes of Gentiles to Jews' in Oeser and Hammond (eds.) *Social Structure and Personality in a City*, London, Routledge and Kegan Paul, 1954

Hansen, I.U. 'Six Victorian Public Schools: Their Nature, Social Function and Ethos', PhD dissertation, Melbourne: Melbourne University, 1969

Hardy, Kenneth R. 'An Appetitional Theory of Sexual Motivation' *Psychological Review*, 71 (1), January, 1964

Harper, Andrew *The Honourable James Balfour, M.L.C., A Memoir* Melbourne: Critchley Parker, 1918

Harris, Dorothy; Hynd, Douglas and Millikan, David (eds.) *The Shape of Belief (Christianity in Australia today)* Homebush, NSW: Lancer, 1982

Harris, Dorothy 'Counting Christians' in Harris et al. (eds.) *The Shape of Belief* Homebush, NSW: Lancer, 1982a, pp. 224–288

Harris, Max 'Morals and Manners' in Peter Coleman (ed.) *Australian Civilisation* Melbourne: F.W. Cheshire, 1962

Heek, F. van 'Roman Catholicism and Fertility in the Netherlands', *Population Studies*, 10 (2), November, 1956

Heer, David M. 'The Trend of Inter-faith Marriages in Canada: 1922–1957'

American Sociological Review, 27 (2), April, 1962

Henderson, Rev. Kenneth T. *Christian Tradition and Australian Outlook* Melbourne: The Australian Student Christian Movement Corporation, 1923
—— 'Religious Institutions and Aspirations' in Caiger, George (ed.) *The Australian Way of Life* Melbourne: Heineman, 1953

Henderson, R. *Ninety Years in the Master's Service* Edinburgh: Andrew Elliott, 1911

Herbert, Martin 'Why Married Couples Grow Alike' *New Society*, 3 April, 1969

Heyer, J. *The Presbyterian Pioneers of Van Diemen's Land: A Contribution to the Ecclesiastical History of Tasmania* Launceston: Presbytery of Tasmania, 1935

Hickman, David C. 'The Social Context of Religious Orientation', unpublished PhD Dissertation, Australian National University, 1969

Higgins, Edward 'Differential Fertility Outlook and Patterns among Major Religious Groups in Johannesburg', *Social Compass*, II (1), 1964

Hill, C.G.N. 'Teacher Trainees and Authoritarian Attitudes' *Australian Journal of Psychology*, 11, 1959

Hilliard, David 'A Church in Decline' *The Adelaide Church Guardian* vol. 73, no. 6, July 1979

Hogan, Michael 'Australian Secularists: The Disavowal of Denominational Allegiance' *Journal for the Scientific Study of Religion* vol. 18, no. 4, 1979, pp. 390–404

Horne, Donald *The Lucky Country* Ringwood, Vic: Penguin 1964

Horsfield, Peter G. 'Christian Television: How Effective is it?' in Harris et al. (eds.) *The Shape of Belief* Homebush NSW: Lancer, 1983, pp. 175–181

Houtart, F. and Pin, E. *The Church and the Latin American Revolution* New York: Sheed and Ward, 1965

'How 50 Million Catholics View their Changing Church', *Sun-Herald*, 19 March 1967

Howe, Renate 'The Wesleyan Church in Victoria: Its Ministry and Membership', MA Thesis, University of Melbourne, 1966

Hubbard, L. Ron *What is Scientology* Los Angeles: Church of Scientology Publications, 1978

'Humanist Funeral' *Viewpoint* 7 (4), April 1969

Hunter, Ian N. 'Sects and Cults I' *St. Mark's Review* no. 107, September 1981, pp. 27–36

Hutch, Richard A. 'The Personal Ritual of Glossolalia' in Hayes, Victor (ed.) *Religious Experience in World Religions* Bedford Park, S.A.: The Australian Association for the Study of Religion, 1980 pp. 78–93

Hynd, Douglas *Christianity in Australia: A Bibliography*, in Harris et al. (eds.) *The Shape of Belief* Homebush, NSW: Lancer, 1982, pp. 201–228

'The Independent Schools of Australia', *Current Affairs Bulletin* 21 (3), 1957

Inglis, K.S., 'Patterns of Religious Worship in 1851', *Journal of Ecclesiastical History* 11 (1), April 1960

Inglis, K.S. 'The Australian Catholic Community' in Mayer, Henry (ed.) *Catholics and the Free Society: An Australian Symposium* Melbourne: Cheshire 1961, pp. 7–32
—— *Churches and the Working Classes in Victorian England* London:

Routledge and Kegan Paul, 1963
—— 'Religious Behaviour' in Davies and Encel (eds.) *Australian Society* Melbourne: Cheshire, 1965
Isambert, Francois A. 'France' in Mol, et al. (eds.) *Western Religion* The Hague: Mouton, 1972, pp. 175–187
Jones, David Charles *The Development of New Christian Schools in Australia: 1975–1981* MEd thesis, University of Melbourne, 1983
Jones, F. Lancaster, 'A Social Profile of Canberra, 1961', *The Australian and New Zealand Journal of Sociology* 1 (2), October 1965
—— 'Social Ranking of Melbourne Suburbs', *The Australian and New Zealand Journal of Sociology* 3 (2), October 1967
Jones, Gavin and Nortman, Dorothy 'Roman Catholic Fertility and Family Planning, a Comparative Review of the Research Literature', *Studies in Family Planning* no. 34, October 1968
Jupp, James *Australian Party Politics* Melbourne: Melbourne University Press, 1964
Kaill, Robert C. 'Ecumenism, Clergy Influence and Liberalism: An Investigation into the Sources of Law Support for Church Union' *Canadian Review of Sociology and Anthropology* vol. 8, 1971, pp. 142–163
Kane, John J. *Catholic-Protestant Conflicts in America* Chicago: Regnery, 1955
Kanter, Rosabeth Moss 'Commitment and Social Organisation: A Study of Commitment Mechanisms in Utopian Communities' *American Sociological Review* 33 (4), August 1968
Kardiner, Abram, *Sex and Morality* Indianapolis: Bobbs-Merrill Co., 1954
Kenny, Denis *The Catholic Church and Freedom* Brisbane: Queensland University Press, 1967
Kiddle, Margaret *Men of Yesterday, a Social History of the Western District of Victoria, 1834–1890* Melbourne: Melbourne University Press, 1961
Kinsey, Alfred C., Pomeroy, Wardell B., Martin, Clyde E. *Sexual Behaviour in the Human Male* Philadelphia: W.B. Saunders, 1948
Knopfelmacher, F. 'The Catholic Church and Totalitarianism' in Mayer, Henry (ed.) *Catholics and the Free Society: An Australian Symposium* Melbourne: Cheshire, 1961
Knopfelmacher, F. and Armstrong, Douglas B. 'The Relation between Authoritarianism, Ethnocentrism and Religious Denomination among Australian Adolescents' *American Catholic Sociological Review* 24 (2), 1963
Köster, R. *Die Kirchentreuen* Stuttgart: Ferdinand Enke Verlag, 1959
Krupinski, J. and Marshall, E. *Analysis of Factors Contributing to Premature Termination of Counselling* Melbourne: Marriage Guidance Council of Victoria, 1967
Lacey, Roderic 'Prophets, Souls and God-talk: a review of some recent explorations of religion in Australia' *Journal of the Institute of Catholic Education* no. 13, November, 1982, pp. 39–53
Latourette, K.S. *Christianity in a Revolutionary Age* vol. 5, London: Eyre and Spottiswood, 1963
Lawlor, Monica *Out of this World: A Study of Catholic Values* London: Sheed and Ward, 1965

Lazerwitz, Bernard 'Religion and Social Structure in the United States' in Schneider, Louis (ed.) *Religion, Culture and Society* New York: Wiley, 1964

Leavitt, I.W.H. (ed.) *Jubilee History of Victoria and Melbourne,* vol. I (2), Wells and Leavitt, 1888

Leavy, Mary Raphael 'The Relevance of St Thomas Aquinas for Australian Education' *Melbourne Studies in Education, 1962–63* (ed. E.L. French), Melbourne University Press, Melbourne, 1964

Leavey, M. Carmel *Religious Education, School Climate and Achievement: A Study of Nine Catholic Sixth Form Girls' Schools,* PhD thesis, Canberra: Australian National University, 1972

Lecomte du Noüy *The Road to Reason,* edited and translated by Mary Lecomte du Noüy, New York: Longmans, 1948

Lenski, Gerhard *The Religious Factor* Garden City, New York: Doubleday and Co., 1961

—— 'Religion's Impact on Secular Institutions' in Brothers, Joan (ed.) *Readings in the Sociology of Religion* Oxford: Pergamon Press, 1967

Lewins, Frank W. 'The Multicultural Challenge' in Harris, et al. (eds.) *The Shape of Belief* Homebush, NSW: Lancer, 1982, pp. 89–94

Lewins, Frank, W. 'Wholes and Parts: Some Aspects of the Relationships between the Australian Catholic Church and Migrants' in Black and Glasner (eds.) *Practice and Belief* Sydney: Allen and Unwin, 1983, pp. 74–85

Lewis, C.S. *Screwtape Letters,* Geoffrey Bles London: The Centenary Press, 1947

Lilley, W.C. *Reminiscences of Life in Brisbane* Brisbane: W.R. Smith and Paterson, 1913

Lippman, Walter M. 'The Demography of Australian Jewry' *Jewish Journal of Sociology,* 8 (2), 1966

Lipset, Seymour Martin 'Religion and Politics in American History' in Raab, Earl (ed.) *Religious Conflict in America* New York: Doubleday, Garden City, 1964

—— 'Political Sociology' in *Sociology* (ed. Neil Smelser), New York: Wiley, 1967

Loane, Marcus 'Foreword' *The Occult: Report of an Anglican Commission of Enquiry* Sydney: Anglican Information Office, 1975

Locke, Ralph. C. 'Who am I in the City of Mammon? The Self, Doubt and Certainty, in a Spiritualist Cult' in Black and Glasner (eds.) *Practice and Belief* Sydney: Allen and Unwin, 1983, pp. 108–133

McCoy, Charles A. 'Australian Democratic Labor Party Support, an Analysis of Two States' *Journal of Commonwealth Political Studies,* III, 1965

McGregor, Craig *Profile of Australia* London: Hodder and Stoughton, 1966

McIntyre, A.J. and J.J. *Country Towns of Victoria, a Social Survey* Melbourne: Melbourne University Press, 1944

MacIntyre, Alasdair *Secularization and Moral Change* London; Oxford University Press, 1967

McLeod, A.L. (ed.) *The Pattern of Australian Culture* Melbourne: Oxford University Press, 1963

Mackle, F. *The Footprints of our Catholic Pioneers, the Beginnings of the*

Church in Victoria, 1839–1859 Melbourne: Advocate Press, 1924

Manley, Ken R. *Baptists: Their Heritage and Faith* Sydney: Baptist Union of New South Wales, 1968

Martin, David *A Sociology of English Religion* London: SCM Press, 1967

Martin, David 'Great Britain: England' in Mol, et al. (eds.) *Western Religion (A Country by Country Sociological Inquiry)* The Hague: Mouton, 1972, pp. 229–247

Martin, Jean I. 'Marriage, the Family and Class' in Elkin, A.P. (ed.) *Marriage and the Family in Australia* Sydney: Angus and Robertson, 1957

Maslow, Abraham H. *Motivation and Personality* New York: Harper, 1954

—— *Religions, Values and Peak Experiences* Columbus: Ohio State University Press, 1964

Mason, Michael (editor) and Fitzpatrick, Georgina (compiler) *Religion in Australian Life: a Bibliography of Social Research* Adelaide: Australian Association for the Study of Religious and the National Catholic Research Council, 1982

Mason, Michael 'Pastoral Leadership for Tomorrow' *Australasian Catholic Record*. vol. 60 (1), Jan. 1983, pp. 29–45

Masterman, C.F.G. *The Conditions of England* London: Methuen, (First published 1909), 1960

Matthews, C.H.S. *A Parson in the Australian Bush* London: Arnold, 1908

Mayer, Henry, 'The DLP Today', *Observer* Sydney: 25 June 1960

—— (ed.), *Catholics and the Free Society: An Australian Symposium* Melbourne: Cheshire, 1961

Medding, Peter Y. *From Assimilation to Group Survival (A political and sociological study of an Australian Jewish Community)* Melbourne: Cheshire, 1968

Meere, Gregory 'The Arguments against a Catholic School System Reassessed' *Dialogue* 2 (1), 1967

Mendelsohn, Oscar 'Unbelief in Melbourne' *Nation*, 25 June 1966

Métin, A. 'Le Socialisme sans Doctrine' in Clark, C.M.H. (ed.) *Select Documents in Australian History* vol. II Sydney: Angus and Robertson, 1955

Middleton, R. and Putney, S. 'Religion, Normative Standards and Behaviour' *Sociometry*, no. 25, 1962

Millikan, David *The Sunburnt Soul: Christianity in Search of an Australian Identity* Homebush: Lancer, 1981

—— 'Christianity and Australian Identity' in Harris et al. (eds.) *The Shape of Belief (Christianity in Australia Today)* Homebush: Lancer, 1982 pp. 29–46

Moberg, David O. *The Church as a Social Institution* Englewood Cliffs: Prentice-Hall, 1962

—— 'Religiosity in Old Age' *The Gerontologist* 5 (2), June 1965

—— 'Theological self-classification and Ascetic Moral Views of Students' *Review of Religious Research* 10 (2), Winter 1969

Moffitt, Ian and Williams, Graham 'A Crisis in the Schools' *Australian* 21 September 1967

—— 'The Catholic Revolution' *Australian* 18 September 1967

Mol, J.J. (Hans) *Church Attendance in Christchurch, New Zealand*, Research

Project 7, Department of Psychology, and Sociology, 1962
—— 'The Decline in Religious Participation of Migrants' *International Migration* 3 (3), 1965
—— 'Pride and Prejudice in Denominational Divisions' in Southall, Ivan (ed.) *The Challenge* Melbourne: Lansdowne Press, 1966
—— 'Collation of Data about Religion in Australia' *Social Compass* XIV (2), 1967
—— 'Religion in New Zealand' *Archives de Sociologie des Religions* no. 24, 1967
—— *Breaking of Traditions* Berkeley: Glendessary Press, 1968
—— *Christianity in Chains* Melbourne: Nelson, 1969
—— *Religion in Australia* Melbourne: Nelson, 1971
—— 'Rejoinder' *The Australian and New Zealand Journal of Sociology* vol. 7 (1) April 1971a, pp. 68–69
—— *Identity and the Sacred* Oxford: Blackwell, 1976
—— *The Fixed and the Fickle (Religion and Identity in New Zealand)* Waterloo, Ontario: Wilfrid Laurier University Press, 1982
—— *Meaning and Place (An Introduction to the Social Scientific Study of Religion)* New York: Pilgrim Press, 1983
—— *Faith and Fragility (Religion and Identity in Canada)* Burlington, Ontario: Trinity, 1985
Mol, J.J. (Hans), Hetherton, Margaret and Henty, Margaret (eds.) *Western Religion (A Country by Country Sociological Inquiry)* The Hague: Mouton, 1972
Molony, John N. *The Roman Mould of the Australian Catholic Church* Melbourne: Melbourne, University Press, 1969
Monahan, Thomas P. and Kephart, William M. 'Divorce and Desertion by Religious and Mixed-Religious Groups' *American Journal of Sociology* 59, March 1954
Moran, P.F. *History of the Catholic Church in Australasia*, Sydney: Oceanic Publishing Company, 1894
Muggeridge, Malcolm *Jesus Rediscovered* London: Fontana Books, Collins, 1969
Murray, Les A. 'Some Religious Stuff I Know about Australia' in Harris et al. (eds.) *The Shape of Belief* Homebush NSW: Lancer, 1982, pp. 13–28
Murtagh, James G. *Australia: The Catholic Chapter* rev. edn, Sydney: Angus and Robertson, 1959
Neuss, Ronald F. *Facts and Figures about the Church of England*, no. 3, London: Church Information Office, 1965
Nichols, Alan 'From Charity to Social Justice' in Harris et al. (eds.) *The Shape of Belief* Homebush, NSW: Lancer, 1982, pp. 140–146
Nowotny, Elizabeth *Young People's Ideas about God, Religion and the Meaning of Life* Melbourne: Dove Communications, 1978
O'Brien, Leslie 'A Case Study of the 'Hare Krishna' Movement' in Black and Glasner *Practice and Belief* Sydney: Allen and Unwin, 1983, pp. 134–153
O'Brien, Eris *Life and Letters of Archpriest John Joseph Therry, Founder of the Catholic Church in Australia* Sydney: Angus and Robertson, 1922

O'Dea, Thomas F. *American Catholic Dilemma: An Inquiry into the Intellectual Life* New York: Sheed and Ward, 1958

O'Donnell, Michael 'Whither Catholic Education' *Dialogue* 2 (1), Spring 1967

Oeser, O.A. and Hammond, S.B. *Social Structure and Personality in a City* London: Routledge and Kegan Paul, 1954

O'Farrell, Patrick 'A History of the N.S.W. Labor Movement 1880–1910', *Journal of Religious History* 2 (2), 1962

—— *The Catholic Church in Australia*, Melbourne: Nelson, 1968

'Old School Tie Chaps' *Canberra Times* 12 September 1968

O'Neill, J.C. 'Letter from Australia' *Theology* 65, September 1962

O'Reilly, Matthew 'Catholics in Uniform', *Australian Catholic Record*, new series 24, 1947

Overacker, Louise, *Australian Parties in a Changing Society, 1945–67* Melbourne: Cheshire, Melbourne, 1968

Parker, David *Fundamentalism and Conservative Protestantism in Australia, 1920–1980* PhD dissertation, University of Queensland, 1982

Parsons, Talcott 'The Theoretical Development of the Sociology of Religion' in Brothers Joan (ed.) *Readings in the Sociology of Religion* Pergamon Oxford: Pergamon Press, 1967

Partridge, P.H. et al. *Teachers in Australia* published for the Australian College of Education Melbourne: Cheshire, 1966

Pawsey, Margaret M. *The Popish Plot: Studies in the Christian Movement* Melbourne: Dove, 1983

Pearlin, Leonard I. and Kohn, Melvin L. 'Social Class, Occupation and Parental Values: A Cross-National Study' *American Sociological Review* 31 (4), August 1966

Phillips, W.W. 'Christianity and its Defence in New South Wales, circa 1880 to 1890', PhD thesis, Australian National University, 1969

Phillips, Walter. W. 'Religious Profession and Practice in New South Wales, 1850–1901: The Statistical Evidence' *Historical Studies* 15, 1972–73, pp. 378–400

—— *Defending 'A Christian Country' (Churchmen and Society in New South Wales in the 1880s and After)* Queensland: University of Queensland, 1981

Pickering, W.F.S 'The 1851 Religious Census—a useless experiment' *British Journal of Sociology* 18, 1967

Pike, Douglas *Paradise of Dissent* London: Longmans Green, 1957

Pin, Emile *Pratique Religieuse et Classes Sociales* Paris: Spes, 1956

Power, John *Politics in a Suburban Community* Sydney: Sydney University Press, 1968

Preston, Noel 'A Christian Response to Aboriginal Australia' in Harris et al. (eds.) *The Shape of Belief* Homebush, NSW: Lancer 1982, pp. 159–174

Price, Charles Archibald 'The Effects of Post-War Immigration on the Growth of Population, Ethnic Composition and Religious Structure of Australia', *The Australian Quarterly*, XXIX (4), 1957

—— 'The Integration of Religious Groups in Australia', *International Migration*, 1 (3), 1963

—— *Jewish Settlers in Australia*, Social Science Monograph no. 23, Canberra:

Australian National University, 1964
—— 'The Migrants' in Venturini, Venturino G. (ed.) *Australia, A Survey* Wiesbaden: Otto Harrassowitz, 1970, pp. 59–75
—— (ed.) *Australian Immigration: A Bibliography and Digest* no. 4, Canberra: Department of Demography, Australian National University, 1979
—— 'Religion and the Census' *St. Mark's Review* no. 107, September 1981, pp. 2–8
Pringle, John Douglas *Australian Accent* London: Chatto and Windus, 1963
Pryor, Robin J. 'Population Changes and Religious Allegiance' in Harris et al., (eds.) *The Shape of Belief* Homebush NSW: Lancer, 1982, pp. 70–77
Pyne, Patricia and Price, Charles A. 'Selected Tables on Australian Immigration: 1947–1978' in Price, Charles A. (ed.) *Australian Immigration: A Bilbiography and Digest* no. 4 Canberra: Dep. of Demography, Australian National University, 1979, pp. A18–A36
Radic, Leonard 'The Men who Bury our Dead' *The Age* 3 December 1968
—— 'A New Set of Graveside Manners' *The Age* 2 December 1968
Rawson, Donald W. *Labor in Vain?* Melbourne: Longmans, 1968
Reilly, J.T. *Fifty Years in Western Australia* Perth: Sands and McDougall, 1908
Reiss, Ira L. 'Premarital Sexual Permissiveness among Negroes and Whites' *American Sociological Review* 29 (5), October 1964
'Report on the Decline in Church-going' Diocese of Newcastle, Australia, 1951
'Report by the Subcommittee on Marriage and Funeral Services' mimeographed NSW Humanist Society, July 1965
Rivett, Rohan 'The Sex Revolution in Print' *Canberra Times* 30 May 1967
Robertson, Yvonne 'Some Religious Practices and Attitudes of Post School Adolescents' *Dialogue* 2 (2), 1968
Roe, Michael *Quest for Authority* Melbourne: Melbourne University Press, 1965
Rokeach, Milton *The Open and Closed Mind* New York: Basic Books, 1960
'Roman Catholic Education' *Conberra Times* 21 January 1969
Roof, Wade Clark 'Traditional Religion in Contemporary Society: A theory of Local, Cosmopolitan Plausibility' *American Social Review*, vol. 41, 1976, pp. 195–208
Ross, C.S. *Colonisation and Church Work in Victoria* Melbourne: Melville, Muller and Slade, 1891
—— *The Scottish Church in Victoria, 1851–1901* Melbourne: Hutchinson, 1901
Ryan, Noel J. 'A Study of Catholic Residences and Tutorials in the University of Melbourne from 1951 to 1961' *The Australian and New Zealand Journal of Sociology* 3 (2), 1967
Ryan, Noel J. 'Sects and Cults II' *St. Mark's Review* no. 107, September 1981, pp. 37–44
Salisbury, W. Seward *Religion in American Culture* Illinois: Dorsey Press, 1964
Saunders, Ross 'The Word on the Wireless' in Harris et al. (eds.) *The Shape*

of Belief Homebush, NSW: Lancer, 1982, pp. 182–188

Schneider, Louis (ed.) *Religion, Culture and Society*, New York: Wiley, 1964

Schofield, Michael et al. *The Sexual Behaviour of Young People* London: Longmans, 1965

Schools for the ACT (Report of the Committee of Review into the Impact of Radford College) Canberra: Australian Government Publishing Service, 1983

Schramm, Wilbur 'The Effects of Mass Communication: A Review' *Journalism Quarterly*, December 1949

Schreuder, O. *Soziographie der Christlichen Kirchen in Europa* Frankfurt am Main: Soziographisches Institüt an der Universität, 1964

Scott, D. and U'Ren, R. *Leisure* Melbourne: Cheshire, 1962

Scott, Ernest *Australia During the War*, (Vol. XI of Bean, C. (ed.) *The Official History of Australia in the War of 1914–1918* Sydney: Angus and Roberston, 1943

Scott, E. and Orr, K. 'Values in the Secondary School—A Queensland Enquiry: Part III Research Findings' *Journal of Christian Education* 10, 1967

Scott, Peter 'The Population Structure of Australian Cities' *Geographic Journal* 131 (4), December 1965

Sharpe, Eric J 'Religion in an Australian Context' *St. Mark's Review*, no. 107, September 1981, pp. 20–36

Sharpe, Eric J. *Understanding Religion* London: Duckworth, 1983

Sharwood, Robin 'Why not Establish a University School of Theology? *The Age* 22 September 1967

Smart, A.J.H. 'Some Religious Beliefs and Attitudes of Students at the Armidale Teacher's College and at the University of New England', *Journal of Christian Education* 7 (1), June 1964

Smith, F.B. 'Joseph Symes and the Australian Secular Association' *Labour History* 5, 1963

Smith, W.G. 'Catholics and Protestants: a Survey', *Social Survey*, 13 (1), Feb 1964

Solomon, David 'A Question of Independence' *Canberra Times* 15 May 1967

Sommers, Tess van *Religions in Australia* Adelaide: Rigby, 1966

Spann, Richard N. 'The Catholic Vote in Australia' in Mayer, H. (ed.) *Catholics and the Free Society: An Australian Symposium* Melbourne: Cheshire, 1961

Spurr, F.C. *Five Years under the Southern Cross: Experiences and Impressions* London: Cassell, 1918

Stanfield, Brian 'The Arguments against a Catholic School System—a Summary' *Dialogue* 1 (2), 1967

Stebbins, Jim 'Historical Models for Christianity in Australia' in Harris et al. (eds.) *The Shape of Belief* Homebush NSW: Lancer, 1982 pp. 47–60

Stewart, Stan *The Church's Ministry with Children* Sydney: Australian Council of Churches, 1976

Stoetzel, Jean *Europe at the Crossroads* mimeographed translation from French Stoetzel, Jean *Les Valeurs du Temps Présent*. L'Europe du

Carrefour, Paris: Press Universitaire de France, 1983

Stouffer, Samuel 'Trends in the Fertility of Catholics and Non-Catholics' *The American Journal of Sociology* 41 (2), September 1935

Suich, Max 'This is what Teenagers Think' *Sun-Herald* 4 June 1967

—— 'Australian Catholic Priest Queries Ban on Pill' *Sun-Herald,* 20 August 1967

Sutherland, R. *The History of the Presbyterian Church of Victoria from the Foundation of the Colony down to the Abolition of State Aid in 1875* London: Nisbet, 1877

Symonds, E. *The Story of the Australian Church*, London: SPCK 1898

Taft, Ronald *From Stranger to Citizen* Perth: University of Western Australia Press, 1968

Television and Religion London: University of London Press, 1964

Therry, Roger, *Reminiscences of NSW and Victoria* London: Sampson Low, 1863

Thomas, John L. 'The Factor of Religion in Selection of Marriage Mates' *American Sociological Review* 16, August 1951

Thompson, A.T. *Australia and the Bible* London: Hodder and Stoughton, 1889

Tien, H.Y. *Social Mobility and Controlled Fertility* New Haven USA: College and University Press, 1965

Trengrove, Alan, 'No Preaching Please, says Dr Gough' *Sydney Morning Herald* 16 October 1965

Trollope, A. *Australia and New Zealand* Melbourne: George Robertson, 1873

Truman, Tom C. 'Catholics and Politics in Australia *Western Political Quarterly*, 22 June 1959

—— *Catholic Action and Politics* rev. ed., Melbourne: Georgian House, 1960

Turner, H.G. *A History of the Colony of Victoria* London: Longmans Green, 1904

Twopenny, R.E.N. *Town Life in Australia* London: Elliott Stock, 1883

Ullathorne, William Bernard *The Catholic Mission in Australasia* Liverpool: Rockliff and Duckworth, 1837

—— *Autobiography* London: Burns and Oates, 1891

UNESCO *Compulsory Education in Australia* Paris: 1951

Vanecko, James J. 'Religious Behaviour and Prejudice: Some Dimensions and Specifications of the Relationship' *Review of Religious Research* 8 (1), Fall 1966

Vellekoop, Cora, 'Social Stratification in New Zealand', PhD thesis, Christchurch, New Zealand: Canterbury University, 1969

Vincent, Clark E. 'Inter-faith Marriages' in Raab, Earl (ed.) *Religious Conflict in America* Garden City, New York: Doubleday, 1964

Walker, A. *Coal Town: A Social Survey of Cessnock* Melbourne: Melbourne University Press, 1945

Walker, R.B. 'Presbyterian Church and People in the Colony of NSW in the late Nineteenth Century' *The Journal of Religious History* 2 (1), June 1962

Ward, Russel, *Australia* London: Horwitz, 1965

Waterhouse, John 'Christian Publishing in Australia in Harris et al. (eds.) *The Shape of Belief* Homebush, NSW: Lancer, 1982, pp. 194–200

Webb, Leicester 'Churches and the Australian Community' in French, E.L. (ed.) *Melbourne Studies in Education, 1958–1959* Melbourne University Press, 1960

Westoff, Charles F. and Ryder, Norman B. 'United States: Methods of Fertility Control, 1955, 1960 and 1965' *Studies in Family Planning* no. 17, 1967

'White Australia—Reform?' *Current Affairs Bulletin* 34 (4) 6 July, 1964

White, C.H., *The Challenge of the Years: A History of the Presbyterian Church of Australia in the State of New South Wales* Sydney: Angus and Robertson, 1961

Wickham, E.R. *Church and People in an Industrial City* London: Lutterworth Press, 1957

—— 'Worker Priests in Britain' in Edwards, D.L. (ed.) *Priests and Workers* London: SCM Press, 1961

Williams, Robin M. Jr. *American Society: A Sociological Interpretation* New York: Knopf, 1956

Williams, Robyn *Stranger Next Door* Englewood Cliffs, New Jersey: Prentice-Hall, 1964

Wilson, Bruce 'The Church in a Secular Society' in Harris et al. (eds) *The Shape of Belief* Homebush, NSW Lancer, 1982, pp. 1–12

Wilson, Bruce *Can God Survive in Australia* Sutherland, NSW: Albatross, 1983

Wilson, Bryan R. *Religion in Secular Society* London: Watts, 1966

Wilson, John, Williams, Norman and Sugarman, Barry *Introduction to Moral Education* Harmondsworth: Penguin, 1968.

Wilson, P.R. and Chappell, D. 'Australian Attitudes towards Abortion, Prostitution and Homosexuality' *Australian Quarterly* 40 (2), June 1968

Winnett, A.R. *Divorce and Remarriage in Anglicanism* London: Macmillan, 1958

Wolf, Richard C. '1900–1950 Survey: Religious Trends in the United States' *Christianity Today* 27 April 1959

Wright, Derek and Cox, Edwin 'A Study of the Relationship between Moral Judgment and Religious Belief in a Sample of English Adolescents' *The Journal of Social Psychology*, no. 72, 1967

Yinger, J. Milton *Religion, Society and the Individual* New York: Macmillan, 1957

—— *Sociology Looks at Religion* New York: Macmillan, 1963

Yule, Valerie 'Group Differences in Problems Presented by Marriage Counselling Clients' *Australian Journal of Social Issues* 2 (2), 1964–1966

Index

242